DEAD BROKE:

LIFE IN THE DUST BOWL IN THE MIDDLE OF THE GREAT DEPRESSION AND BEYOND

Darrell Dempster

4/9/2017

Revision 1
September 2017

Photograph Front Cover:
Dempster Farm, Offerle, Kansas: Dad, John,
Darrell, Wilma, Mom and Phyllis, 1936

Publisher and Distributor:
Three D Dynamics
2212 Chesapeake Harbor Drive East, Suite 1002
Annapolis, MD 21403
ThreeDDynamics@gmail.com

Prologue

In 2014, I first heard Hillary Clinton say, "We were **dead broke** when we left the White House." I said to myself, "Did she really mean they were **dead broke**?" I grew up hearing **dead broke** and many variations, such as "dirt poor," "needy," "don't have a nickel to my name," "bankrupt," "flat broke," "bread-line busted," and "penniless" many times. I thought I knew what **dead broke** really meant. It turns out that Hillary wasn't using **dead broke** to describe her family as penniless or facing the bread line. Apparently, she was using the term **dead broke** to evoke compassion and to deny or justify the immense wealth she and her husband, ex-President Bill Clinton, had accumulated since leaving the White House.

I decided to write a book about myself and show what **dead broke** really means. Since I was born in Kansas in 1929, my focus will be on my family, the Great Depression, the Dust Bowl, Pearl Harbor, and then I will travel through my other experiences, including a career in the United States Navy.

I don't know where I'm going, but I'll know I'm there, when I get there.

TABLE OF CONTENTS

CHAPTER 1: THE DUST BOWL AND THE GREAT DEPRESSION

The story of my early life, during the Great Depression and the Dust Bowl storms from 1929 to 1937, is not about me. It is about my parents, Edwin Dempster and Catharine Boehme Dempster. I have come to understand the resilience and perseverance of my parents, as they struggled to survive during their early married life from 1928 to 1941. Mom and Dad were married in 1928, when Mom was 17 and Dad was 21. I was born in 1929, and my sister, Wilma, was born in 1931. We lived in Hutchinson, Kinsley, Dodge City, Great Bend, Offerle, and Ford, Kansas, before moving to the Dempster farm, nine miles southeast of Offerle, Kansas, in 1932. The Dempster farm was originally 240 acres, but 160 acres had been sold in 1928, and the farm was now 80 acres and called the "80."

These were hard times. I can think of no other way to describe the years of 1929 to 1939 in the Midwest states of North Dakota, South Dakota, Nebraska, Colorado, Kansas, Oklahoma, and Texas.

This story will start with my early years in Kansas where I lived from 1929 to 1948. The economic and environmental disasters that defined 1929 to 1939 were the Great Depression and the Dust Bowl. The Great Depression affected all of the United States, but the Dust Bowl disaster was unique to these Midwest states. The Dust Bowl was the worst ecological disaster in the history of the United States.

The Great Depression began with the stock market crash of October 1929. The market crash was the beginning of a decade of high unemployment, bankruptcies, hunger, and migrations from one state to another. Most people in the Midwest knew little of the stock market, as they were living day-to-day and had no assets to make investments. The effect in their world was a decrease in the prices of farm products they sold and an increase in the prices of items they bought.

Industries that suffered the most, as Dust Bowl conditions commenced in 1932 and continued until 1935, included construction, agriculture, shipping, mining, logging, and the sale of automobiles and appliances. The economy reached bottom in the winter of 1932–33. In late 1933, there was some growth for about four years, but very few people in the Midwest would agree there was growth, as they were now in the middle of the Dust Bowl — a double whammy.

Many farmers prospered in the 1920s, as crops were generally very good. The farmers converted this prosperity into the purchase of more land and farming machinery. They also took on debt by mortgaging their property. When the Dust Bowl drought hit them, they were not able to get enough income to buy seed for the next year's crop, let alone pay mortgages. Consequently, many farmers lost their farms.

Bread line during the Great Depression

"It was the best of times, it was the worst of times" are the opening words from **Tale of Two Cities** by Charles Dickens. These were the worst of times — were there any best of times? My parents settled in Hutchinson, Kansas, in 1928, where my grandfather, Ben Dempster, operated a sandwich shop. Dad worked at odd jobs, including nights at a pool hall. When I was about three months old, my Dad decided that he needed to "Go West" in order to earn money. Work in Kansas was hard to find. My Dad and Jerry, a schoolmate who had a brother in California, left Kansas by car and traveled to California where they found work near Fresno picking grapes and plums. Meanwhile, my mother worked in the Dempster sandwich shop. Mom was paid three dollars per week; she worked the day shift with my grandmother, Ethel Dempster. My Dad's sister, Opal Dempster, worked the night shift with Grandpa. Aunt Opal was paid five dollars per week, although she said she didn't always get the money.

When Dad left for California, I was taken to Kinsley, Kansas, near my mother's hometown, to live with my mother's sister, Thelma Quisenberry. Dad wrote letters to Mom during his absence, and it is reported that he was "terribly homesick." He didn't earn the money he had hoped to earn, so he and Jerry sold the car, and with some additional money sent by Grandma, Dad returned by bus to Kansas. Mom met Dad at Midway, a small town southwest of Hutchinson. They drove out to Kinsley, picked me up from Aunt Thelma, and returned to Hutchinson. Dad needed a new pair of shoes after the ardors of traveling to California, laboring in the vineyard, and returning to Kansas. Mom bought a pair from her savings – The cost was probably about two dollars. Dad was **Dead Broke.**

In the winter of 1929, my parents moved to Dodge City to help my grandfather operate a small restaurant on Front Street, near the famous Long Branch Saloon of frontier days. Years later, in 1959, my wife, Sally, our four-month-old son, Eddie, and I were traveling cross-country from Annapolis,

Eddie and Darrell in Dodge City en route to Japan in 1959

Maryland, to San Francisco on our way to Japan for Navy duty. We stopped in Dodge City, and I finally had a chance to see the famous Long Branch Saloon — Eddie did not enjoy it as much as I did.

In the fall of 1930, Dad worked for Uncle Irwin Armstrong on his farm south of Great Bend, Kansas, shucking corn and doing other farm work. Grandpa Ben Dempster and Irwin's wife, Nellie, were siblings. Mom and I were with Dad at the Armstrongs that winter.

The next summer and fall of 1931, Dad worked for his cousin, Wilbur Armstrong, on a farm south of Ford, Kansas. While Dad was working for Wilbur, Mom and I stayed with Grandpa and Grandma Boehme (John and Luella) in Offerle. My sister, Wilma, was born in the hospital in Spearville, Kansas, while Mom and I were staying with the Boehmes.

Other accounts confirm my impressions of life at that time, as well those recounted to me. **Wessels Living History Farm** website reported: "The most visible evidence of how dry the 1930s became were the dust storms. Tons of topsoil were blown off barren fields and carried in storm clouds for hundreds of miles. Technically, the driest region of the Plains — southeastern Colorado, southwest Kansas, and the panhandles of Oklahoma and Texas — became known as the Dust Bowl, and many dust storms started there. But the entire region, and eventually the entire country, was affected."

Timothy Egan wrote the following in his excellent book **The Worst Hard Time**: "March and April were the worst months of the year — a two-month block of steady wind throwing fine-grained dirt at the High Plains. The cold snap had killed what little wheat that had been planted the previous fall. There was an expanse of fallow land (ploughed but left unseeded) nearly half the size of England, no pasture for cattle, and no food for other animals. The year 1933 was called the worst growing season ever. The dust made both people and animals sick. It was also very difficult to keep things clean. Windows had to be covered as well as any small crack. The dust entered machinery parts making some equipment inoperable or hard to start. Cars just stopped on the roads and highways because the engines were choked with dust. People left their vehicles to find shelter. When they were stopped in a familiar area, the wind and dust blew so hard they had to crawl along the ground and try to find landmarks, such as fences to find their way to shelter."

In 1932, 14 dust storms were recorded on the Plains. In 1933, there were 38 storms. By 1934, it was estimated that 100 million acres of farmland had lost all or most of the topsoil to the winds. By April 1935, there had been weeks of dust storms, but the cloud that appeared on the horizon on Sunday, April 14, 1935, a day that would be known as "Black Sunday," was the worst.

Again, Timothy Egan wrote: "When the big roller crossed into Kansas, it was reported to be two hundred miles wide, with high winds like a tornado turned on its side. In Denver, temperatures dropped twenty-five degrees in an hour, and the city fell into a haze. The sun was blocked. That was just the western edge of the storm. The front edge had charged into Kansas carrying soil from four states.

A telegraph inquiry around 2:30 PM came by Morse code from northern Kansas to the railroad depot in Dodge City, about 35 miles from the Dempster farm:

> *Has the storm hit?*
> The reply came a few minutes later tapped
> from the Dodge City depot:
> *My God! Here it comes!*

Dodge City went black. The front edge of the duster looked two thousand feet high. A few minutes earlier, there had been bright sunshine and a temperature of eighty-one degrees, without a wisp of wind. Drivers turned on their headlights and could not see ahead of them, or even the person sitting next to them. It was like three midnights in a jug, one old nester said. Cars died, their systems shorted out by the static. People fled to tornado shelters, gymnasiums, fire stations, and church basements. There was a whiff of panic, not felt in earlier storms, as fear took hold that the end was near."

A series on **Public Television**, titled "American Experience" depicted in stark reality the power of the dust storms, and the trials of the people in their struggle to survive. The storm on Black Sunday was the last major dust storm of the year, and the damage it caused was not calculated for months. Coming on the heels of a stormy season, the April 14 storm hit as many others had, only harder. "The impact is like a shovelful of fine sand flung against the face," Avis D. Carlson wrote in a **New Republic** article. "People caught in their own yards grope for the doorstep. Cars come to a standstill, for no light in the world can penetrate that swirling murk. The nightmare is deepest during the storms. But, on the occasional bright day and the usual gray day, we cannot shake from it. We live with the dust, eat it, sleep with it, and watch it strip us of possessions and the hope of possessions. It is becoming **Real**. The poetic uplift of spring fades into a phantom of the storied past. The nightmare is becoming life."

The Dust Bowl got its name on April 15, 1935, the day after Black Sunday. Robert Geiger, a reporter for the **Associated Press**, traveled through the region and wrote the following: "Three little words, achingly familiar on a western

Dust Storm, Texas, 1935

farmer's tongue, rule life in the dust bowl of the continent — if it rains." Geiger's term "Dust Bowl" stuck, spreading to radio broadcasts, publications, private letters, and public speeches. Geiger intended for the emphasis to be on the generally used phrase "if it rains" but the words "Dust Bowl" were what people remembered.

Chapter 2: The Dempster Farm, 1932, Offerle, Kansas

Mom and Dad decided they had enough moving and staying with relatives, so in the summer of 1932, they moved to the Dempster farm south of Offerle. The house was built by Grandpa Dempster in 1920. At least, they could grow farm products for their fare, and they expected to find some kind of work. By the time I was three years old, I had lived in six places. You can see how important it was to have the support of family during these hard times. The house hadn't been lived in for some time, so Mom and Dad had a lot of work to do. The barn had burned, and all that was left on the farm was the house, a granary, and a chicken house. Mom's father, John Boehme, gave us a Holstein cow, and Dad built a shed for the cow alongside the granary. Shortly after moving to the farm, Uncle Earl Lightcap, who lived on a farm about three miles away, gave us chickens. This brood of chickens was the start of the Dempster egg business.

Mom and Dad did not know that the dust storms, now moving across the Kansas prairie, would become a way of life for them. We were not pioneers, but we lived like pioneers. The only advantage we had was an automobile. My mother's life was different from the life she lived before she was married. Grandpa Boehme was a successful farmer, and the family lived in a comfortable house on Highway 50, a half mile east of Offerle. Dad had previously lived on a farm and was accustomed to rugged farm life, but neither of my parents had previously experienced the environmental and economic disasters of the 1930s. We had a place to live, and I am sure that was a comfort to my parents, but being **dead broke** must have been disheartening for them.

Both of my Boehme grandparents were very charitable, helping those in need. An example of this is found in an article that appeared in the **Kinsley Mercury** of November 12, 1925.

> "SERVICE MONEY COULD NOT BUY: Offerle Man Does Work for Strangers and Refuses Pay.
>
> Unlimited praise has been given to John Boehme, a farmer living just east of the city, for the unselfish help he rendered to Price Wheller, field manager of the Garden City Sugar Co. and Willard Welsh, farm editor of the **Hutchinson News and Herald** during the blizzard.
>
> The two men left Kinsley Friday morning in the storm, expecting to be able to drive through to Dodge City before the roads became blocked. They stated that the only way they could tell where the road was, was by the rows of telephone poles stretching along each side. There were two inches or more of snow on the ground and the air was full of the flaky icicles, which were driven by a strong wind.
>
> Mr. Wheller, who was driving his Ford coupe, had to open the window of the coupe in order to see the road ahead. The snow fell so thick that when about a mile and a half from Offerle, the car went through a snow drift and sank down in a deep ditch. The two men were unable to budge it, so taking a sheepskin coat to hold over their heads, they hiked through

> the storm for a mile to the home of Mr. Boehme.
>
> He had just located his own home after being lost in the pasture for nearly three hours, on the way home from his brother's farm, where he went to care for some cattle. He was riding his saddle horse and discovered he was riding in a circle. He stated that he was so cold he could not tell which way the wind was blowing. Finally he got off his horse, and let the animal loose, believing that the horse's instinct would lead him to the stable. By following the animal, Mr. Boehme reached his home in safety.
>
> In spite of his face being nearly frozen, and his eyelids being decorated with icicles, Mr. Boehme offered to hitch up his team and help the two stranded strangers get the car out of the ditch. It took three hours to accomplish this task because the snow had drifted almost entirely over the car.
>
> After the job had been completed, Mr. Boehme refused to accept payment for his assistance. He declared that he wouldn't have gone out in that storm for any man's money but still he did it because he felt it his duty to assist any fellow man he found in trouble."

On Christmas Eve 2016, at our church, St. Martin's Lutheran Church in Annapolis, Pastor Dave Oravec opened his sermon by citing my grandfather's saga: Darrell's grandfather rode on horseback to his brother's farm to care for some cattle. He did this despite an encroaching blizzard. When this job was completed, he pointed the horse towards home, but by that time the storm was at full tilt with almost zero visibility. Mindful of his family and responsibilities at home, he set off into the storm. However, he soon came to the frightening realization that he was lost and traveling in circles. His very life was in danger. Thankfully, he had a brilliant idea. He decided that if he stopped trying to navigate, if he got off the horse and simply followed his horse, his trusty friend might just know the way home. So he dismounted and followed his horse that evening, and sure enough, the horse knew the way. It led him home — all the way back to the stable.

Pastor Dave then talked about the busyness of the season and how people are called to "dismount, let go of the reigns," and let the power of the Christmas story lead the way. When we do this, we will be led back home, back to the stable where the Christ child was born. God changes everything.

I am not surprised that Grandpa Boehme would perform a good deed such as this. He was a very giving person, as was Grandma Boehme. My mother told me that during the Great Depression, Grandpa often gave gasoline from his gas storage tank to travelers, mostly going west, who were stranded on Highway 50 with no money. Grandma also gave them food. When hoboes stopped and were willing to work for food, Grandma would help them. There were also gypsies on the highway and when they stopped and wanted food, one had to be wary because they were not always honest. They sometimes stole from the farmers. I was told a story that one day gypsies stopped at the farm, and when Grandma turned her back, the gypsies stole a pie and left. This seems to be a small price to pay for someone in need.

Grandma Dempster (Ethel) lost her job as a cook for the jail in the Hutchinson Courthouse, so Grandpa and Grandma Dempster and their daughter, Geraldine, came to live with us on the farm for the winter of 1932. Geraldine, who was in the 11th grade, said that the Dempsters stuffed me, Darrell, with grapes, bacon, and Rice Krispies. I would have both hands and mouth full of grapes, with juice running down my chin, and would manage to ask, "Dot more drapes?" Since Geraldine was in high school, she lived with Mrs. Sams in Offerle, worked for her room and board, and went to school there during the week.

Grandpa liked to tell the story about Darrell going to the mail box with him, which was about a quarter mile down the lane, and saying, "Grandpa, yet me get the yetters." It was also during this time that I learned lessons in sharing. Grandpa Dempster would buy a Hershey bar for me, and I would break off pieces and go around the room saying, "This piece has your name on it." Before long, I had given away all the pieces and had none left for me. The next year, 1933, Grandma got her job back at the courthouse, so Grandma, Grandpa, and Aunt Geraldine moved back to Hutchinson.

As previously mentioned, dirt and sand were blowing across the plains of Kansas and thistles and dirt piled up against fences. Wilma and I were sometimes sent to the Mathes' farm, about a quarter mile away, to get milk. For us, this was not a chore as the Mathes family had two girls about our ages, and we would linger and play with them for a time. When we went across the field, we would climb up a pile of dust and over the fence.

Dust Bowl — Kansas hills

The dirt blew through the doors and windows of the farmhouse, and each day Mom would have to clean and sweep the dirt from the house. Swarms of locusts would cloud the sky, swoop down, and eat every leaf from the few trees on the farm. Mom left a freshly baked pie on the counter one night, and the next morning, it was covered with dust.

My brother, John, was born in 1934. When he was a baby, Mom would wet a sheet and put it over John's crib, so the dust and sand wouldn't pile up on him. John was small and his first two years were hard as he was sick so much. In the winter of 1935–1936, when I was in the first grade, John was sick, and

Mom and Dad took him to the hospital in Spearville, about 10 miles from our farm. John was seen by young Doctor Spears who could not determine a specific diagnosis. Mom and Dad were about to leave the hospital when the older Doctor Spears came into the hospital and asked what was wrong with John. Mom and Dad explained the situation. After examining John, he said that John might have polio. Doctor Spears gave John blood from a known polio victim. John recovered from this illness and did not have similar problems in the future, except that he did not walk until he was two years old.

It must have been very difficult for Grandma and Grandpa Boehme to watch our family struggle in such difficult times. It must have also been difficult for Grandpa and Grandma Dempster to see us live through these times, but they were almost destitute themselves and could not help us as much as the Boehmes. I can almost see us visiting the Boehmes and returning to our farm with vegetables and meat.

Aunt Geraldine has some memories of the dust and sand storms. "I walked south to school from Mrs. Sams' house and the wind blew sand so hard that it was like tiny needles striking you. The wind did not have to be blowing, as one time we were on our way to Kinsley and the dust was so thick, like fog, that we could hardly see. Many times I held a wet washcloth over my mouth and nose to filter out the dust. The next two or three years after we moved back to Hutchinson, the dust would just roll in like a cloud. The downtown merchants covered their merchandise with sheets and closed their stores. Those dust storms were a real phenomenon."

A major financial crisis occurred about this time. The Dempster cow suffered calf-birth complications, and Dad raced into Offerle to get the "vet." On the way, he took Mom, Wilma, and me to the Boehmes in Offerle. This was a Sunday and he had trouble rounding up the "vet." When he returned to the Boehmes, he brought news that the cow and calf had both died. Grandpa Boehme gave us another Holstein cow.

One day, Mom found that the milk had turned sour. The milk was cooled by placing it in the cattle water tank and letting the water from the windmill cool it. Since Mom needed milk for John, she milked the Holstein to get enough milk to feed John. This was the only time that Mom ever milked a cow. Dad did most of the milking, but when I was about five years old, sometimes that chore fell to me, although I never considered milking a cow to be a chore.

My sister Phyllis was born in the Spearville hospital in 1936, so by the time my mother was 24 and my father was 28, they had four children.

Dempster farm,
Offerle, Kansas, 1936
Darrell, John, and Dad

We had some income from farm products, and we always planted a big garden. Mom took eggs, chickens, butter, and cream to the grocer in Offerle where they would be sold or traded for other food (barter economy). Saturday was the day to go to Offerle to shop and discuss the "affairs of state" with the other farmers from around Offerle. This group was called the "spit and whittle" club — from the fact that they chewed tobacco and whittled sticks with pocket knives.

There was a Saturday night movie shown on the side of Joe Basgall's General Store. Car seats were taken out of cars and placed on the ground for seating. There was no sound, so we had sub-titles. Some people could not read from a distance, or could not read at all, and some could not hear well, so someone read to them. For the nearly deaf, the speaker had to speak loudly. Mom said this was very distracting, and she tried to sit as far away from them as possible.

We saw Charlie Chaplin movies, as well as western movies. We were almost in cowboy country, and the movies depicted, in a way, our way of life. These movies included well-known stars: Gene Autry, Roy Rogers, and William Boyd (Hop-Along Cassidy), and their sidekicks — Andy Devine, Gabby Hayes, and, of course, The Sons of the Pioneers. I didn't see a movie with sound until my family moved to Kinsley in 1937.

One day, we went to the Arkansas River, about one mile distant, probably for a picnic. The river was very shallow and about 10-feet wide. I went into the water for a dip. I remember that I thought that if the current took me down the river, I might fall off the end of the earth. Since Kansas was "flat as a pancake," I must have thought the earth was also flat.

Speaking of flat, is Kansas really as flat as a pancake? Three researchers from Texas State University and Arizona State University did scientific research on this question and made a report in the **Annals of Improbable Research**. Their findings, based on digitized data and mathematical techniques, determined that Kansas was considerably flatter than a pancake. The authors further stated that the flatness might be described, mathematically, as "damn flat."

I went to see the Arkansas River south of Offerle near the old Dempster farm in 2013. There was not a drop of water in the river. The big cottonwood trees had died because the water table was so low that they had no moisture.

Dead cottonwood trees,
Arkansas River, 2013

There is a large flow of water from the source of the Arkansas River at Leadville, Colorado, in the Rocky Mountains to Pueblo, Colorado. The website for Pueblo, Colorado, advertises their European-style River Walk featuring outside dining. The Pueblo environs also have white water rafting. Wichita, Kansas, down river from Offerle, has water in the Arkansas River — Wichita also has a River Walk.

Where does the water go between Pueblo and Offerle, and where does the water come from before the river reaches Wichita? There is significant irrigation from the Arkansas River, and the water is significantly depleted by the time it reaches southwest Kansas. There has been conflict between Colorado and Kansas regarding the use of the Arkansas River water. Lawsuits have been filed and argued in the Supreme Court. To this day, there is still conflict.

The Arkansas River is the sixth-longest river in the United States and the 45th longest in the world. It originates in the Rocky Mountains of Colorado and runs through Kansas, Oklahoma, and Arkansas before it reaches the Mississippi at Napoleon, Arkansas, a distance of about 1,450 miles. A system of dams was constructed on the Arkansas River from Tulsa, Oklahoma, to the Mississippi River, to make the Arkansas River navigable for 445 miles. So, you can see there is plenty of water available, but not in a large portion of Kansas.

During the 1980s, I flew over Kansas many times on a route that passed over the Arkansas River basin starting at Great Bend, Kansas, and continuing through western Kansas to Colorado. Starting at Kinsley, Kansas, and continuing through eastern Colorado, the landscape is covered with fields of irrigated crops visible in each section (640 acres=one square mile) going on for endless miles. Since irrigation is conducted by sprinklers that rotate in circles, each portion of a section has a circle of green with mostly brown at the corners where the water does not reach.

Although the Arkansas River was dry, water was being pumped from the underground Ogallala Aquifer. The crops were a verdant green, but the river was dry. At this time, it looked from the air as if western Kansas and eastern Colorado were getting a lot of irrigation water, but at what cost? In recent years, the aquifer water level has decreased significantly, and replenishment will take thousands of years. This decrease is ongoing despite efforts to be more efficient with the use of water. In conclusion, my home state of Kansas is damn dry as well as damn flat.

Regarding my time of "swimming" in the Arkansas River and my fear of the "Great River" taking me downstream to who knows where, I did some research on where the river goes. I found that the mouth of the Arkansas River was near Napoleon, Arkansas, or should I say **was** near where Napoleon, Arkansas, used to be!

In **Life on the Mississippi**, Mark Twain tells us that he was already "in a pretty sour humor" before he ascended to the hurricane deck and told Captain McCord, "I have come to say good-bye, captain. I wish to go ashore at Napoleon." The captain glanced up at the pilothouse and said, "He wants to get off at Napoleon! Why, hang it, don't you know? There isn't any Napoleon any more. Hasn't been for years and years. The Arkansas River burst through it, tore it all to rags, and emptied it into the Mississippi!"

Twain reports being flabbergasted. "Carried the whole town away — banks, churches, jails, newspaper offices, courthouse, theater, fire department, livery stable, everything?" "Everything," came the reply. "Didn't leave hide nor hair, shred nor shingle of it, except the fag-end of a shanty and one brick chimney. This boat is paddling along right now where the dead-center of where that town used to be; yonder is the brick chimney — all that's left of Napoleon."

What Twain then squinted at was the remains of the history of a town that saw La Salle's participation in America's first Catholic mass; the destroyed dreams of a French officer, Frederick Notrebe, who was in exile from Napoleon Bonaparte's France and named the town after his former commander; the Trail of Tears; and the destruction of Napoleon precipitated by the Civil War. The Trail of Tears was the forced removal of Indian tribes from their homes in the Southeastern US to areas west of the Mississippi that had been designated as Indian Territory. Many Indians died during this migration.

Napoleon's demise began in the winter of 1862–63 when Union forces occupied Napoleon. The narrow Beulah Bend in the Mississippi River was guarded by Confederate cannon on the Mississippi side (the side opposite Napoleon) that could easily fire on Union gunboats. In order to protect their travel on the river, Union troops dug a canal from the Mississippi River to the Arkansas River. The canal not only diverted the river away from the bend, but in time, directed the flow of the Mississippi towards Napoleon. The diverted river slowly eroded the river bank and Napoleon crumbled into the Mississippi River. (From "Death Comes For Napoleon" by Mitch Gould; Desha County Historical Society Journal, "River Towns, River Boats, River People," Spring, 1977)

The demise of Napoleon, Arkansas, is another example of a federal program intended to serve the public good, in this case protection of Union shipping, but having unintended, disastrous, and tragic results. This story may as well be titled "Destruction of Napoleon, Arkansas, by Union Army — a Man-Made Disaster."

The Dempster farm was very near the Santa Fe Trail that connected Missouri and Santa Fe, New Mexico. Between 1821 and 1880, it was used by Mexican and American traders. In 1846, the Mexican-American War began. The Army of the West followed the Santa Fe Trail to invade the territory of New Mexico. When the Treaty of Guadalupe Hidalgo ended the war in 1848, the Santa Fe Trail became a national road connecting the United States to the new southwest territories. Commercial freighting along the trail continued, including considerable military freight to supply the southwestern forts. A stagecoach line was established on the trail. Thou-Thousands of gold seekers used the stagecoach as they headed to the California and Colorado gold fields. Adventurers, fur trappers, immigrants, and gamblers also used the stagecoach. In 1880, the railroad reached Santa Fe, and the trail faded into history.

Dinner Station, Santa Fe Trail marker

The wet route of the Santa Fe Trail was about one mile from the Dempster farm. Though longer, the wet route had the benefit of being near the Arkansas River and a supply of water. The dry route was shorter, but the risk was greater because of lack of water.

When our family went to the Arkansas River, we were on land that had been traveled about 50 years earlier by settlers taking part in the Great Western Migration. The dry route passed near Offerle. Uncle Elmer Boehme had some acreage south of Offerle that still had what looked like original sod when I worked on the Boehme farm in the 1930s and 1940s. I liked to imagine that I saw the ruts of wagon wheels — maybe I did, maybe I didn't. This acreage was very near Mule Head

Hill where a Santa Fe Trail marker denotes the spot as "Dinner Station." I would show a picture of Mule Head Hill, but it is only a few feet above the rest of the landscape. It is surmised that meals were served to stagecoach passengers at Dinner Station. Also, the Hixon homestead was very near Dinner Station.

My great-grandmother, Sarah Hixon, who married William McChesney Lightcap in 1881, lived on this homestead, and her five children, including my grandmother, Luella Lightcap Boehme, were born there. The Hixon family migrated from Illinois in 1878, when Sarah was 16 years old. The

My grandmother, Luella Lightcap Boehme, age 40, my mother, Catharine Boehme Dempster, age 18, myself, and my great-grandmother, Sarah Catherine Hixon Lightcap, age 67, in 1929

Hixons traveled by train to Kansas and settled on a farm about four miles southwest of Offerle. The Hixons established an orchard on the farm and planted numerous trees.

I started school in Offerle in 1935, and I walked down a lane about a quarter mile to catch the school bus. I was the last to be picked up. I had to be at the road at the end of our lane when the school bus came. I could not wait in the house and look for the school bus and then run down the lane. In the heavy snow storms of the winter, I got pretty cold waiting for the bus that was often delayed due to the nine miles of snow-covered roads it had to travel from Offerle. Sometimes the roads were closed, and eventually I realized I had to return home. The next year, Betty Mathes, who lived on the next farm farther away, started school, so I could wait for the bus to pass on the way to her farm, before I walked down the lane.

At the beginning of the 1935 school year, there were six students in my class: Sonny, Marvin, Tommy, Beatrice, another girl, and myself. Beatrice was deemed too advanced to be in the first grade, so she was moved to the second grade. The other girl had a learning problem, and she was sent to another school, now called an alternative school. So, there were just us four boys in the first grade. The first and second grades were in the same classroom.

1920s–1930s school bus

Arriving home on the school bus was the most anticipated part of my day. I would rush up the lane to our house and turn on the radio to hear afternoon radio serial programs. My favorite was "The Lone Ranger" with his sidekick "Tonto" and the great stallion "Silver." The Lone Ranger was to have more significance to me later when I was stationed on the US Navy aircraft carrier **USS Ranger (CVA-61)** from 1969–1971. That duty included two eight-month deployments in the Tonkin Gulf between Vietnam and the Chinese island of Hainan. Almost every day at sea, we had underway replenishment of supplies, provisions, fuel, and ammunition from another ship, as we sailed alongside each other. We had a life-sized replica of the great horse, Silver, the ship's mascot. During the replenishment, one of our sailors, dressed as the Lone Ranger, rode Silver, mounted on an aircraft tow tractor, as the "William Tell Overture," the Lone Ranger theme song, blared over the ship's loud speakers. Silver had a registered brand, Top Gun Bar None, signified by the letters "TG" over a bar with the numeral "0" under the bar. We were also known as "Top Gun of the Pacific Fleet." It was a great celebration and an expected event by all ships that came alongside.

Another radio show that I listened to was the "Green Hornet" with his super-powered car "Black Beauty" and his multi-talented valet, "Kato." The "Green Hornet" was a thrill-packed radio adventure, and it was a great pastime listening to the exploits of this crime-fighting hero. In addition to the daily drama, I listened to the advertisements in amazement at the wonders of the world — maybe it was just the United States or Kansas. Secret rings, secret codes, and disappearing ink were some of the items I ordered. The items were paid for with postage stamps; the cost of each item was about 25 cents. After placing an order, I would check the mail box when I arrived home from school, and hopefully, my order had arrived, and I would be able to communicate with my friends secretly or decipher codes I heard on the radio. Of course, to communicate with friends, they also had to have the same code.

I experienced rejection very soon after school started when I was not selected as the music leader — of course, we were also competing against the second grade, as we were in one classroom. The music leader was the one who would wave the baton in front of the class. I don't remember who was selected, but it wasn't me. Perhaps the teacher was evening things out and I had forgotten any triumphs I may have had. My musical ability continued on a downward trend, as in the eighth grade, when we were living in Wichita, Kansas, I received a grade of "D" playing the French horn. This was too much, so I quit the music class. I probably added woodworking or typesetting that was more suited to my ability.

I had fair grades in the first and second grades, the lowest being a grade of C minus in citizenship. I have no idea what attributes made up citizenship, but, apparently, I was not in possession of these attributes, or, at least, I could not express them. I had mostly C pluses in music, and as I later learned, this was a direct result of my lack of musical ability. I was absent from school only two days during my first two years of school despite the often severe weather conditions and the distance I had to travel from the farm to Offerle. I attribute my excellent school attendance record to the school bus driver and the efforts of my parents and grandparents in getting me ready and off to school.

President Franklin D. Roosevelt (FDR) proposed to Congress on March 21, 1933, a public works employment program to help alleviate poverty. The program included projects for the public good, such as prevention of soil erosion, forestry, and flood control. Congress enacted the law that established the Civilian Conservation Corps (CCC) on March 31, 1933 — an interval of ten days.

The CCC was a public works relief program that operated from 1933 to 1942 for unemployed, unmarried men from poor families, ages 18–25, as part of Roosevelt's New Deal. The CCC provided unskilled, manual-labor jobs related to the conservation and development of natural resources in rural lands owned by federal, state, and local governments. The CCC was designed to provide jobs and relieve families who had difficulty finding jobs during the Great Depression, while at the same time implementing a general natural resource conservation program in every state and territory. Maximum enrollment at any one time was 300,000. In nine years, three million young men participated in the CCC which provided them with shelter, clothing, and food, together with a small wage of $30 a month. The young men were required to send $25 of their monthly pay home to their families. They were often the family breadwinners.

The American public made the CCC the most popular of all the New Deal programs. Principal benefits of an individual's enrollment in the CCC included improved physical condition, increased morale, and increased employability. The CCC also led to a greater public awareness and appreciation of the outdoors, the nation's natural resources, and the continued need for a carefully planned, comprehensive national program for the protection and development of natural resources. My brother John, a long-time Boeing Aircraft Company employee, told me in 2016 that many of his supervisors, when he started at Boeing in 1956, were graduate engineers in the 1930s and worked for the CCC in designing and supervising projects.

In 1965, when I was stationed at the Naval Postgraduate School in Monterey, California, we went on a weekend camping trip to the Pinnacles National Monument. I read in a Pinnacles brochure of the many projects that the CCC had completed there. We went on a hike, and as we crossed a ridge, we descended to a valley on steps that had been hewn out of rock by the CCC. A hand rail had also been installed.

Today, when I see idle youth and young men and women standing on street corners throughout neighborhoods, wandering in and out of public housing projects, and engaged in illegal pursuits, I wonder why the President doesn't establish a program similar to the CCC. Of course, there would be adverse comments from self-interest groups as Roosevelt encountered when he established the CCC, but the public good would outweigh the perceived detrimental effects. The program could achieve the same benefit of individual self-worth that the CCC achieved in the 1930s, and also serve the public good by completing public projects long needed but not funded.

Pinnacles National Monument, California, CCC trail project

There were many movies depicting life in the CCC. The main one that I remember was **Pride of the Bowery**, a 1940 movie starring Leo Gorcey as Muggs McGinnis. The primary theme of the Bowery Boys' movies was always redemption. The movies gave me a view of life in the big city, a life in vivid contrast to our lives in the wide-open spaces of Kansas. I could not imagine living in the crowded conditions of the tenement dwellings of a big city. Would I have been "tough" like Muggs and been able to survive as he did? Of course, the movies also provided entertainment and taught life values of redemption and comradeship.

There were many prominent members of the CCC including Hyman G. Rickover, Four-Star Admiral, and CCC Area Commander; Raymond Burr, actor; Archie Moore, light-heavyweight boxing champion; Robert Mitchum, actor; Chuck Yeager, test pilot (first human to break the sound barrier); Stan Musial, baseball player; Walter Matthau, actor; and Red Schoendienst, baseball player/manager. Stan Musial and Red

Schoendienst were players with the St. Louis Cardinals who I remember well from listening to their games in the 1940s. The games we listened to were all played during the day — night baseball was very rare.

The Pearl Harbor attack of December 1941 inspired many of the CCC members to join the Armed Forces. Also, a majority of the members, being of age and physically fit, were drafted. Due to their CCC discipline and military-like experiences, these men had a significant head start and provided the Armed Forces with instant leadership. They significantly contributed to the defense of our country and victory in World War II.

During the operation of the CCC, volunteers planted nearly three billion trees to help reforest America, constructed more than 800 parks nationwide, upgraded most state parks, updated forest fire-fighting methods, and built a network of service buildings and public roadways in remote areas. One of the major CCC projects was the construction of shelterbelts in the Midwest states of North Dakota, South Dakota, Nebraska, Kansas, Oklahoma and Texas. A shelterbelt is a windbreak built on the side of a field, and, generally, by a road or highway with larger trees in the middle and gradually smaller trees towards the sides, forming an upside down "V." There were also single lines of trees planted around individual grain fields and pastures. The plan was to diminish the velocity of the wind along the ground by the configuration of the trees. There would then be fewer tendencies for the soil to be carried away by the wind, thereby avoiding what happened during the Dust Bowl. Farmers were also paid to plant trees and to maintain shelterbelts on their property.

I saw these shelterbelts planted in the mid-1930s, and the name shelterbelt became a part of our vocabulary. If you had to stop your car while traveling, it was best to stop by a shelterbelt. The shelterbelt provided a wind break and shade. If it was your duty, as a child, to roundup the cows and drive them home for milking, and it was hot, you would often find the cows in the shade of the shelterbelt.

When we lived in Wichita and drove to Offerle for a holiday, I saw many shelterbelts along Highway 50. The shelterbelts remain to this day, but in many cases, the original scheme of planting the trees to form a windbreak has been overtaken by the death of the original trees and the growth of trees not suited to form a windbreak. It was up to individual farmers to maintain the shelterbelts on their properties.

Dad borrowed a truck from his father-in-law, John Boehme, and along with his father, Ben, hauled sand from the riverbed for road projects on Highway 50 and county roads. Dad was not eligible to join the CCC because he was married and had children, but he provided sand for CCC projects. Dad also surveyed land by means of a large wheel that was operated by a person sitting on a tractor seat installed on the rear of a car. I helped Dad, sometimes, by riding on the tractor seat and handling the large measuring wheel. The land was measured to determine the total acreage that could be planted by each farmer. This restriction on acreage planted was to prevent over production of crops, and the consequent reduced prices of crops sold by farmers.

Were we poor? If we were, I didn't know it. There were people poorer or less well off than we were. There was a large family in Offerle who lived in a dugout house with about half the house below the ground. I remember seeing some of the children on the street and in school with ragged, patched clothing. They were a nice family and didn't seem to mind their plight — there was absolutely no bullying or disdain shown to them. My parents would have never allowed this to happen. Since I was the oldest in my family, I didn't wear hand-me-down clothing, but I wore patched clothing. I wore trousers I had outgrown, and I wore clothing that was too big for me so I could grow into them.

I remember asking my mother if Uncle Earl Lightcap was rich (remember Uncle Earl gave us a brood of chickens when we moved to the Dempster Farm). I was very familiar with Uncle Earl's farm that was about three miles from our farm. Uncle Earl's youngest son, Gerald, was six months younger, and I visited his farm often, frequently staying overnight. Uncle Earl lived in a very nice house and had several out buildings, including a spring house for use as cool storage for food items that today would be stored in a refrigerator. Thus, I thought the family was rich. I don't remember Mom's exact answer, but it was along this line: "No, they aren't rich. They are a family just like we are."

Great Grandfather Alex, Great Grandmother Lizzie Thorn Dempster, Great Aunt Nellie and Grandfather Ben Dempster, about 1890

Dad and sisters, Geraldine and Opal, about 1925

Offerle, Kansas girls basketball team, 1927, Mom front row left, Cousin Mozelle Quisenberry, back row, 2nd from right

Darrell and sister, Wilma, 1933

Mom and Dad, 50th wedding anniversary, 1978

Boiler, Threshing Machine, and Cook House and horse with buggy in front of Cook House, Dempster farm near Great Bend, Kansas, about 1913. From right on Cook House steps, Grandma Dempster, Opal, and Dad. Grandpa Ben Dempster is second from left with white shirt and tie.

Chapter 3: Move to the City, Kinsley, Kansas — 1937

In 1936, John Boehme was elected county commissioner and one of his most important acts was to use the political spoils system to appoint Dad as janitor of the Edwards County Courthouse in Kinsley. I wonder what kind of an agreement Grandpa made to get us this privilege. Dad's wages were $90 per month — his first regular and steady job. My family rented a house and moved to Kinsley in early 1937, and I stayed with Grandma and Grandpa Boehme, so I could finish the second grade in Offerle.

Grandma and Grandpa's house was full of people again — Uncle Elmer was 22, and living at home, and Aunt Donna was three years old. I walked to school most of the time, except for real bad weather. I had a short walk across a field, where I crossed Highway 50 and the railroad tracks, and then had a half mile walk to school. As I walked on the road beside the railroad tracks, I passed a row of one-story concrete houses that were homes to the families of railroad workers, called section hands. They were called section hands because they were responsible for maintenance of a certain section/distance of the railroad. The section hands were of Mexican heritage. The concrete buildings were divided into about four housing units. Each unit was one or two rooms — the housing units were sparsely furnished. There were Mexican children living there, but none of them were in my school classes. One of my first-grade classmates, Beatrice Basgall, reported in her oral history that there were some Mexicans in the Offerle School. Beatrice graduated from Offerle High School, whereas I attended only the first and second grades there. I do remember playing with some Mexican boys on my way to and from school. Perhaps I can remember this because they taught me to say "dirty" words in Spanish.

Darrell and Wilma (sister), Dempster farm house,
Kinsley, Kansas, 2013

For a short time we lived across the street from the courthouse in Kinsley. We later rented the Jenkins' house a short distance away. Dad moved the Dempster farmhouse to Kinsley in 1938 and this became the Dempster home the remaining time we were in Kinsley. Moving the farm house was a big deal, requiring a ten-mile trip, over a quarter-mile dirt lane, a five-mile gravel road with three turns, a steep railroad crossing, about four miles on Highway 50, and seven blocks through the streets of Kinsley. The house came through in good shape.

The first thing Dad did was to install water, electric lines, and a bathroom, although I remember the first few days we lived in the house, we took baths in the kitchen in the tin tub we used on the farm. There wasn't much bathing privacy. When my sister, Wilma, and I saw the house in 2013, it was a beautiful house with a well-manicured lawn and shrubbery with some additions to the old square farm house that had been built in 1920.

Mom supplemented the family income by washing cloth mops for the courthouse. She washed about 10 mops per month at 50 cents per mop. Wouldn't you think Dad would dirty more mops, so Mom could make more money? Perhaps he was concerned that others would think there was a bit of nepotism involved, and he thought this was all the "market could bear." After all, we were already benefiting from nepotism — it was a good job and Dad didn't want to take any unnecessary risks.

I began collecting postage stamps. I was fascinated by colorful foreign stamps and would search for these countries on world maps and globes. Dad received many visits from traveling salesmen selling janitorial supplies. One of these salesmen heard about my stamp collecting and said he would send me a stamp album. At that time, I was organizing my collection on notebook paper and in envelopes. I waited for weeks and never received the stamp album. Perhaps he was disappointed that Dad didn't buy supplies from him.

We "helped" Dad around the courthouse — or as we say now, we hung out with him. I cleaned the spittoons. They were made of brass, and to the uninitiated, they were used as cigarette and cigar ash trays and as receptacles for discarding chewing tobacco juice. The chewers often missed the spittoon if they spat from a distance. But, of course, it was a source of pride to a "spitter" if he could hit the spittoon from a distance. There were many misses and it was my job to clean up this mess. The finished job was a highly polished brass spittoon — an enviable accessory for the office of a "gentleman," especially for the judge. There were many scenes in cowboy movies of law-abiding citizens and the "bad guys" spitting into spittoons, especially while playing card games.

One of the playtime activities Wilma and I enjoyed was to go a couple blocks south to the railroad siding and climb to the top of the railroad cars loaded with sugar beets. These car loads of sugar beets were being transported from western Kansas to the sugar beet processing plant in Kansas City.

We would always look through the courthouse trash each evening to find "useful" items. One of the useful items we looked for every January was leftover Christmas decoration stamps — the size of a postage stamp in sheets of 100 each. We used these stamps to decorate items such as cardboard boxes — great fun.

Dad took up woodworking during this time. He used discarded wood and a space in the courthouse basement to manufacture furniture and toys. He surprised us with many Christmas gifts, including a small desk and chair, that all of us kids used. The courthouse front steps had a brass rail and it was our job to polish it. We were playing on the courthouse steps on a cold winter afternoon and there was frost on the rail. My sister, Wilma, licked the rail with her tongue and her tongue became stuck to the rail. Mom came to the courthouse with hot water and loosened Wilma's tongue. Wilma's mistake was a practice that none of us ever repeated — you never touch a hot stove twice to see if it is hot.

I also have memories of fresh-cut grass on the courthouse lawn — the lawn mower didn't have a catcher and Dad raked the grass into piles. We then ran and jumped into the piles of grass and, of course, Dad had to rake the grass again.

During these last two years, our family had moved from just barely surviving to what we considered a comfortable, but austere way of life. During the early 1930s, our family chose to be survivors rather than victims, subsisting entirely on the welfare of others. I use this survivor/victim example from a recent Bible study comment by our pastor, who commented about an American civilian who stepped on a land mine in Israel and had part of his foot blown off. This "victim" went through a rigorous rehabilitation and transformed himself from a victim to a survivor by taking the "bull by the horns" to become a productive and useful citizen of this great country. My parents, albeit with help from my grandfather and others, were moving a bit up the food chain.

Chapter 4: Reelection — The Big Fights, 1936 and 1938

The reelection campaign of my grandfather as Edwards County Commissioner in the summer and fall of 1938 was underway, and one of the reelection events was a chili supper at our house in Kinsley. It was scheduled for the evening of the second "Big Fight" between the American, Joe Louis, and the German, Max Schmeling. Louis and Schmeling had their first boxing match in 1936.

Joe Louis, an African-American known as the Brown Bomber, had a record of 23 wins without a loss leading to the first Joe Louis-Max Schmeling fight. Max Schmeling, a German, was 30 years old and many people thought he would not be a serious threat to Joe Louis. At the time of the fight, there were serious concerns about the direction that Germany was taking. Hitler had taken control of Germany and began persecution of the Jewish people. Suffice it to say that there was a growing tension between the United States and Germany. The fight took place at Yankee Stadium in New York on June 19, 1936. Louis was a hero to most Americans, but especially to the African-American community. Schmeling began the fight with a barrage of blows and had Louis in trouble from the beginning. Schmeling won by a knock out in the 12th round and Louis suffered his first knockout and his first loss. There was sadness in the hearts of Americans as they listened to their radios or read the news of Schmeling's defeat of Louis.

In the two years following the first fight, the United States economy had continued to decline. At the time of the rematch between Louis and Schmeling, Hitler had occupied Austria and tensions were high between the United States and Germany. Schmeling came to the United States amid a flood of anti-German sentiment. The German propaganda was overwhelmingly anti-Jewish and anti-black while touting Schmeling as a purebred Aryan. Schmeling did not like being a part of Nazi propaganda.

The Nazi propaganda insisted that a black man could never defeat Schmeling. Louis met with President Roosevelt and the President told Joe that the entire country was behind him. Louis understood that the fight was more than a boxing match; it was a battle between the United States and the evils of Nazi Germany. Everyone I knew was rooting for Joe Louis, although there were some in America who would rather have seen a white person win, even though he was a German, just because of their relationship with black people. I knew none of this in Kinsley — all schools and facilities were integrated. We wanted a red, white and blue American to win.

The John Boehme reelection supper required a lot of preparation — it was not catered. It was prepared by the Dempster and Boehme women with the help of the wives of friends. The women were busy all day preparing chili, bread, and side dishes. I doubt that the hosts furnished whiskey and beer, although it is probable that some of the guests brought their own "beverages." I never saw my parents or grandparents drink alcohol, although I was told recently that my grandfather, John Boehme, drank alcohol whenever his son-in-law, Ernie, visited from Arkansas in the 1960s and 1970s.

Kansas banned the sale of alcohol from 1881 to 1948, and was the last state to allow the sale of alcohol. Kansas continued to ban the sale of alcohol by the drink until 1986. At the end of 2012, Kansas still had 13 of its 105 counties that prohibited the sale of alcohol by the drink. In addition to being damn flat, you can also say that some of Kansas is also damn dry —yes, dry weather but also dry in the sense of absence of alcohol. Kansas has still not ratified the 21st Amendment to the United States

Constitution. The 21st Amendment repealed the 18th Amendment, which had mandated nationwide prohibition of alcohol on January 16, 1920. The 21st Amendment was ratified December 5, 1933. It is unique among the 27 amendments for being the only one to repeal a previous amendment.

The prohibition of alcohol sales did not stop the consumption of alcohol. The availability continued through sales by bootleggers, a term used in the late 19th century in the western states to describe the practice of concealing a bottle of liquor in the top of a boot and under the trousers when trading with Indians. Bootleggers obtained liquor from Mexico, Canada, and from medicinal liquor sold in drugstores by prescription. These prescriptions were written by doctors, but some of the time they were forged. Does this sound like the illegal drug problem we have today? Also, as law enforcement began to crack down on the import of foreign liquor, bootleggers began to rely on local liquor made in homemade stills, the quality of which varied from awful to poisonous.

There were many deaths caused by consuming this illegal liquor. Again, does this sound like a problem we have with illegal drugs today? The illegal liquor was called "moonshine," because it was safer to operate the still at night under the light of the moon. The US government agent enforcing the ban of liquor was called a "revenoor." The local revenue authorities disposed of confiscated liquor in a vacant lot behind our house. The liquor bottles were broken and the liquor ran into the ground, or most of it did as there was talk that the local sheriff or revenoor often kept a few bottles for themselves. Even at the age of nine I was aware of what a revenoor was. My Uncle Gene Quisenberry told a joke about the revenoor who was standing on a railroad platform. The revenoor spotted a man carrying a bag and saw a stream of liquid coming out of the bag. He went up to the man holding the bag and touched the liquid with his finger, tasted it, and said to the man, "You have two bottles of Jack Daniels liquor in the bag." The man opened the bag, showed the contents to the revenoor and said, "It is not liquor — they are two poodles."

The supper was set up in the yard under a big tree with tables and chairs borrowed from the Christian Church and other churches, a common practice in those days. The attendees began to arrive with their children about 6 PM. For an event like this, if the parents came, the children came as there was no one at home to care for them. The children were left to fend for themselves with the older ones taking care of the younger ones. Iced tea was served and visiting commenced. Grandpa worked the crowd and listened to suggestions and guests complain about issues. It is likely that there were complaints about ex-President Herbert Hoover and FDR. Although Roosevelt had made a lot of progress to alleviate the effects of the Great Depression, there were many who reviled FDR because of some of his social and economic programs, and simply because he was a Democrat. Obviously, if his program helped you, then you were for him and if it hurt you, you were against him. As with many programs today there were often unintended consequences.

The Louis -Schmeling fight started at 9 PM, a late hour for the "early to bed, early to rise" attendees. The men and boys surrounded the radio to listen to the pre-match hoopla at about 8 PM. The women were busy washing the dishes and doing other clean-up chores. The fight lasted just over two minutes. Louis won by a technical knockout and was the heavyweight champion. There was jubilation all over America as the American had defeated the German.

Louis and Schmeling in 1971

Louis was a sports hero and an American celebrity. Louis served in the United States Army in World War II, but did not see combat. Louis defended his title 25 times, retiring in 1949. Louis had financial problems, and one of his last jobs was as a greeter at the Caesar's Palace Hotel in Las Vegas, Nevada. Schmeling served briefly in the German Luftwaffe. After retiring from boxing, Schmeling did very well as a businessman and due to his rejection of Nazi methods; he was highly respected in post-war Germany. Perhaps more remarkable than the two big fights was the friendship that developed between Louis and Schmeling after the war.

Schmeling visited Louis every year and sent Louis money. Joe Louis died in 1981. Schmeling was a pall bearer at Louis' funeral and paid part of the funeral costs. Schmeling died in 2005, just shy of his 100th birthday.

Grandpa won the reelection and my Dad served another two years as the Edwards County Courthouse janitor.

I tried my hand at raising chickens as part of the Victory Chick program. This article was in the Kinsley newspaper April 9, 1940, my 11th birthday:

"Time is Short For Obtaining Chicks:"

> This is the last week for registration in the Wolf Milling Company's Victory Chick Program. Each farm boy or girl who registers for the program will receive 25 of the best baby chicks money can buy and a sack of feed Saturday, April 18.
>
> Registration for the program must be made this week so that the mill can order sufficient chicks to fill the demand. Registrations will be received at the mill office, or at the Wolf Premium Feed store on the highway just north of the mill up to and including Saturday, April 11.
>
> The mill gives the chicks and feed to start them free. The only return the mill asks is that each boy and girl registering to return five roosters to the mill next October. Prizes will be given for the best roosters returned.
>
> This year, when the government is asking for big increases in chicken and egg production, the mill program could prove unusually popular. If you have not registered to date be sure that you get your name in before registrations close this weekend.

We had a fence around the back yard and that area became the chicken pen. I bought the chicks more food and took care of them. Also, Grandpa Boehme gave me some chicken feed. In October, when the chicks were grown, I returned my five prized roosters, and won a few ribbons in the mill contest. Maybe, in the old days, like today, everyone got a prize, but I prefer to think that my roosters were really prize quality. The mill got a good deal — five roosters for 25 chicks and a bag of feed. But, I got a better deal — all my remaining chickens to feed the family and a great experience in the responsibility I had in caring for the chicks. Now it came time to eat the chickens and it was up to me to select one, take the head off by putting my foot on the neck, and pulling the chicken by the legs. It would flop around on the ground until the blood had drained. Another method of killing the chicken was to hold it by the head and swing it round and round until the head came off. I never used this method — it was hard enough for me to kill the chicken by any method as I had cared for the chickens for a few months and they were my friends. I was a chicken farmer for only one year. To this day, chicken is not my favorite meal.

I was getting around Kinsley by walking, and decided I would be more efficient in getting things done, if I had some transportation. I found an old rusty-broken bike on the Boehme farm. I was trying to get it in condition to ride, and Grandpa must have realized it was a hopeless case, so he gave money to my folks (probably about $20 — now these were big bucks, as my father's salary at the court house was $90 per month) to buy a new bike. The bike was purchased in Hutchinson when Mom and Dad took a trip to see Grandpa Dempster. Grandpa was very sick during the end of his life. He died in November 1940. It was certainly a big surprise to me when my folks returned home with the bike.

The bike gave me great mobility. I worked for Wimpy Rehmert delivering the Kinsley paper. I used it to ride downtown to set pins at the bowling alley, and best of all, I rode it the eight miles from Kinsley to Offerle to visit Grandma and Grandpa. By this time I was doing odd jobs around the farm and being trained by Grandma and Grandpa to really do farm work.

Kinsley, Kansas, earned the name "Midway USA" by being exactly 1,561 miles from San Francisco to the west and 1,561 miles to New York in the east, inspiring a 1939 **Saturday Evening Post** cover showing two cars, starting in Kinsley and going in opposite directions, both bearing a sign saying "World's Fair or Bust." In 1939, there were two "World's Fairs" — one in New York, and one in San Francisco.

In 1939, the midpoint sign was located about two miles west of Kinsley. A boy from Kansas could only read or dream about these two great cities. Who could have imagined that in 1948, I joined the Navy, and in that year, I was in both San Francisco and New York. What a country! In 2013, Eddie and I were in Kinsley, and we posed for a photo at the midpoint sign.

Eddie and Darrell Dempster, Kinsley, Kansas, 2013

During the summer, I rode my bike to Offerle and stayed for a week or two with Grandma and Grandpa Boehme. I was given jobs around the farm; basically my job was Grandpa's "sidekick." Aunt Donna, about six years old, and Aunt Ramona and her son, Keith, about three years old, were also living on the Boehme farm. Ramona's husband died in 1938.

Ramona worked at the Offerle drugstore, and my favorite spot there was the soda fountain where I spent my earnings on ice cream sundaes and ice cream sodas created by Aunt Ramona. After the evening meal on the farm, I would ask Aunt Ramona to make fudge. She frequently made fudge, but sometimes she would tell me that she did not have one of the ingredients. That was her way of denying me the joy of instant gratification. She did not really succeed. Fudge and ice cream are still my favorite sweets. I now make my own fudge and share it with anyone who wants it, but I keep a small portion in the refrigerator to raise my spirits.

Even though Dad had a steady job at the courthouse, we were still in pretty bad shape financially, and we took advantage of "commodities" (free food) that were distributed by the government. I used my Red Flyer wagon to pick up our commodities at either a warehouse or from a truck in Kinsley. I don't remember taking any type of form or any other eligibility information with me. I just appeared and picked up the commodities. My favorite was grapefruit — probably the first grapefruit we ever had. Dad said that there was some sort of canned meat that he ate so much during the Depression that now he wouldn't eat it. I am not sure that we received spam with the commodities, but I know we ate spam and I always liked spam. On my 60th birthday, I asked for a menu of spam and cherry pie and that's what we had. The younger generation liked it.

My sister, Wilma, remembers a family across the street who received commodities, and she was jealous because they had apples and oranges. I didn't pick up commodities many times — it was not a regular occurrence. Maybe we stopped getting commodities because we became ineligible or my parents didn't want them anymore. I don't remember feeling embarrassed about getting free food. I just went downtown and picked it up, and I enjoyed eating it. There was a term "being on relief" that I remember hearing a lot where families received assistance from the government, but I never heard my parents talking about us being on relief, although maybe we were as we received free government food.

The commodity distribution program began during the 1930s economic depression that brought widespread unemployment for many American families. With no means to support their families, many sought help through public assistance programs.

During the Depression, farm production created surplus food supplies without adequate markets. Limited family income left school children hungry and the danger of childhood malnourishment became a national concern. The Federal Surplus Commodities Corporation was created to procure and distribute surplus foods to schools and needy families. Items distributed included cheese, butter, canned meat, flour, fruits, and vegetables. Our grade school did not have a school lunch program. I lived close enough to school that I went home for lunch. However, there were many farm families who attended school in Kinsley — they took a bus to school and packed a lunch.

We returned to hard times in 1941 when Dad lost his job at the courthouse as a consequence of Grandpa Boehme not running for reelection for county commissioner. Dad was able to find some work with the Works Progress Administration (WPA) building a bridge across the Arkansas River on Highway 50 on the outskirts of Kinsley. When I talked to Aunt Geraldine (97 years old) in September 2014, she told me that Dad was able to work only two or three days a week, since there were so many unemployed, and one position had to be shared among two or three workers. She also told me that Dad had told her that some of the men were so desperate that they brought potato peels in their lunch boxes for a noon meal. I'll have to fry some potato skins, as I like the crunchiness of the skin of a baked potato.

There were jokes about the WPA worker. Some people called them "leaners," because when you drove on the highway and saw a WPA crew, you would sometimes see them leaning on their picks and shovels. I remember hearing the term, but I don't think my family used it. I think it must have been used by those who had work and thought those working for the WPA were getting paid by government largesse, not remembering that they were benefiting from the projects completed by the WPA.

The WPA was a relief measure established in 1935. The WPA offered work to the unemployed on an unprecedented scale. The programs included projects on highways and building construction, slum clearance, reforestation, and rural rehabilitation. This gigantic undertaking was inevitably attended by confusion, waste and political favoritism, yet it stimulated private business during the Depression years and inaugurated programs that states had been unable to fund.

Most families supplemented their food supply by canning fruits and vegetables. One of the fruits we canned was sand hill plums. These plums grew wild in the sand hills south and east of Kinsley. Saturdays and Sundays were plum picking days. Dad would drive us to the sand hills and all of us would pick plums. They grew on thorny bushes and walking to get to them was difficult because of the sand, but they were free and we picked them. They were canned as jelly, although some people made wine from them.

In 2013, when I was in Offerle for a family reunion, I went to Kinsley on a Saturday and bought some sand hill plum jelly from a Vietnamese woman. She told me that it was a good year for sand hill plums and this reminded me that, just like the wheat crops, there are good and bad years for sand hill plums, with rain, at the right time, the main determinant.

We canned many other fruits and vegetables. I remember Mom taking all of us to her Cousin Maxine's house, about fifteen miles away, for a canning day. It was a mass production, with everyone assigned a duty. It was an all-day affair. Most people stored their canned goods in a basement or storm cellar, but since we had neither, ours were stored in the kitchen.

I joined the Boy Scouts when I turned 12 in April 1941. I was also a Cub Scout, although about the only thing I remember was going with my mother to a meeting at a house on the "other side of the tracks." A Boy Scout trip was planned for July and I needed to pass my Tenderfoot tests before I could go. I did pass, but I also had to earn the money for the trip. I can't remember the cost, but it was probably about $25. The scouts had several sponsors, and I was lucky to be assigned to work for the owner of the movie theater. My job was cutting the grass at his home.

When I was thirsty I could go into his unlocked house and get a drink of water. It was one of the nicer homes in Kinsley and, of course, more richly furnished than our house on the "other side of the tracks." There were some dollar bills on the kitchen table, and I couldn't help but think that this was a test to see if I was "trustworthy"— one of the Boy Scout laws. I can still recite these laws today: A scout is trustworthy, loyal, helpful, friendly, courteous, kind, obedient, cheerful, thrifty, brave, clean, and reverent.

The trip to Camp Birch, in the Rocky Mountains near Pueblo, Colorado (south of Colorado Springs), was to me, at that time, the thrill of a lifetime. About twenty Boy Scouts and leaders traveled in a flatbed truck that had boards placed crosswise for seating. We left Kinsley in the morning for the 300-mile trip on Highway 50 to Camp Birch. Highway 50 was two lanes, and, although paved, I'm sure it was a bit bumpy. I remember grabbing hold of the bench occasionally, as we rolled along. I imagine we averaged no more than 20 mph with all the pit stops for a group of boys. As we traveled through the night, the pit stops were on the side of the road. I don't remember where we slept in the truck, but some of us must have been on the benches and some on the floor bed of the truck. The route took us through Dodge City, Garden City, and Syracuse, Kansas, and Lamar and La Junta, Colorado, to Pueblo, Colorado.

We must have taken food and drink for dinner and supper as we called those two meals in Kansas. Of course, now in the East we call those two meals lunch and dinner. It wasn't until I was in my 20s that I finally became used to using the terms "lunch" and "dinner." I was confused when I was invited to dinner, as to whether I was to arrive at noon time or in the evening.

I do remember that when we arrived in Pueblo, we stopped in a restaurant to have breakfast. I ordered pancakes, and the waitress remarked to me that I was one of the few of us that ordered a real meal — something substantial. I don't remember what other boys ate, but my meal must have cost no more than twenty or twenty-five cents. I probably had about three dollars spending money for the trip. To this day, I do not skip breakfast, even though now it is mostly a bowl of cereal with fruit, a glass of orange juice, and a cup of coffee.

Camp Birch was in the Rocky Mountains, in a rustic and pioneer setting. I don't remember much about the food, but it was probably some of the best food, except for reunions and special meals, that I ever had.

The swimming pool was fed by a mountain stream. Even at that exuberant age, the water felt like it was ice cold. That is where I learned to swim. I also remember the campfire stories. It seemed like the sole intent was to scare us with stories of wild beasts and imaginary predators. The stories did scare me and my dreams of those stories remained with me for awhile.

In 1940, I worked setting bowling pins in the Kinsley Bowling Alley. It was a manual operation, as I set the pins on a spot in the lane. It was a bit tricky to keep from being hit, because I set pins in two alleys at the same time. The pay was one or two cents per line. I was lucky if I could make 30 cents in an evening. This was a big wintertime activity in a rural community. I remember riding my bike home on cold, icy nights and slipping and sliding, as I crossed the railroad tracks. My pay was subject to Social Security withdrawal, and I obtained my Social Security number at that time.

The Social Security System was proposed by President Franklin D. Roosevelt in 1935 and was operational in 1937. This job, along with a summer working at Beech Aircraft, working as a teamster in a warehouse, and two years part-time work at the **Wichita Eagle** newspaper were the only jobs where my work

Roosevelt signs Social Security legislation

was covered by Social Security. My Social Security record shows that my total pay covered under Social Security from 1937 to 1948 was $1,509.

I was definitely a summer time farmhand by now. Grandpa bought two new Allis Chalmers self-propelled combines, which were not pulled by a tractor. During the harvest, he drove one and Uncle Elmer drove the other. At 12 years old, I was given a very important job — driving the truck that hauled the wheat to the granary elevator in Offerle. The truck was an old International that had no driver's side door, and a blanket was used to cover the springs in the seat. I was not allowed to back up the truck — I could only go forward. Consequently, I stopped in the field and the combine full of wheat came to me.

We worked from daybreak to almost dusk. We took about two hours off for dinner, starting about 11:30 AM. The first thing we did, when we got in from the fields, was to wash our hands and face. We did this in the stock tank that was fed water by the windmill. There was a soap dish by the stock tank — we would throw cool water on our faces to cool off and then wash up. We never washed inside for the noon meal. This was the main meal of the day and almost always included meat and mashed potatoes with gravy and generally a baked dessert. Grandpa and I would then take a short nap on the floor while he listened to noon commodity reports (wheat, corn, and cattle prices). Refreshed, we would get back to work with the harvest. We generally worked until about 6 PM, unless we expected rain the next day, or Grandpa wanted to complete a particular field.

In addition to the long hours working in the wheat fields, I was trying to keep up with the regular games of our national pastime — baseball. I learned this from my father, a real baseball fan. Our family mainly followed the St. Louis Cardinals and St. Louis Browns. The games were day games, and we listened to the games on the radio, but, of course, everyone followed the Yankees.

The big baseball news in 1941 was the hitting streak of the "Yankee Clipper," Joe DiMaggio. I regularly read the morning news in the **Wichita Eagle,** almost always reading the sports news first. By the time I left Wichita, probably about June 15, to "work the harvest" in Offerle, the hitting streak had reached 27 when Joe had a hit off the Cleveland Indians' pitcher, Bob Feller.

As we did regular farm work and prepared the equipment for the harvest, it was not easy to keep up with the sports news. I didn't get sports news on the radio as I was the only one interested in sports. The others probably considered this interest in sports as the amusements of a "city boy."

When Grandpa listened to the radio, it was usually to get updates on farm product prices. I got my sports news in Offerle from the Hutchinson daily newspaper that was delivered by the noon Santa Fe train that came through Offerle. I would watch for the train's arrival from the fields or, most generally, from Grandpa's farm that was across Highway 50 from the railroad tracks. After the train had passed through Offerle, on the next trip to town, I would run to the post office to get the paper and nervously look to see if Joe had a hit the previous day.

Joe continued to get hits and his streak continued. It was probably about July 1 when we started harvest that Joe's streak had reached 42. The timing of my trips to take the wheat to the grain elevator in Offerle was random, and sometimes I would dump the load of wheat and head back to the field just before the train passed through Offerle. This was the most anxious time, as I had to wait until the next trip, sometimes over an hour. I would finally get the paper, and hopefully, he got another hit — time after time he did get the hit.

I began to consider myself responsible for Joe continuing to get hits. I had to be on my best behavior — not to do anything wrong. Finally, as I read the paper on July 18, Joe failed to get a hit — the STREAK was over at 56, and I could find nothing that I did to contribute to Joe's failure — it was over.

In researching the specifics of this vignette, I came across a story from **Baseball Almanac** by Joe DiMaggio. In the story, Joe states, "Now this is over thirty years later and the guy said he was the cab driver who drove me to the game on July 17th. He apologized for telling me that he thought the streak would end that day, and he was serious. I felt awful. He might have been spending his whole life thinking he had jinxed me, but I told him he hadn't. My number was up." I didn't know this at the time, but the baseball story is an example of control — we can only control what we do — not what others do.

I had another baseball experience while living in Kinsley. I was hanging around the sandlot baseball diamond, hoping the older boys would let me play. They began organizing a trip to Lewis, Kansas, to play an early afternoon game — they said I could go with them. I probably ran home and told my mother where we were going. The Kinsley team drove to Lewis in a flat-bed truck, and most of the team was in the back of the truck. When we arrived, I learned that I was to be the umpire on the bases (the regular umpire did not show up, and they needed a sub, and I was it). The home team umpired behind the plate. They told me to stand behind second base and call the plays and, of course, try not to get hit. There was a close play at second base, and I called one of the Lewis players safe. Our manager came running out and yelled, "He was out!" I explained that the second baseman didn't touch the runner with the ball. Our manager said, "You don't have to touch him with the ball — you just have to touch the runner with the glove as long as the ball is in the glove." I said, "OK, he is out!" But, the Lewis team would not let me change the call. I finished the game as umpire. I don't remember where I rode in the truck on the way home, but I definitely did not have any friends. That was the end of my baseball experiences at the sandlot baseball field in Kinsley. I wasn't expelled — I was rejected.

Another job I had, about this time, was cultivating the maize. I drove the tractor between the rows, and the harrow that was pulled by the tractor turned the earth between the rows. Of course, at 12 years old, I wasn't a very good driver, and I knocked down a bit of maize. Grandpa later bragged that the maize crop was one of the best he ever had, because the crop was thinned, and there was better growth. This most likely was not true, but it was Grandpa's way of giving me a pat on the back. I didn't become a farmer, but the lessons I learned from Grandma and Grandpa are still with me after 70 years.

In the early afternoon, on December 7, 1941, I was walking across town to church to practice for a Christmas pageant, when someone gave me the news that the Japanese had attacked Pearl Harbor. From all the excitement, I knew this was a serious situation. I did not know where Pearl Harbor was, but when I got home, my family was listening to the radio. There was talk of war. The next day, at 12:30 PM, President Roosevelt gave his "Day of Infamy" speech: "Yesterday, December 7, 1941 — a date which will live in infamy — the United States of America was suddenly and deliberately attacked by naval and air forces of the Empire of Japan." He further requested that the Congress declare war on Japan. Forty minutes later at 1 PM, Congress declared war on Japan as follows:

> **JOINT RESOLUTION Declaring that a state of war exists between the Imperial Government of Japan and the Government and the people of the United States and making provisions to prosecute the same. Whereas the Imperial Government of Japan has committed unprovoked acts of war against the Government and the people of the United States of America: Therefore be it Resolved by the Senate and House of Representatives of the United States of America in Congress assembled, That the state of war between the United States and the Imperial Government of Japan which has thus been thrust upon the United States is hereby formally declared; and the President is hereby authorized and directed to employ the entire naval and military forces of the United States and the resources of the Government to carry on war against the Imperial Government of Japan; and, to bring the conflict to a successful termination, all the resources of the country are hereby pledged by the Congress of the United States.**

Maybe my teacher let us listen to the news on the radio. I don't remember, but I have heard this speech so many times over the years that it feels to me that I was there and heard the speech on December 8, 1941. You would expect that all of us in Kansas were just like everyone else in the United States. We were mad as hell and we weren't going to take it anymore. I do remember a patriotic pageant we had at the Lodge Hall on June 3, 1942. We formed a V for Victory in front of the American flag and the Statue of Liberty.

Patriotic pageant, Lodge Hall, Kinsley, Kansas, June 1942

My siblings, Wilma, John and Phyllis, my cousin Keith, and Aunt Donna are in the picture. I am the fourth back on the right side of the V. You can see that I am peering around a tall girl. Yes, it is also the case in Kansas — seventh grade girls are taller than seventh grade boys. I didn't mind it at the time, but as I look at the picture 73 years later, why didn't they put me in front of the tall girl?

Yes, we were patriotic. Each week we purchased war savings stamps. We placed these stamps in a booklet, and when we had $18.75 worth of stamps, we could purchase a $25 war savings bond. The bonds accumulated interest and were worth $25 after ten years. I purchased two of these bonds and, after about 40 years, when they were no longer drawing interest, I cashed them in for about $75 each.

Dad must have read or heard about employment opportunities in Wichita, because in January 1942, he started commuting from Kinsley to Wichita and began working in the aircraft manufacturing industry. He stayed in Wichita during the week and commuted to and from Wichita with my mother's cousin, Junior Lightcap. We benefitted from the World War II need for military aircraft, as Dad had a steady job again, and my parents made plans for a permanent move to Wichita.

Kinsley, Kansas, High School, seventh grade, Darrell, second row middle behind boy in black

Aunt Tillie with Mom and her daughter, Gladys Harkness, 1998. Aunt Tillie is about three months shy of her 109th birthday.

A sad bunch, Darrell, Dad, John, Mom, Phyllis, and Wilma, Kinsley, Kansas, 1938

CHAPTER 5: WICHITA, KANSAS — 1942-1948

Mom and Dad bought a house in Wichita at 2232 N. Minnesota and moved in August 1942. The move to Wichita must have looked like some "Okies" moving to California during the Depression. The furniture was stacked high on a truck that had been borrowed from Jesse Dugger — a friend from the Christian Church in Kinsley.

Our house was a giant upgrade from our Kinsley house. We had two bedrooms, a garage, and best of all, a bathtub. Our sleeping arrangements were about the same as in Kinsley. Mom and Dad had a bedroom, Wilma and Phyllis had the other bedroom, and John and I slept on a day bed in the living room (the daytime couch was opened and John and I had a bed). The main problem was that John and I couldn't go to bed until everyone else went to bed, and we had to get up when the first person in the house got up. Nevertheless, we were all happy and pleased to be in Wichita.

Dad worked for Unit Tool at 2500 N. Broadway, when he went to Wichita in January 1942. The company later moved to North Hillside. Dad went to work for Beech Aircraft in 1942 and worked for Beech until 1947. During World War II, he also had a second job at a tool shop at 18th and Broadway. I went with him to the shop in the evening and helped him make aircraft parts. He went to work for Boeing as a tool and die maker in 1947 and worked there until he retired in 1972.

My sister, Wilma, remembers a situation in September 1942, when I was in the eighth grade, Wilma was in the sixth grade, John was in the third grade and Phyllis was in the first grade. Wilma says that Dad's boss noticed that he looked despondent at work, and his boss asked him if something was wrong. Dad responded that he had four kids starting school, and he didn't have money to buy books for them. His boss bought the school books for us. Wilma said that, at that time, we were **dead broke**.

I started school at the Horace Mann Intermediate School in September 1942. The school was about 2 ½ miles from our house with no direct public transportation. The fastest route was to walk to the Stockyards about three quarters of a mile west on 21st Street. I could catch a bus from there to the school. In the winter time, I could wait for the bus in the stockyard lobby. I reversed this route to return home. Sometimes when I had the time, I walked the whole distance by taking a short cut on the railroad tracks to North Broadway, a street near the school. I worked in the school cafeteria washing trays and utensils in return for a free lunch. The price of the bus was five or ten cents, and the lunch probably cost about 25 cents. I don't remember feeling like the new boy on the block or unwelcome at Horace Mann.

I joined a scout troop near our home in 1942. We met at the nearby Skinner Elementary School. I earned the rank of First Class Scout on April 1, 1946, just shy of my 17th birthday. I was not as rigorous in trying to advance my scouting career as my grandson, Cody Dempster, who is a Life Scout at age fourteen. Two other grandsons, Jason Stanko and Mitchell Dempster earned the rank of Eagle Scout. My scouting experience ended in 1946, partly due to our dwindling troop numbers and my pursuit of other adventures. While I failed to attain the rank of Eagle Scout, I had many wonderful experiences that have served me in good stead. Attaining the rank of Eagle Scout is an outstanding accomplishment reserved for the very few.

One of the evaluations considered for entry into the United States Naval Academy is the Eagle Scout award. Two of my most outstanding Naval Academy classmates are Carl Trost and Ross Perot. Carl attained the rank of Four-Star Admiral and was the Chief of Naval Operations. He stood number one academically and was the Academy Brigade Commander (senior midshipman). Ross, after a stint in the Navy, became an extremely successful businessman with many accomplishments, and, at this date, is still performing at a high level. Ross was also the president of our class and served with distinction on the Academy Honor Committee. Both are outstanding gentlemen and scholars. I am sure that both of them would say that the lessons they learned while progressing through all the steps to earn the rank of Eagle Scout were lifetime lessons and served as the groundwork for their many accomplishments.

In addition to the Boy Scout law, I learned to have confidence in my daily efforts. This confidence came, in no small part, from the Boy Scout motto "Be Prepared" — be ready to perform the task. I also learned self-reliance from being prepared to perform at a reasonable level in the world around me. Of course, I really didn't do this on my own. I owe a deep debt of gratitude to my scout leaders and the leaders in the business community who sponsored us. What a great Country! Just remember "Be Prepared" — be ready. When the student is ready, the teacher will appear.

Not long after we moved to Wichita, I began caddying at the Wichita Country Club, about three miles from our house. I walked a mile north on 21st Street, and then caught a bus to Eighth Street, where I walked about four blocks north to the Wichita Country Club (now MacDonald Golf Course, a public course). After some training, I was assigned to a player by the caddy master. The rate of pay was one dollar per round, and sometimes I received a twenty-five cent tip. I had to arrive at the course by about 8 AM to have the best chance of getting an assignment. Sometimes I went to the course in the morning and did not get on the course until the afternoon. After paying the bus fare, my take home pay was generally less than a dollar.

By the time I was about 14, I had become a Class "A" caddy, and I was often requested by specific members. I carried two bags, and most of the time, I received a 50-cent tip, so I earned three dollars. I can tell you that the weather was hot under the summer sun on a golf course on the plains of Kansas — often reaching 100 degrees. On rare occasions, I would caddy for two rounds and would earn six dollars. Also, I often rode my bicycle, thus saving the bus fare.

One of my favorite days at the golf course was doctors' day, Wednesday afternoon. They teed off at 1 PM, and I generally caddied for the same doctors. One of them was Dr. Smith, father of one of my classmates, Marilyn Smith. Marilyn was one of the first female professional golfers and had a long and storied career, winning more than 20 tournaments. Marilyn was one of the founders of the Ladies Professional Golf Association (LPGA).

Caddies were permitted to play golf on Monday mornings. After a few lessons from the other caddies, I obtained some used clubs and began a lifetime love of the game of golf. After I stopped caddying, I generally played at Sim Park public course, sometimes playing 36 holes and one time 45 holes in one day.

In the summer of 1959, my wife Sally, son Eddie (four months old), and I were traveling cross-country from Annapolis to San Francisco to catch a plane for our new duty station in Yokosuka, Japan. On our cross-country trips, we always stopped for a visit in Wichita. There was a city tournament scheduled, and I decided to enter. I had to be a member of a Wichita Golf Club, so I joined Echo Hills, the least expensive club, but it had sand greens. Sand greens were about 24 feet in diameter. A smooth path, about two feet wide, was rolled with a roller. The hole was in the center of this path. Players were responsible for rolling the path after they finished the hole. I played Echo Hills once and then played in the tournament at the Crestview Country Club, where I had also caddied. I placed second in the "B" bracket. I guess Sally was wondering what kind of a guy she had married — one who left her and our son with my folks, while I played golf, but after all, it was a tournament. I tried to be a little more careful with my sports activities after that.

When we arrived in Wichita, we became subject to the local regulations regarding "Blackout," part of the Civil Defense effort, where all shades were to be drawn at night and no light was to be seen from the street. All street lights were turned off, although this didn't apply to us, as we didn't have street lights. It was probably in 1943 that Dad became our "Air Raid Warden," and I was his helper. When darkness came, we would walk the street and be sure that no light was showing from the houses. If we could see light, we would knock on the door and ask the resident to darken the window. I don't remember ever having any trouble with the residents in our neighborhood complying with the rules. I think that after a year or two, the Blackout was discontinued. Associated with the Blackout was the use of aircraft spotting cards. Cards that had silhouettes of German, Japanese, and US aircraft were distributed. We were informally trained (I received my training in the Boy Scouts) to identify (spot) enemy aircraft. Some entrepreneurs printed the silhouettes on playing cards. I had a deck of these cards. Of course, it was most unlikely that German or Japanese aircraft could have flown to the center of the US, but we were ready.

World War II aircraft spotting cards

I earned some money as a gas station attendant near our house. My pay was 20 cents per hour. I pumped gas and checked the oil and tires. We collected gas ration coupons for the gas. It was a good job, and I worked about 15 hours per week, earning about three dollars per week. The pay was actually better than a beginning caddy, but I liked golf and the chance to make more money when I became a class "A" caddy.

Rationing commenced in 1942, and some of the items rationed were tires, gasoline, fuel oil, kerosene, shoes, sugar, coffee, cheese, and some other food items. The only rationed item that affected us was gasoline. The ration for regular car drivers was three gallons per week. Since Dad was a factory worker, he received eight gallons per week, but that would have been barely enough to drive the eight miles each way to work, plus driving the family around, so he was forced to carpool. I do remember waiting to get shoes, but this was no real hardship. At times, Dad may have been classified as an "essential war worker," and this category had no rationing restrictions. The maximum highway speed limit was 35 mph. This was done, not only to conserve gasoline, but also for safety, as many drivers were driving with smooth tires due to tire rationing. Retreading tires was common.

It was probably about 1943 that I seized an opportunity to make a few dollars. There was an oil storage facility on the bank of a small creek near our house. After several exploration trips to the site, I observed that several 50-gallon oil drums were discarded there. A fire was occasionally set to burn the residue from inside the drums. I determined that they would serve as trash cans, so I would pick up one at a time, load it on my wagon and go door-to-door and sell the drum for 50 cents. Since the fires were set in the winter, this was a cold-weather activity. I would sell two or three drums a day. My business was word-of-mouth, as a satisfied customer would tell a neighbor where to buy the can. We didn't have a telephone in those days, so the buyer would have to come to our house or stop me in the street. I didn't have any competition, and I never saw anyone at the site getting their own drum.

I had the choice of either of the two public high schools, East or North, and I chose Wichita East. I started at Wichita East High School in 1943. It was a bit of a chore to get to either high school. North was near my intermediate school, so I would have had a three-quarter mile walk and then a bus. East required about a one-mile walk and then a bus. I enjoyed high school. East was a large school of about 1,000 classmates. The competition for a sports team was beyond my athletic capabilities, although I did play junior-varsity golf for all of my four years.

I also played church basketball. We formed a team at the Christian Church that met at the Skinner Elementary School near our house. My father was the coach. We didn't have a very good team, as we had a very small church membership. We played against other churches, and I played against some high school classmates. One of my friends, Jack Stannard, asked me to join his church and play with him, so I attended a Congregational church and played basketball with them.

In addition to playing against Wichita churches, we played games in Hutchinson, Kansas. Jack's father was a contractor, and he purchased uniforms and sweat suits for us. Another of my friends on the team joined the Navy after high school and attended the Naval Academy with me. Playing organized basketball was a great way to learn teamwork, while being physically active and extending my circle of friends.

As Wichita grew and nearby farms were developed into housing areas, some rabbits lost their habitat, but that didn't stop them from multiplying. They just moved to other farm land and became a nuisance to farmers, as well as gardeners in nearby housing. As a result of the rabbit over-population, rabbit drives were held. I joined one of these rabbit drives.

We congregated about three miles from the city limits and formed a line for the drive. As we walked in lines, we drove the rabbits ahead of us, and funneled them into an enclosure, where men with clubs beat the rabbits to death. This sounds cruel, but that's the way it was. I was on the outskirts of the group and never saw what happened as the rabbits approached the enclosure. During the Dust Bowl, rabbit drives were common in the western counties of Kansas.

Why didn't we have a telephone? I guess my folks didn't consider it a priority item, given the income and other needs. We made emergency calls and received calls at a neighbor's house two doors away. We had a good relationship with them, and when a call came in for us, they would come to our house and tell us we had a call. I don't know what the monthly cost of a phone was, but it was probably about five dollars per month. We got our first telephone about 1944.

The best paying job I had in Wichita was my job at the **Wichita Eagle** newspaper. I worked Wednesday putting all advertisement flyers together inside the comics. On Saturday evening, when the Sunday paper was printed, I would stuff the ads and comics inside the Sunday paper. These were then packaged in bundles of about twenty papers for distribution. Some workers were selected to work in another room where the papers were counted and grouped for each delivery point. I worked in this room the last few months of my employment. I sometimes wrapped a Sunday newspaper and addressed it to one of my relatives in another city.

Lawrence-Dumont Stadium was built in 1934 as a WPA project. My family was very familiar with the stadium as we regularly attended baseball games there; however, our seating was unique — on the top of railroad cars. The railroad obliged us by placing their cars on a siding near the center field fence. I don't know how my Dad learned of this "reserved" seating — probably another baseball fan told him as they talked about baseball. This was 1943 and 1944. Phyllis was only nine years old when we started going to these games, but my parents felt comfortable with her climbing up the side of the railroad car. We also took food and drinks, so Dad and I had a burden to carry to the top of the railroad car. You might say we were in on the beginning of the knothole gang where men and boys saw free baseball through the knotholes in the wooden fences. Wichita hosted a semi-professional baseball tournament in the summer that lasted about three weeks, and we attended about half the games.

When I was about 15, and not attending games with my parents, I worked off and on for about two years selling cold drinks, hot dogs, popcorn and peanuts at the Lawrence-Dumont Stadium and at the Forum, an indoor arena in downtown Wichita. I sold whatever was assigned to me for the evening. My earnings ranged from a dollar to ten dollars. It was hard work walking up and down the steps, especially carrying 24 bottles of soft drinks with ice in a bucked hooked to my arm; however, I made the most profit on the soft drinks. In the fall and winter, I sold the same items at wrestling and basketball events at the Forum. It was a long evening, as after the events, we were obligated to pick up all the empty bottles.

When I was making "all" this money, I couldn't just hide it under the mattress, so I opened a savings account. I never had much money in the account, but I enjoyed watching the savings grow.

During these years, there was total support of our war against the Axis powers, mainly the Germans and Japanese. There were many servicemen on the streets of Wichita. I observed them, particularly when I rode the bus home from downtown.

During the evening hours, the bus extended its route to go to the Shadowland Night Club on North Hillside. There were always servicemen on the bus going to Shadowland, and they usually had several girls with them. There were no alcoholic drinks served in Shadowland, but the servicemen usually had a package with them in case they were thirsty during the evening. I wondered about the evening entertainment and I envied the life of a serviceman.

Navy recruiting poster

All young men were patriotic and most of us were waiting for the day when we were old enough to join the Army, Navy, or Marines. There were recruiting posters in the downtown store windows and I particularly remember those in the Kress five and ten cent store at Broadway and Douglas, in the center of Wichita.

I would stop and look at the posters as I passed the store. I found out that you could join the Merchant Marine with your parents' permission when you were sixteen years old. I tried to join the Merchant Marine, but my mother would have nothing to do with it.

In the summer of 1945, I worked in the wheat harvest. This was the beginning of my wanderlust. I started about mid-June and gradually moved north as the wheat ripened. The wheat ripened in Texas and Oklahoma in June and gradually ripened to the north, with wheat ripening in North Dakota in August. I started in Lewis, Kansas, working for the parents of Aunt Joyce Carroll Boehme, my Uncle Elmer's wife. Elmer had taken over the Boehme farm when my Grandfather Boehme turned 65 in 1944.

The Carroll farm was located about five miles south of Lewis. My job was driving the truck. I hauled wheat from the combine to the granary on the farm. I had a lot of dead time. After I unloaded the truck, I would wait in the field for the next load. I discovered large stacks of old magazines in one of the storage sheds. I selected **Collier's** and put some under the seat in the truck and read them while waiting for the next load of wheat.

The following information about **Collier's** is taken from the **Collier's** website: **Collier's** was launched as a magazine of fiction, fact, sensation, wit, humor, and news. **Collier's** became known widely for its investigative journalism and social reform-seeking values. The writers included Winston Churchill, Ernest Hemingway, Sinclair Lewis, Jack London, F. Scott Fitzgerald, J. D. Salinger, John Steinbeck, Pearl S. Buck, and Kurt Vonnegut. They reported on historical events, such as World War I and the Spanish Civil War, and political events. They wrote short stories or serialized novels. Some of the most famous articles published were "The Great American Fraud" and Upton Sinclair's "Is Chicago Meat Clean," which eventually led to the Senate Meat Inspection Act of 1906. All of these articles and stories have shaped and contributed to **Collier's** ultimate goal — to seek the truth.

In October 1905, **Collier's** initiated the "The Great American Fraud," an 11-part **Collier's** series that analyzed the contents of popular "patent medicines." **Collier's** pointed out that the companies producing these medicines made false claims about their products, and some products were health hazards. **Collier's** launched the series with the following editorial:

> In the present number we print the first article in 'The Great American Fraud' series, which is to describe thoroughly the ways and methods, as well as the evils and dangers, of the patent medicine business. This article is but the opening gun of the campaign, and is largely introductory in character, but it will give the reader a good idea of what is to come when we get down to peculiarities. The next article, to appear two weeks hence, will treat

> those concoctions which are advertised and sold as medicines, but which in reality are practically cocktails. Since these articles on patent medicine frauds were announced in Collier's some time ago, most of the makers of alcoholic and opiated medicines have been running to cover, and even the Government has been awakened to a sense of responsibility. A few weeks ago the Commissioner of Internal Revenue issued an order to his Collectors, ordering them to exact a special tax from the manufacturer of every compound composed of distilled spirits. Booze is booze and the government is going to get their take.

Patent medicine promoters initiated many advertising and sales techniques that were later used for other products. The promoters used endorsements from so-called experts or celebrities that were likely not true. Patent medicine advertising deluded the buyer into believing that the miracle "medicine" contained all sorts of exotic ingredients and could cure their malady.

Some sellers of these medicines claimed their product contained snake oil, thus making "snake oil salesmen" the memorable words for a charlatan. I heard the term patent medicine enough times in my teen years to now believe that my extended family and friends likely fell for this ruse. The advertising industries use of "experts" and celebrities to promote their "amazing products" is very much alive and well, in fact, it is even more prevalent today! There is a sucker born every minute.

Earlier in 1938 to 1942, while in Kinsley, my family regularly attended the annual county fair held at the city park. There were a few animals, a carousel, sideshows starring weird things, and salesmen. One of the salesmen, a huckster, stood on a platform on the back of an enclosed trailer and hawked a patent medicine called Hadacol that would cure everything. I saw these Hadacol salesmen every year. They had a spellbinding spiel that mesmerized the crowd, and many were eager to part with their money to buy a supply of this miraculous "medicine." Hadacol cost about a dollar a bottle. It was supposed to cure many diseases, including hay fever, high blood pressure, cancer, gall stones, heart trouble, ulcers, and strokes. It made people think they felt better; of course, they were drinking alcohol, and it cured none of these diseases.

Hadacol "medicine"

The label on the tonic's bottle stated that the recommended dosage (one tablespoonful taken four times a day) was to be taken in a half glass of water after meals and before retiring. However, some pharmacies in dry counties were known to sell it by the shot glass, and some bars sold cocktails with Hadacol as an ingredient. Some states and counties limited Hadacol sales to liquor stores. The 12 percent alcohol was added as a "preservative." In summary, the laws regarding patent medicine had little effect on these peddlers of an ineffective and sometimes dangerous "medicine." Since Hadacol and other "medicines" contained alcohol, customers used these products as a substitute for alcohol, thus violating the prohibition laws.

Collier's published many other serials including "Fu Manchu" that starred the master villain Dr. Fu Manchu and his associate, a villainous Chinese seductress. Opposing these villains was the long arm of a lawman and a bumbling assistant who always got the better of the evildoers. Of course, there was a pretty woman who was often kidnapped or fell into some other suspenseful trap. Each serial end-

Fu Manchu mask

ed with one of the good guys in the hands of Dr. Fu Manchu awaiting imminent death. The reader was thus trapped and had no other choice but to wait for the next installment. The challenge I had, after reading one installment of a serial, was to find the other magazines that included the serial. There were about 20 years of **Collier's** — about 250 magazines, so sorting them into order was difficult, but well worth it, as the pastime provided an education about "somewhat" current events — the magazines were old! I had something to look forward to each day. This education reminds me of a term used about some older people in the 1940s who did not have much schooling. They were educated by reading **Readers Digest**.

My bedroom at the Carrolls was on the second floor. I don't remember reading at night. We worked long hours, and were so tired that we went to bed at dusk and got up to have breakfast at first light. The meals were very good. The Carroll family was very religious — a prayer was said before every meal. There were just three of us, Mr. and Mrs. Carroll and myself. The Carroll harvest lasted about two weeks. I was paid five dollars per day, and that was pretty good money for a 16-year-old, but I thought I was worth more.

When the Carroll harvest was finished, I went to Offerle, 18 miles to the west, to visit Grandma and Grandpa Boehme. It was a Saturday night, and as usual on Saturday night, the Boehme family was in Offerle for the evening. Grandma sat in the car parked perpendicular to the one-block main street (Highway 50) where she observed the town's people on the sidewalk. I sat in the car with her and bemoaned my "meager" pay by the Carroll family. Grandma would never criticize the Carroll family, nor would she judge anyone else. She consoled me and gave me a "pat on the back" for my industriousness.

I continued my summer job as a migrant worker. I hitched rides from Offerle to Goodland, about 230 miles to northwestern Kansas near the Colorado and Nebraska borders. I stayed in Goodland with my mother's brother, Clifford, and his wife, Sammy. By word-of-mouth and the help of Uncle Clifford and Aunt Sammy, I was able to obtain work as an assistant to a truck driver who hauled wheat on a custom basis. Again, I was paid five dollars per day but only got my noon meal from the farmer. I had to manage breakfast and supper on my own. The truck driver had a small trailer, and we slept in the trailer and had some meals there, but there was no refrigeration, so we ate some meals in Goodland. This work lasted about 10 days, and it was time for me to move on. I think Aunt Sammy did my laundry before I left, as she would have insisted that I be prepared for the next part of my journey.

For the next part of the harvest, I had to head north. I went to Wray, Colorado, in the northeastern part of the state. This was my second time in Colorado, and it was not mountainous as before in the Rocky Mountains, but it was certainly hilly — not like Kansas. I went to downtown Wray and inquired about harvest work and landed a job. Work was not too hard to find, as most of the farmhands either enlisted or were drafted into military service. Again, the family I worked for was very religious — prayers before every meal and no swearing. I didn't have to be told this — it was obvious in the demeanor of the farmer and his family. I heard the farmer say "my gosh" or "golly darn" a few times when something happened to the equipment. My sleeping quarters were in a utility shed that contained the cream separator, milk and cream storage, and storage of other items relating to milking cows. It was very clean and comfortable.

I was a general handyman — I did anything the farmer wanted me to do. The main job was to ride the combine and keep an eye on all parts of the combine to make sure it was operating correctly. As usual, the first thing we did each morning was grease all necessary parts. Since I had not operated this type of combine before, the farmer was very careful in explaining every part to be greased and what parts to watch during operation.

The farmer did not work on Sundays. This was very unusual, even for religious families, as rain could delay the harvest, and the farmers wanted to "make hay while the sun shines." I probably spent my Sundays reading, or I went into Wray to sightsee. I didn't go to church with the farmer — probably because I had no Sunday clothes with me. This job lasted about two weeks. Since it was now early August, I headed home to start my junior year in high school. But, first I had to visit Denver.

I hitched rides south and west to Denver and stayed a couple days to sightsee in the biggest city I had seen to date. I was impressed by the big buildings and hills in and around Denver. I was surprised to meet one of my former supervisors from the **Wichita Eagle** on the street in Denver. He was taking a smoke break from his new job with the Denver newspaper. I stayed a couple days and began hitchhiking home. I stopped in Goodland to visit Uncle Clifford and in Offerle to visit Grandma and Grandpa Boehme and to tell them of my adventures. When I look back, I am amazed that I can't remember anyone trying to discourage a 16-year-old boy from going on this adventure. I wrote postcards to keep my family informed of my whereabouts. The travel west and east was fairly easy, as they were the main travel routes. Travel north and south was more difficult, as the roads were often not paved with asphalt, and there was less traffic with much shorter rides. I traveled about 1,300 miles during this venture.

In about March of 1946, I read an advertisement in a magazine or newspaper looking for lumbermen in Missoula, Montana. I submitted an application and anxiously waited for an answer. By the time school was out for the summer, I did not have an answer, so I applied for summer work at Beech Aircraft and got a job installing floorboards in the Beech Bonanza aircraft. I carpooled to and from work with Dad. About a week after I started work at Beech, I received an answer from Montana offering me a job. Dad advised me to decline the offer, and I worked through the summer at Beech. The work at Beech was enjoyable and rewarding, although I did the same thing every day. My first task, when a new aircraft came my way on the assembly line, was to vacuum the area under the floor board. I knew this was important, as any loose item that was left could cause damage to the control wires inside the bottom of the aircraft. I was instructed on where the hidden pockets were and how to thump an area to see if I could hear any loose items. I then screwed the floor boards into predrilled holes. I used a tool similar to an ice pick to align the hole in the floor board with the hole in the aluminum brace in the aircraft. My tenure as a factory worker ended when I started my senior year at East High.

After graduation from high school in 1947, I visited my friend Delbert, who was working at a grain elevator in Wichita. His job was unloading wheat from rail cars. A mechanical shovel was used to scoop out the wheat, after about half a car load was released into a pit when the rail car doors were opened. The remainder had to be scooped out by walking up the piles of wheat in the corners and lowering the shovel into the wheat. Lowering the shovel activated a pulley that moved downward and out of the car. The operator maintained a downward pressure on the shovel as it dragged the wheat. I decided that I could do this, and Delbert and I decided we would travel to Omaha, Nebraska, to find work. We traveled on my Cushman scooter that I had purchased the previous year to facilitate my transportation in and about Wichita. The main roads were two lanes and most of them had a small ridge on the side to warn drivers if they strayed from the road. We rode the scooter as far to the side of the road as we could to allow traffic to pass us and to keep from being clipped by passing cars. If we hit the ridge, we were suddenly jerked to the left and into the path of passing cars and trucks. This was not a good thing and we had many close calls. We found work when we arrived in Omaha and found lodging in a boarding house.

The business of scooping wheat from rail cars was more difficult than I expected. The main problem was the dust generated by the movement of wheat in a confined space. We wore masks, but the dust was too much for me, as I hacked repeatedly after every downward scoop. I lasted two days and quit the business of scooping wheat. We remained in Omaha a few days to see the sights, including a trip across the Missouri River to Iowa.

When we left Omaha for home, we stopped at Father Flannigan's Boys Town near Omaha. Boys Town was the subject of the movie "Boys Town" starring Spencer Tracy and Mickey Rooney. Father Flannigan started Boys Town in 1917 to provide a home for orphans and juvenile delinquents and care for their growth by means of social preparation. The movie was released in 1938. The captivating story was about

Father Flannigan (Spencer Tracy) and his relationship with the delinquent Whitey Marsh (Mickey Rooney). It was the typical story of a fall from grace by a troubled youth and redemption with the help of a devoted mentor. The story gave hope to troubled youth and parents alike that the youth might mend their ways and become socially acceptable and productive citizens. I saw the movie about 1942 and was anxiously awaiting my visit to Boys Town. It was a beautiful campus with many large buildings, dormitories, and athletic facilities and definitely brought the story to life for me.

Boys Town movie with Spencer Tracy and Mickey Rooney

After leaving Boys Town, we headed for Valley Falls, a small town in northeastern Kansas. My mother's sister, Ramona, and her husband, Edgar Jackson, were farming and raising cattle in Valley Falls. My cousin, Keith Jackson, was about ten years old and my cousin Judy Jackson was just a baby. Edgar was remodeling the farm house, and we helped him for a few days before returning to Wichita. By then, I had pretty much used up the summer and didn't have much to show for it except for some sightseeing. I now had a decision to make — what would I do with the rest of my life?

After discussions with my parents and others, I decided to attend the University of Wichita, located about one mile from my house. I passed the university on the way to high school and was a sports fan of all the university sports teams. Registration was not a big deal. I filled out some forms, showed my high school diploma and grades, paid about $50, and I was a college student. It seemed like the thing to do. Maybe I was putting off the decision about what I would do with the rest of my life.

My college costs were minimal, as I generally packed a lunch and used my reliable Cushman scooter as transportation. I took two math classes and the usual freshman classes, and I joined the Army Reserve Officer Training Corps. I also tried to join a fraternity, but was not voted in as a pledge. I was rejected, but I don't remember being downcast about it. I thought it was the thing to do, but I knew it was a long shot. At the time I didn't know how important it was to form a basis for membership by networking, as we call it today. I was from the wrong side of the tracks, and did not prepare myself in high school by forming the necessary friendships.

I caddied about once a week on Wednesday afternoons at Crestview Country Club for two members who requested that I be their caddy. I earned three dollars for each 18 holes. I also went back to my old job working weekends at the **Wichita Eagle**.

I formed a friendship with a football player who had been recruited from Pennsylvania. He had served in the Marines at the end of World War II, and between classes, he regaled me with his experiences in the occupation of Japan. He told me about his Japanese girlfriend, his Japanese house, and all his exploits in Japan. I started thinking about what he had told me, and I thought to myself, "I have to get out of Dodge" (a term used by unsavory individuals in Dodge City in the late 1830s, who had used up their welcome in Dodge City). I don't know whether it was because of his influence or a yearning for foreign travel, but at the end of November 1947, I went to the Navy Recruiting Office in Wichita to discuss the different opportunities for me in the Navy.

One of the opportunities was a position as an electronics technician. This was a relatively new field at the time, and I took a test based on the skills required of an electronics technician. I did well on the test. It included many of the principles I was studying at the university. If I joined the Navy, I was guaranteed to be promoted to Seaman from Seaman Recruit after I finished recruit training. I would then attend a 42-week course at the Navy Electronics School at the Naval Station, Treasure Island, San Francisco, California. If I performed well in electronics school, I would be promoted to Second Class Petty Officer. This sounded like a wonderful opportunity, and I agreed to join the Navy after I finished my first semester at the university in January 1948.

CHAPTER 6: US NAVY — THE BEGINNING

I departed Wichita by bus for Kansas City, Missouri, early in the morning on Tuesday, January 27, 1948, with about ten other recruits. We picked up another ten recruits in Kansas and arrived in Kansas City after lunch. With about 20 more recruits from the Kansas City area, making about 40 recruits in all, we took physical examinations and were sworn into the United States Navy. Then we waited and waited and finally left Kansas City by train in a private car in the early evening. For a reason I cannot fathom, I was appointed to be in charge of the recruit group. My responsibilities were few, mainly to take a daily muster and to distribute meal coupons. After traveling overnight, we were supposed to have breakfast at a Harvey's restaurant in Oklahoma, but we were four hours late, so we had breakfast at noon. We missed the regular dinner (lunch), but we had a good supper (dinner) in the diner furnished by the US Navy — what a life! We were on a paid sightseeing vacation.

On January 28, I reported to my parents by a penny postcard posted by the Kansas City and Tucson Railroad that I was tired of sightseeing in Oklahoma, and we would soon be in Texas. We traveled through Texas and New Mexico, where we were put on a siding for a short time, while we were switched to another train. I wrote another postcard on Thursday, January 29, about our six hours on a siding in Yuma, Arizona. We had a day in the sun, and we walked around Yuma to see the sights, including the hoboes who had a camp near our siding. We enjoyed talking to the hoboes. We called them hoboes, but maybe they were tramps or bums. A hobo is a migrant worker, who sometimes goes without work, or takes a "vacation" for a while. A tramp works only when someone forces him to work. A bum does not work at all. He sleeps in the open and bums or begs for his food. To us, they were all hoboes.

The rail route from Yuma to San Diego was the most scenic of the trip, with the route passing twice through Mexico. Prominent citizens of San Diego had been trying for years to build a rail route to the east to connect the port of San Diego to the farm and mineral products and tourist trade of the rest of the US. In 1906, John D. Spreckles, sugar heir and entrepreneur, formed the San Diego and Arizona Eastern Railway to build a 145-mile line from San Diego to El Centro, California, the central city of the Imperial Valley.

Railroad through Mexico

Railroad bridge over Carizzo Canyon

The most difficult construction was in the Carizzo Canyon of California with steep grades, deep canyons, falling rocks, and many tunnels and trestles. Hence, this railroad was called the "impossible railroad."

The construction faced many obstacles including extremely rugged terrain, transportation of supplies, cold weather, extreme heat, Mexican bandits, labor strife, housing and food for workers, hurricanes, landslides, and a World War I work stoppage. The rail line was completed in 1919 and was in operation until 1951. Portions of the line were later reopened for tourist excursions, but now the line is entirely closed.

We left Yuma in the morning and passed across the Colorado River with a short stretch into Mexico. We passed through El Centro, the desert, and into the mountains. Not only were we excited about our last day of travel, but we were overwhelmed by the breathtaking scenery. Those who have

Railroad in distance by side of canyon

ridden in a car around sharp mountain curves with deep drops will understand that some of us were reluctant to sit on the side of the railcar nearest the cliff. Some people moved to the other side of the car.

We entered Mexico at Tecate, and re-entered the US at Tijuana, a distance of about 50 miles by train, as there were many switchbacks. The train stopped a couple times in Mexico, and I, with a few others, got off the train to buy souvenirs. I didn't know how to haggle then, so I paid the asking price. I could now say that I had been in my first foreign country. We had just been on a four-day paid sightseeing vacation — what a life!

When I was in San Diego in March 2015, I drove about 75 miles east to Jacumba, California, where the impossible railroad ran next to the Mexican border. Jacumba is a town of about 50 houses. The old railroad depot is now a private home, as are two of the Pullman cars. There are several abandoned Pullman railroad cars there. All the furnishings have been removed, but looking at the inside brought back memories of my travel.

1940s Pullman railroad car, Jacumba, California, 2015

US/Mexico Border fence, 2015

The US/Mexico border is about a half mile south of the Jacumba railroad depot. In 1948, you could simply walk across the border. In 2013, there was a border fence/wall, about 20-feet high. What a contrast!

We arrived at the San Diego station in the late afternoon on Friday, January 30 and were taken by bus to the San Diego Naval Training Center. Saturday was induction day. We had our hair cut, another physical, signed more paperwork, and were issued uniforms. We were in companies of 120 recruits quartered in one building with 60 of us on the first deck and 60

San Diego, California, Railway Depot, 1940s

on the second deck. Recruit training lasted about 12 weeks. Of course, there was a lot of marching on a big open space called the Grinder. It was a bit of a walk across the Grinder to the mess hall. We had good food. It was probably a benefit to grow up in the Depression — all the food, except liver, suited my simple taste. I never learned to eat liver, but there was always mashed potatoes served with the liver. I could eat the liver gravy with the potatoes, and we always had a dessert.

Occasionally, I was assigned to work in the mess (dining) hall. The only task I remember doing there was peeling potatoes. We also had guard duty, called being "on watch" or "having the watch." We had training in many skills and we had some free time for sports. I organized a company volleyball team and we had a great time being away from the constant discipline.

Our team won the recruit championship. You can see from the picture that we had a couple tall shipmates, including my good friend Harold Buck (back left) from Wichita. It was not

Recruit Training Volleyball Champions, 1948 – Darrell, center

difficult to win, as all we had to do was get organized and pass to the "setters" and then the "spikers."

We had a couple Saturdays when we could go on liberty (time off) to San Diego. Although we could go to Tijuana, Mexico, I did not know anyone who went. The main reason no one went to Mexico was a training class depiction of what would happen if one got a venereal disease.

I had one weekend liberty in Long Beach, California. The main place I saw was the amusement pier at San Pedro. I encountered many men in uniform, including groups that looked to me as if they were officers. In recruit training, we were taught to salute anything that moved, and I was constantly saluting these "officers." It turns out they were midshipmen, but they returned my salute. All in all, the San Diego recruit training experience was OK — you can't beat the weather. Since it was winter, the weather was better than the other Recruit Training Station at Great Lakes, Illinois. We graduated about mid-May and after a short leave in Wichita, I was on my way by train to the Electronics School at the Naval Station, Treasure Island, San Francisco, California.

Darrell, guard duty

I had a nice train trip to San Francisco with all my belongings in a "sea bag." I caught another train across the San Francisco Oakland Bay Bridge. I got off the train halfway across at Yerba Buena Island and then took a short ride on a Navy bus to the Treasure Island Naval Station.

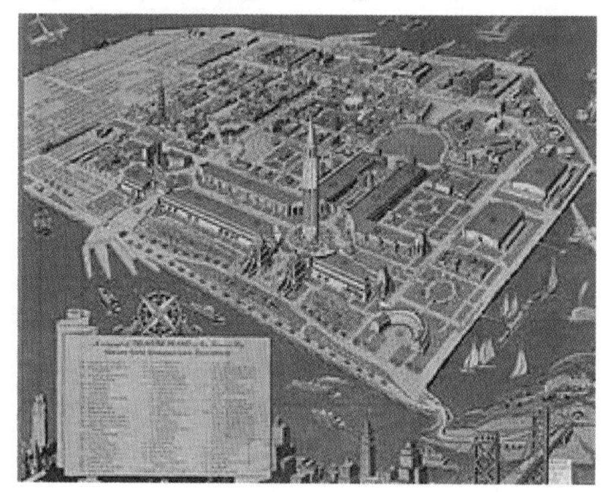

1939 View of Treasure Island World's Fair

I knew I was in a special place. I was at the place I had dreamed about in 1939, when I rode my bicycle past the mid-point between the San Francisco and New York World Fairs. Treasure

Treasure Island and Yerba Buena Island

Island is a man-made island constructed for the 1939 San Francisco World's Fair (1939 San Francisco Exposition).

When the fair was over, Treasure Island was to serve as the San Francisco International Airport. In 1942, the Navy exchanged Mills Field, on the San Francisco Peninsula, for Treasure Island. The San Francisco International Airport was built on the new site. Two large hangars and a seaplane harbor were located at Treasure Island, as Pan American World Airways was to use Treasure Island as a base for its Pan American Clipper fleet. Many other elegant buildings were constructed, including the inspiring World's Fair Administration Building, used later as the airport terminal, exhibit halls, and the "Tower of the Sun." This 400-foot tower was featured on the 1939 World's Fair postage stamp.

Postage stamp, San Francisco World's Fair, 1939

After checking in at the administration office, I was assigned to a barracks dormitory. We had double-decker bunk beds. Electronics School consisted of electronics theory, math courses, and electronic laboratories. The course was not difficult, especially after the math courses I had recently studied at Wichita University.

When we did not have the duty, we could travel to San Francisco, Oakland, and other cities. I had some friends that always wanted to go to the movies in San Francisco, but I didn't want to be cooped up in a dark theater, so I usually went sightseeing. I was on the golf team and drill team. We had weekly golf matches and went to different cities to march in parades about once a month.

I went to San Leandro a few times to a Christian mission where we had meals, coed companions, and could stay for the night. Perhaps the coed companions were the reason I traveled all the way to San Leandro. In the evening, we would have a religious service in a large room, where we slept on the floor on thin mattresses. One evening, I dozed off and was suddenly awakened by water being poured on my face. I was reminded to pay attention to the service.

Alcatraz

One place I never visited and didn't want to visit was Alcatraz. Alcatraz is about two miles from Treasure Island and is visible from the west and north sides. The athletic fields were on the north side of Treasure Island, so when we played touch football or softball, Alcatraz was always in our sight.

In mid-August, I had watch duty from midnight to 4 AM. Our duties were to patrol the perimeter of the island and to inspect certain buildings. While walking through the administration building, I read the bulletin board which had a notice about the Naval Academy. The notice said that if we had an interest in attending the Naval Academy, we should sign a list in the administrative office. The deadline was midnight on the very night I was reading the notice — I was late. I gave this opportunity some thought. I knew nothing about the Naval Academy, but I did know enough to think it was a pretty good deal. Now, I had to think of a way to get my name on the list.

One of the members of the golf team was the school executive officer, a Navy commander. I went to see him the next day, and he quickly agreed to grant me an interview. I was interviewed by a board of three officers, perhaps one or two were Naval Academy graduates, but I was not in a position to know this. The only question that I remember being asked was to define a "tetrahedron." I knew the answer from high school geometry. A tetrahedron is a four-sided solid figure in the shape of a pyramid. The interview was concluded, and I went about the business of studying electronics and seeing the sights of the San Francisco area.

I went to Santa Cruz to see the beach, but I got more than I bargained for. I spent too much time in the sun and got sunburned, especially on the top of my feet. Being fresh out of recruit training, I knew that it was against Navy regulations to get sunburned, because I might not be able to perform my duties. Consequently, I did not get medical attention and endured the pain in silence. The worst part was sleeping and walking. Our bedding was a small mattress enclosed by a pillow-like cover with a wool blanket. The wool blanket irritated my sunburn, so I removed the cover from the mattress and slept in the mattress cover. I endured the pain of wearing shoes, and thankfully, we did not have any parades or marching while I was recovering from the sunburn.

I went on one weekend trip with a friend to Reno, Nevada. We hitchhiked to Carson City, Nevada, on Highway 50, a highway that I knew well, then north to Reno. We selected Reno for the excitement of its gambling history, although we definitely didn't have enough money for serious gambling. We arrived in Reno late in the day, and had to be prepared to return to Treasure Island early the next morning. The coin for the Reno slots was the silver dollar. We exchanged our greenbacks for about five silver dollars and that was our gambling pot. We played the slots for awhile and ended up with about ten silver dollars, a significant win. I retained those silver dollars for several months, but later I spent them all.

In early September 1948, I received word that I had been accepted for studies at the Naval Academy Preparatory School. I was transferred to the Naval Training Station, Bainbridge, Maryland, about 35 miles northeast of Baltimore,

Maryland. I had been at the Electronics School for 20 weeks, and I needed to have 27 weeks to be promoted to Petty Officer Third Class, so I left Electronics School as a Navy Seaman. I checked out of the electronics school, and with a full sea bag, I took a train to Oakland. I caught the train from Oakland to Wichita, a distance of 1,880 miles, traversing California, Arizona, New Mexico, Texas, Oklahoma, and into Kansas. A large portion of the travel was over the same rail line I had traveled previously from Kansas City to San Diego. The travel time was a little more than 39 hours with two overnights on the train. The Navy paid for my train ticket and also paid me about $20 for meals.

I left Oakland in the afternoon, and after passing the Oakland hills, I saw farmland all the way to Fresno, California, when darkness fell. When the sun rose the next day, I was in Kingman, Arizona. The travel through Arizona was very scenic with high mountains to the north before Kingman and very high mountains farther to the north and south of Flagstaff. The slope of the railroad was gentle, making for a smooth ride. I had my meals in the deluxe dining car. My meals ranged from ham and eggs for breakfast, to a hamburger for lunch, and a nice dinner. The cost ranged from 25 cents for the hamburger to about three dollars for the dinner.

Railroad dining car, 1940s

The dining cars were equivalent to a top quality restaurant. The men wore suits, and the women wore nice dresses, and I wore my uniform. When we arrived in New Mexico, it was dark and we traveled through New Mexico, Texas, and Oklahoma during the night. I arrived in Wichita, Kansas, early in the morning. I stayed in

Wichita about three days to visit my family and friends and then continued my way east to Bainbridge, Maryland.

My train trip from Wichita went through Kansas City and Chicago, where I changed trains for Baltimore. The trip took about 33 hours, with one overnight on the train. I traveled through Missouri, Illinois, Indiana, Ohio, West Virginia, and Maryland. I had now been in 14 different states. My subsistence on this part of the trip was quite good, as I was well fortified with sandwiches, fruit, dessert, and candy bars provided by my mother. My sea bag was becoming a part of me, as I trudged from one train to another and to the bus that took me from Baltimore to Perryville, Maryland. I took a taxi from Perryville on Route 40 to the Bainbridge Naval Station.

The Bainbridge Naval Station had been a major Recruit Training Center during World War II, but was closed in 1947. The Naval Academy Preparatory School (NAPS) was the only activity left at Bainbridge. Our campus was the former Tome School.

Bainbridge Navy Training Center, Tome School building

The school was perched at the top of steep cliffs above the small town of Port Deposit. The former Tome School for Boys, with its sweeping views of the Susquehanna River, was at its peak in the 1920s, considered one of the most beautiful boarding school campuses on the East Coast. The school was named for Jacob Tome, a Port Deposit lumberman and banker. In 1942, Tome School and several nearby farms became the Bainbridge Naval Training Center. Port Deposit is between the Susquehanna River to the west and cliffs to the east. Port Deposit is about 35 miles from Baltimore and has a population of about 800.

We started school immediately after I arrived at Bainbridge. We were assigned to two-man dormitory rooms that were quite nice. My roommate was John Godek, from Dubois, Pennsylvania. John was an All-Navy wrestling champion and my polka teacher — I don't know why we thought learning the polka should be a part of our education, but that is what we did. The dining hall was located near the dormitory, and the classes were held across the quadrangle in the principal Tome School building that was dominated by a clock tower. Our campus was much the same as it was when it was a boys' school.

It was a good life, and I was excited about the school and my preparation for entering the Naval Academy. We had good meals and plenty of exercise, as we were all expected to participate in some sort of varsity or intramural sport. Also, I was looking forward to seeing some of the sights of the East Coast of the United States.

I became acquainted with Dick Gantt, one of my classmates, and Dick invited me to his home in Wilmington, Delaware. I accepted, and Dick and I made our way to Perryville and hitchhiked on Route 40 to Wilmington, a distance of 37 miles. There were about five of us, all strangers to the area, who were frequent guests at the Gantt home — it was a wonderful experience and just as important to my development as my prep-school education. Mrs. Gantt was a good teacher, and she continually pressed us to do our best, both academically and culturally. Most of us didn't realize that this was happening, but it happened.

It was sometime around Thanksgiving that my classmate, Ken Fortney, from my hometown of Wichita, and I went to New York. We visited all the sights, including a New York Giants football game against the Los Angeles Dons to see our fellow Wichitan, Linwood Sexton, play professional football. It was Linwood's last game, as he was injured during the game. Linwood was a senior during my freshman year at Wichita

University in 1947. One of my memories of Linwood was that he could not play against Tulsa in Oklahoma, since he was a Negro. He was a hero to many and our best player, and it cost us the game — Wichita lost to Tulsa 7–0. If Linwood could have played, he could have surely turned the tide.

Ken and I went to New York again to see the New Year's Eve celebration at Times Square. It was very cold with a freezing rain, and the icy mush was so deep that it ran over our shoe tops. We held out and stayed in Times Square until midnight. After the celebratory cheering, we immediately went to the bus station and caught a bus back to Perryville and on to Bainbridge. The warm bus thawed and dried us, and we suffered no complications, as we rolled into our bunks at about four on Sunday morning.

I was on the NAPS cross-country team. I had never run cross-country before, but I thought that since I didn't have any bad habits, at least not too many, I might be a good runner. It turns out that I was just an average runner. One of our meets was against an Army team at Ft. Belvoir, Virginia. We arrived at Ft. Belvoir on Friday night for a Saturday morning meet. I went to the mess hall for breakfast and ate a little bit of everything they had. This was a mistake, as at the start of the race, I upchucked my whole breakfast. I ran OK though, and finished near the head of the pack. We had free time after the meet.

My classmate, Fuzzy Knight, and I went to Washington, D. C. to see the sights. We were overwhelmed by the monuments of this great city.

Darrell, unauthorized ride on monument horse at US Capitol, 1949

One of our guard duties at Bainbridge was to inspect the whale-boat storage facility on the Susquehanna River. This duty required a long walk down steps hewn into the cliff leading to Port Deposit. It was a rigorous climb back up the cliff. Making sure these boats were secure gave me the desire to do some boating on the Susquehanna. I rented a small boat with oars and launched it into the Susquehanna. It was easy going downstream, but when I had gone far enough and turned the boat upstream, I found that I could not make any progress. I then turned toward shore and tied the boat to some rocks. I waited there, and finally a helpful boater towed me back to the rental facility. The Susquehanna has a swift flow, especially below the Conowingo Dam, about six miles upstream from Port Deposit. That was the end of my solo boating.

It is sad to note that on September 21, 2014, the landmark of the Tome School, the vacant Georgian-style school building with a clock tower, burned, probably by arson. The chapel inside this building was also destroyed.

Bainbridge Naval Academy Preparatory School Chapel fire destruction, 2014

The school had several prominent attendees including R.J. Reynolds, Jr. and members of the Mellon and Carnegie families. The Tome School was a landmark that was visible from Route 95, as it crossed the Susquehanna River. In the 1960s through the 1990s, we traveled this highway many times and our children, as well as my wife, Sally, grew weary as I always pointed out the clock tower while stating, "That is one of the places where I went to school."

In the early spring of 1949, my classmate, Ken Fortney, and I made a three-day trip to Quebec, Canada. It was a long way to Quebec, but we had a desire to see new things. We traveled by bus and tram around Quebec to take in the French atmosphere and see the city. We visited the Plains of Abraham, which was the principal site of the Battle of Quebec (Seven Years War) between the British and the French. It was a beautiful area overlooking the St. Lawrence River. Another beautiful sight was the majestic Chateau Frontenac. We stayed two nights in a very comfortable French inn and headed back to Bainbridge. I had now been in two foreign countries.

My roommate, John Godek, and I heard that you got one free weekend a month if you sang in the NAPS chapel choir, so we joined the choir. The choir leader was Mrs. Henry, the wife of Ensign Henry, who had been a wrestler at the Naval Academy. Ensign Henry was John's wrestling coach. Neither of us could really sing, but Mrs. Henry tried her best to teach us.

I took the Naval Academy entrance exam in May, and in late May, I was notified that I had passed the exam. I was on my way to becoming a Midshipman at the United States Naval Academy. My NAPS shipmates and I were transferred June 12, 1949, to the **USS Block Island (CVE-106)** docked at the Naval Station, Annapolis, across the Severn River from the Naval Academy. The **Block Island** was a training ship for Midshipmen. The ship was fairly new, commissioned in December 1944. The **Block Island** sponsor was the mother of the Marine hero, Major Pappy Boyington, who had been a Japanese Prisoner of War. Some of us had never been on a Navy ship, and it was exciting to be aboard ship, even if it was solidly tied to the Naval Station pier. We weren't assigned any duties, and all we had to do was wait to enter the Naval Academy.

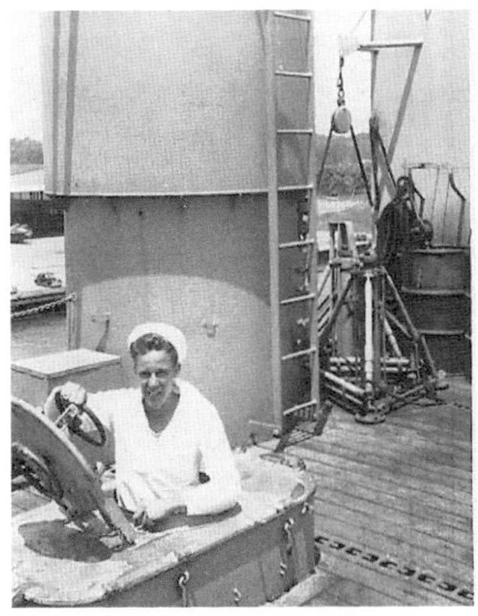

Darrell, **USS Block Island**, June 1948

CHAPTER 7: UNITED STATES NAVAL ACADEMY

We left the **Block Island** on June 15, 1949, and crossed the Severn River to the Naval Academy on Navy boats. We were sworn in as midshipmen, United States Navy — we were Naval Academy plebes. According to the dictionary, a plebe is "one who is considered to be inferior." It is derived from "plebian," the working class of ancient Rome. At the time, I did not know how low on the ladder I was. I was happy to be where I was. Plebe summer was our indoctrination into the military way of life. Being among the approximately 100 former members of the military, with about 1,000 other midshipmen entering from civilian life, some of the rules we had to follow were familiar to me. However, the overall training was intense, and I was busy trying to keep up with all the new rules and regulations.

We marched, we exercised, and we were yelled at by Marines on the rifle range. We rowed 12-man-whale boats and also learned to sail. It was a tough regimen, but was even tougher with the return of the upperclassmen at the end of the summer.

When we started the academic year, we were given only one option in the courses we were to take — the foreign language. My short exposure to the French language, during my visit to Quebec, influenced my decision to choose French as the language I would study during my first two years at the academy. Other than our foreign language, everyone took the same courses the entire four years.

Plebes were required to "brace up" — stand straight, walk straight, sit on the front of a chair, and sit straight when sitting for meals. Sometimes at meals, we were allowed to "carry on" — relax and sit comfortably in our chairs.

We had reveille at 6 AM and taps at 10 PM. We had classes from 8 AM to 4 PM each day and on Saturday morning. We marched to all classes, and we formed as companies and marched to all meals. We marched to mandatory church services each Sunday.

The highlights of the fall were the Saturday afternoon football games. We attended two-away games: Notre Dame, at the old Memorial Stadium in Baltimore, and the Army/Navy game in Philadelphia. We traveled to Baltimore by bus, about 75 buses in all. We traveled to Philadelphia, first by bus to Baltimore, and then by train to Philadelphia. If we won the Army/Navy game, we were allowed to "carry on" through our Christmas break. We lost to Army 38–0, so I never experienced a long "carry on" time during plebe year.

In January, the Brigade of Midshipmen was called to march in the funeral procession in Washington of General of the Air Force and General of the Army (both five-star ranks) Henry Harley "Hap" Arnold. General Arnold was Commander of the Army Air Corps during World War II and one of the first military aviators. The day was sunny, but very cold, with temperatures in the teens. It was extremely cold during the march down Constitution Avenue. We were carrying our M1 rifles at "right shoulder arms" all the way past the Lincoln Memorial. Just before we crossed Memorial Bridge, we were given the order "left shoulder arms." Shifting my rifle to my left shoulder was not very military, because I had very little movement in my right arm; it hung in the air, as if I still had a rifle on my right shoulder. We continued to march across the Memorial Bridge and into Arlington Cemetery to the Memorial Amphitheatre, where we were dismissed. We then boarded busses and returned to Annapolis; it was a long, cold day, but a privilege to honor an American hero.

I was very busy with my studies and keeping up with the constant discipline, and time passed quickly. It was soon the end of plebe year, and I was ready for the third-class summer cruise.

I was assigned to the battleship, **USS Missouri**. Our ports-of-call were New York City, Boston, Guantanamo Bay, Cuba, and Cristobal, Panama. We lived in the crew's quarters and performed the duties of enlisted sailors. My battle station was in a 16-inch gun mount. There were three 16-inch gun mounts, each mount had three guns — nine guns in all. The gun was prepared for firing by placing six powder bags into the spanner tray and then lowering the projectile into the spanner tray. My duty was to load three of the powder bags, weighing about 80 pounds each. There was a rumor that the cost of each projectile was equivalent to the cost of a new Cadillac — about $3,000. On one occasion, all nine guns were fired at the same time as a broadside. From inside the mount, we could feel the ship move to the side. I never saw the guns fired when I was topside.

World War II Japanese surrender, **USS Missouri**, 1945

The job we seemed to perform every day was holy stoning (cleaning) the teak deck. We would all get in line and scrub our way across the deck. Five years earlier, in 1945, the deck was the site of the World War II Japanese surrender, so the deck was treated with reverence.

Mrs. Gantt, the mother of my Bainbridge classmate, Dick Gantt, often came to Annapolis to visit Dick. I generally met with her when she was in Annapolis. We would sit on the benches in front of Bancroft Hall and talk about our progress at the Naval Academy. On a few occasions, we would have a Sunday lunch with one of her acquaintances, Mrs. Stone, who lived near the Annapolis hospital in the historic district. Mrs. Stone lived on the second floor above her son and his wife, who lived on the first floor. Mrs. Stone's daughter-in-law later worked with my wife, Sally, at the Annapolis Health Department. Mrs. Stone was a cousin of Admiral Arleigh Burke, the famous fleet commander of World War II Pacific battles against the Japanese. Mrs. Stone often referred to Admiral Burke as little "Billy." Mrs. Stone's husband graduated from the Naval Academy in the class of 1894. Mrs. Stone gave me Commander Stone's dress uniform including his epaulettes and cocked hat. The latter two items were packaged in form-fitting black metal containers. The cocked hat was discontinued as a uniform item in 1940. Commander Stone's classmate at the Naval Academy was Winston Churchill, a famed American novelist, later overshadowed by Winston S. Churchill, the British Prime Minister. The two Churchills met and communicated early in life. After the prime minister became aware of the writings of the American novelist, Winston S. Churchill agreed to sign his books Winston Spencer Church-

Cocked hat and epaulettes of Commander Stone

ill to differentiate the two authors. The prime minister later changed his writing name to Winston S. Churchill.

Winston Churchill was a superb athlete at the Naval Academy, an expert fencer, and he started the first eight-oared crew team that he captained for two years. Winston Churchill resigned shortly after graduation to pursue a writing career. His second novel, Richard Carvel, an eight volume compendium, became a best seller. The story covered American/British history during revolutionary times, as well as history of colonial Annapolis. The last volume brings Richard Carvel, the main character, to England to follow his neighbor and sweetheart, Dorothy Manners. In England, he is abducted by highway bandits and taken prisoner on a pirate ship. The pirate ship fights a British brigantine and sinks. Richard is rescued by the brigantine, captained by John Paul, who later changed his name to John Paul Jones. Carvel returns to America and at the beginning of the Revolutionary War decides to fight for his country. John Paul Jones has decided to oppose the British and has joined the American Navy. Carvel serves with Captain John Paul Jones on the **Bonhomme Richard** when the **Bonhomme Richard** fought the famous battle against the British ship, **Serapis**. Carvel is wounded and during his recovery is cared for by his former sweetheart, Dorothy. Carvel later becomes master of Carvel Hall and is married to his childhood sweetheart, Dorothy Manners.

Churchill likely got the name of his novel from Carvel Hall, a hotel in Annapolis across the street from the Naval Academy. Carvel Hall was a favorite lodging for the girlfriends of Midshipmen who were in Annapolis for the weekend. As a Midshipman, I often went to Carvel Hall. The last time I went there was in 1958. I attended a presentation by my classmate, Bob Kassel. Bob served on the US nuclear submarine **Nautilus** when she made the first undersea voyage to the geographic North Pole on August 3, 1958. The **Nautilus** was constructed under the supervision of Captain (later Vice Admiral) Hyman Rickover who became my protagonist when I was interviewed by him in 1961

My third-class year started in September, and so did the football season. Again, the Army/Navy game was the highlight of our season. There was a custom between the Army Cadets and the Navy Midshipmen to bet their distinctive bath robes that their team would win. Since Army entered the game undefeated and the number two collegiate football team in the nation, and Navy had a record of two wins and six losses, it seemed that the game was out of reach for the Navy team. Since we were such a heavy underdog, the cadet that I made the bet with, gave me 21 points. Navy played a great game and won 14 to 2, and I had an Army bathrobe.

Academics were getting more difficult for me, probably because I had now finished the subjects I had previously studied in college, at the Navy Electronics School, and at the Naval Academy Preparatory School. I was two years older than many of my classmates, and this gave me a small advantage, or maybe it just allowed me to keep up with the class.

I was in my second year of junior-varsity soccer. I had tried fencing during plebe year, but did not continue during my third-class year. I also played intramural volleyball and tried out for the golf team, where I never advanced beyond junior varsity. Our physical training included wrestling and boxing, so I had a chance to imitate Joe Louis. It was mandatory that every midshipman play either varsity or intramural sports. Again, our academic year seemed to pass quickly, and we were soon on another summer training cruise.

The second-class summer training was a combination of amphibious and aviation training. The amphibious portion was held at the Naval Amphibious Base at Little Creek, Virginia, near Norfolk, Virginia. Our quarters were in Quonset huts. With the metal roof and no air conditioning; it was very hot in the Virginia summer climate. Almost every day, we went to sea in amphibious ships, practiced climbing down rope ladders into landing craft and landing on the beach. There was a lot of waiting for something to happen, but I always had a pocket book to read.

We left Little Creek and went to the Naval Aircraft Rework Facility in Norfolk to observe the process of overhauling aircraft. It was in Norfolk that I observed some of the customs of the "Deep South." The water fountains were marked "For Colored Only" and "For White Only."

We then went to the Naval Air Station, Pensacola, Florida, where Navy pilots were trained, and then to Barksdale Air

Force Base in Shreveport, Louisiana. It was excellent summer training, with some shipboard experience and a lot of flying. While we were in Shreveport, I visited with my Aunt Geraldine and her husband, Phil Collins.

October 3, 1951, of my second-class year, was a cold, blustery day at Hospital Point on the banks of the Severn River. Hospital Point contained several athletic fields. I was in the locker room, near the Naval Academy Cemetery, dressing for soccer practice. The New York Giants and Brooklyn Dodgers were playing the decisive game three which would decide the winner of the National League pennant. It was about four in the afternoon, and I was listening to the game on my ever-present transistor radio. I had been listening to the game since about 3:30 PM, as I was walking from our dormitory, Bancroft Hall, to Hospital Point. The score was Dodgers 4, Giants 2 in the bottom half of the 9th inning. Ralph Branca relieved the Dodgers' starting pitcher, Don Newcombe, with one out, two men on base, and Bobby Thompson at the plate. Thompson was a great hitter, who had hit 31 home runs for the season, but the Dodgers opted to let him hit rather than give him an intentional walk because the dangerous Willie Mays was the next batter. Thompson took a called strike, and then hit a fast ball over the left field fence and the Giants won the pennant 5 to 4. It was the "shot heard around the world" — a reference to the first shots fired in the American Revolution at Concord, and also, perhaps, to the servicemen stationed in Korea listening to the game on Armed Forces Radio. It was one of those days that I will never forget, and it was much better to listen to the game on the radio, than to read about it in the newspaper. The game is often referenced in news reports, and although I wasn't at the game, I was there!

For first-class summer training I was assigned to the destroyer **Putnam (DD-757)**, and we embarked at Norfolk for a North Atlantic cruise with port calls at Londonderry, Northern Ireland, and Le Havre, France. The North Atlantic seas were rough, and it took some time to get used to the pitch and roll of a small ship. My shipboard duties were in the engine room. It was a great experience, and I learned a lot about the propulsion system of a destroyer. Londonderry, in the northern latitudes, had very long periods of daylight. The sights and people of Northern Ireland were fantastic, and we were on our way to Le Havre. We had shore leave in Le Havre and a group of us took a train to Paris. Of course, we enjoyed the sights and excitement of Paris: the Eiffel Tower, Notre Dame Cathedral, the Champs Elysées, the Arc de Triomphe, and the Follies Bergère (an extravaganza featuring young women in various states of dress, or should I say undress).

"How Ya Gonna Keep 'em Down on the Farm (After They've Seen Paree?)" This was a popular World War I song, referring to the young soldiers of rural America, who might not want to return to their roots, after experiencing the culture and glamour of Paris. We were back in Le Havre for the French national holiday, Bastille Day, July 14, although I did not get to enjoy the celebration as I had watch duty.

The Bastille, a fortress/prison, constructed in the 14th century and used for holding political prisoners, symbolized the tyranny of King Louis XVI and his regime. Revolutionaries stormed the Bastille on July 14, 1789, freeing all political prisoners. This was the beginning of the French Revolution, a decade of terror. Thousands of French citizens were executed, many by the guillotine, including the king and his famous wife, Marie Antoinette.

We did have a little excitement on January 30, 1953, as the Brigade of Midshipmen marched in President Eisenhower's inaugural parade. It was a long day, as we left Annapolis very early by bus, and then waited a long time in Washington before the parade began. The day's temperature was a mild 50 degrees. The parade lasted about four hours, and fortunately, we were near the beginning of the parade. We finished by dark and returned to Annapolis.

During first-class year, we made our selection of service assignments. Since there was no Air Force Academy, and the Air Force was in need of qualified officers, about 25 per cent of our class went into the United States Air Force. My eyesight had begun to fail at the end of plebe year, but I was not tempted by the lure of Air Force blue and the generous 60 days of leave (vacation). I decided to go into the Navy Supply Corps.

In April of 1953, I purchased my first car, a 1953 red Chevrolet convertible. I graduated on June 5, 1953, and my brother, John, and I traveled to Philadelphia, where we saw the Phillies play baseball at the old Connie Mack Stadium. We continued north to see the sights of New York and then further north to Montreal and Quebec, Canada. After enjoying the sights of these two great cities, we drove to Wichita, Kansas, for a visit. After a short visit in Wichita, I traveled to Bayonne, New Jersey, to attend the Navy Supply Corps School.

Darrell driving his new Chevrolet, Times Square, New York City, 1953

Chapter 8: Navy Supply Corps School, Bayonne, New Jersey

The Navy Supply Corps School was located on the New Jersey shore of the Hudson River with magnificent views of the Statue of Liberty and the New York City skyline. The school was on the site of the World War II Military Ocean Terminal. Bayonne was a solid working- class all-American city. Since there were limited military quarters at the Navy Base, three classmates and I rented a house for three months in Staten Island, New York, and then rented an apartment in Jersey City, New Jersey, for three months.

Statue of Liberty and New York City skyline from Bayonne, New Jersey, 1953

We studied the duties of a supply officer, which basically are all areas of support, including stocking and supply of repair parts, pay of crew, food services, resale services, such as personal hygiene items and snacks, laundry services, and management of contracts for goods and services. The Supply Corps studies always emphasized strict adherence to rules and regulations. These rules required accounting for cash and other funds to the penny — no rounding of numbers.

One particular study that I remember was the reimbursement of claims for official travel that involved crossing the International Date Line. In this computation, it was necessary to either add or subtract a day from the calendar depending on which direction one was traveling.

I might have learned then, but I certainly learned later on, that there would be conflict between the need for a quick response and the time needed to "get every signature on every dotted line." The career of the supply officer was often decided by the skill with which he treaded the narrow gap between these, sometimes, opposing forces.

We had a lecture on the consequences of enhancing one's fortune by using government funds for personal use or accepting "favors" from contractors. The "reward" for this malfeasance was a tour of duty in the "Big House" — the Navy prison at Newport, Rhode Island. You could add a visit to another state to your count. We were shown pictures of a person in a striped suit chopping rocks — "making little ones out of big ones." During my Naval career, I did not always follow the strict rules and regulations, but I managed to balance the needs of the Naval service and these rules and regulations.

School was not all study. There were too many things to see in the New York environs. When I lived on Staten Island, I took the ferry from Staten Island to the New York Battery waterfront. I walked the streets of New York from the Battery to Central Park, passing through Chinatown, Greenwich Village, up Broadway to Times Square and past Rockefeller Center to Central Park, a distance of seven miles. You might say I experienced the "wonders of the world" in those seven miles.

For night life, we couldn't beat Sammy's Bowery Follies. The Follies were a vaudeville show featuring "older" women and comedians. The ladies, some of whom were former Broadway show girls, danced like "can can" girls, kicking their legs high. They were a big hit. The customers ranged from the serious-alcoholic derelict to the New York upper class. It was a real destination. You could get a meal for about four dollars or a hamburger for a dollar.

I came across the Follies while returning to Staten Island. My route that night took me down Third Avenue under the elevated train and through the Bowery District. In the evening, there were always several men sleeping in doorways. It was a seedy area, but in those days, not a frightening walk. I saw the posters outside when I passed Sammy's. They looked interesting, so I went in. The older women on stage looked a bit different, but I stayed and saw a fantastic show. Sammy's was both a daytime and evening home for the drinking man/alcoholic. They waited outside Sammy's early in the morning to get in out of the cold and to have a little refreshment. They were part of the décor. I returned to Sammy's a few times with some of my classmates from Bayonne.

Sammy's Bowery Follies,
New York City, 1953

Men in line for food,
New York City

The Statue of Liberty was very close to Bayonne, but we had to cross the Hudson River via a tunnel or use the Staten Island Ferry to get there. The statue was easily accessible from the New York Battery. There were no entry lines and Lady Liberty's crown was easily accessible. At the current time, there is high security for Liberty Island entry, and reservations must be made months in advance for access to the crown.

Despite all the distractions of New York City, I graduated from Supply Corps School in December 1953, and after a short Christmas leave in Wichita, I reported to the aircraft carrier **USS Randolph (CVA 15)** on New Year's Eve 1953.

CHAPTER 9: THE MEDITERRANEAN SEA

Early in the New Year, 1954, **USS Randolph** departed Norfolk for a six-month deployment to the Mediterranean (Med). The **Randolph** was assigned to the US Navy Sixth Fleet in the Med. The responsibility of the Sixth Fleet was to conduct air operations in various sections of the Med in support of the Cold War.

Our first stop was Gibraltar. The main attractions were the climb up the "Rock" and the abundance of monkeys. They are Barbary macaques, native to Algeria and Morocco. They are the only wild monkeys in Europe and probably came to Gibraltar from North Africa with the Moors in the 8th century.

The main street of Gibraltar had a British ambiance, and the locals were used to seeing a large number of Navy people. The border to Spain was open to us, and I walked across the border to La Linea, Spain. Although it was not typical of the real Spain, it certainly had the atmosphere of the people of Spain, especially my excursion to the bull fights.

Other ports we were to visit during our time in the Mediterranean were Thessaloniki, Greece; Genoa, Naples, Livorno and Taranto, Italy; Palermo, Sicily; Algiers, Algeria; Valencia, Spain, and Cannes and Marseille, France.

We left Gibraltar, transited to the eastern Mediterranean, and went north in the Aegean Sea to Thessaloniki (Salonika),

Greece. Salonika is the second largest city in Greece. We were there in February, and it was very cold. I met an older man, and he invited me to his house, where he offered me a small glass of ouzo. I learned that ouzo is the favorite alcoholic drink of Greece. It has a licorice taste and to the faint of heart, it must be sipped with moderation. I wanted to be a good guest, but I finished only about a third of the drink. I did my best.

I went with a friend to a Greek night club. We were invited to sit at a table with some young Greek men and women. They were drinking beer. Thankfully, it was not ouzo. When one of the women went to the restroom, she was accompanied by a man, not a woman — an unusual custom. The restroom consisted of a hole in the floor with two imprints for placement of the feet in front of the hole — not uncomfortable for me, but what about the women?

When we left Salonika, we headed to a warmer climate. Our main port of call in the Med was Naples, and we were there three times. We visited Rome, Pompeii, the Amalfi Coast, and the Isle of Capri. During one stay in Naples, I was sent to Livorno (Leghorn) to get some aircraft parts from another Navy aircraft carrier. We made the short trip north on a Navy aircraft. We were there overnight, and after I obtained the parts, I had a chance to travel to the not-too-distant Pisa to see the Leaning Tower of Pisa. The view from the top of the

Leaning Tower of Pisa, Pisa, Italy, 1954

Darrell grips rail on high side of Leaning Tower of Pisa

Leaning Tower was beautiful, but I took some time getting used to standing on the low side and looking down. At the edge, I had the sensation, if I leaned too far, it might topple. You can see in the picture that I am holding on to the rail on the high side. The tower definitely leans.

Algiers was my most exciting port of call. The panorama of Algiers, as seen from our anchorage, was a wonder to behold. At the center of the panorama was an oval of tightly-clustered white buildings, vividly demarcated from the surrounding buildings. I learned that this white scene was the Casbah or Citadel of Algiers. It was a Muslim area, and we were warned to be very careful about entering the Casbah. A group of us had a guide when we made a short excursion into the Casbah. It was very crowded and all the women wore veils.

Casbah (white area), Algiers, Algeria, 1954

We were one of the last US Navy ships to visit Algiers. The Algerians were aggressively demonstrating and beginning to fight for independence from the French in 1954. The insurgents later had a safe haven in the Casbah in their battles against the French.

I was the manager of the **Randolph** softball team. A French sports club allowed us to set up a softball field on one of their soccer fields. We played against teams from other ships that were in port in Algiers. We always had a good attendance of the locals at our games.

The year 1954 was not too long after the end of World War II, and there were black markets in most of the ports we visited. The biggest selling item was cigarettes. I didn't smoke cigarettes and was never tempted to make a profit in this manner, but some people did engage in this nefarious transaction. One was a shipmate, a reserve officer. He went ashore in Algiers with several cartons of cigarettes, and was caught by the French Gendarme while making a transaction. They put him in a French slammer. He called his father in the States. His father had some connections overseas, and after a few calls, my shipmate was released, but not before he spent the night in the slammer. Maybe he paid a sizable fine, but for what he did, he got off easy. He still had to face the Military Justice system, but as I remember, his punishment back on the ship was not serious. For a career officer, an incident such as this could have ended his career. The release of the offender was paramount, as the captain of the **Randolph** would not have wanted to report that he had left an officer behind in a French jail when the **Randolph** departed Algiers.

When we went on shore leave (liberty) in the Med, the officers were allowed to wear civilian clothes, but we were required to wear a coat, a tie, and a hat. A lot of us bought hats in Naples that could be folded. Once we were off the ship, we could fold our hats and put them in our luggage or pocket.

Marseille was a great port. I met some legionnaires who had served in the French Foreign Legion in Africa. They were mostly French with some Germans. I had read and heard about the rigors of service in the French Foreign Legion, but

French Foreign Legion Post, Marseille, France

the tales they told seemed bigger than life. One of them had just been discharged, and I traded some of my US Navy insignia for his epaulettes. Their service, at that time, was particularly difficult. Throughout French Africa, there was unrest as the locals were battling for independence.

One of my jobs, in addition to aviation stores' officer, was assistant disbursing officer. When we left the US, the supply officer and disbursing officer estimated that the **Randolph** would need $2,000,000 in cash to handle the exchange of dollars for foreign currency, i.e. Gibraltar pounds, Greek drachma, Italian lire, French francs, Algerian francs, and Spanish pesetas. Two million dollars in cash is a lot of bulk, requiring two large safes. The bulk of the cash was $20 dollar bills in bundles of $80,000. The disbursing officer was audited on a surprise basis by the supply officer once a quarter. The cash was counted by a group of supply officers. It was no more difficult to count two million dollars than it was to count $200,000 since all we had to do with the larger amount was to count about 23 bundles of 20 dollar bills and then the remaining cash.

The disbursing officer took shore leave when we were in Marseille, and I was the acting disbursing officer. When I took over as disbursing officer for a short time, I counted all the cash, as did the regular disbursing officer when he returned. The first day in Marseille, I wrote a government check for $80,000 and took a small boat from our anchorage to the dock in Marseille. I was accompanied by a disbursing clerk, and we both wore unloaded side arms. I carried a large attaché case attached to a float. The clerk and I walked up the wide boulevard Rue Canebiere. I presented a United States government check to the bank and received $80,000 worth of French francs. We retraced our route back to the dock and by boat back to the **Randolph**, successfully completing the transaction. Although I knew well that Marseille was a port city and had its share of criminal mischief, I don't remember having any anxiety about walking the streets with $80,000 in French francs. My next job back on the ship was to enlist the help of other supply officers to provide the crew with French francs in exchange for US dollars. In summary, you can see that we did not expend US dollars in that I wrote a government check for francs, and I then exchanged these francs for dollars that we had previously paid the crew. At the end of the cruise, we had about the same amount of dollars as at the start of the deployment.

The most difficult of the currency exchanges we made was the Greek drachma, with a conversion rate of 30,003 drachma per dollar. After obtaining about $100,000 Greek drachma, we packaged them in million-drachma packages as follows:

One million drachma = $ 33.35
Two million drachma = $ 66.70
Five million drachma = $166.75

One might ask, "Why not let the crew exchange dollars for drachmas in Greece?" This was certainly their option, but being unfamiliar with the process, some of the crew may not have been able to make a fair exchange ashore. The intent was to make it convenient for the crew. Of course, some veterans of foreign deployments used the illegal black market and negotiated a more favorable rate of exchange, but to their peril.

I had started reading **The Count of Monte Cristo** by Alexandre Dumas. The hero, Edmond Dantes, is falsely accused and condemned without trial to life imprisonment in the Chateau d'If. The Chateau d'If is an island in the harbor of Marseille and was a short distance from our anchorage. The drama of the novel added to the excitement of my time in Marseille, as I could easily see the Chateau d'If from the deck of the **Randolph** and could imagine the life of Edmond Dantes during his imprisonment there.

Harbor of Marseille, France, Chateau d'If Island

I went on a day trip to Arles and Avignon. Avignon is famous for the Pont d'Avignon (Bridge of Avignon), built in the 12th century over the Rhone River. Due to flooding of the Rhone, the bridge has been destroyed several times and only four of the original 22 arches remain today. The city and bridge are known for the song "Sur le Pont d'Avignon — On the Bridge of Avignon." It has been 63 years since I was there, but I still remember the first stanza in French. We learned it on the bus going from Marseille to Avignon. Avignon is also famous as the residence of the Popes in the 14th century. The French Pope Clement V was elected in 1305. He moved his papal court to Avignon, where it remained under a succession of French popes for 67 years before returning to Rome. The Papal palace was a magnificent structure with many paintings and other adornments.

Pont d'Avignon, Avignon, France, 1954

There were also Roman ruins in Avignon. Those Romans really got around. It seemed like there were Roman ruins everywhere we went. Arles is famous for its Roman Coliseum as well as a nearby aqueduct and flour mill. The engineering and construction of these facilities, as well as Roman roads, are a tribute to the advanced engineering ability of the Romans. One might say that the Romans of almost 2,000 years ago were cleverer than the Midwest farmers of early 20th century America, in that the Romans made sure they had water for their people and fields before they "moved in." They didn't hope and pray for water, they planned for water.

Cannes, France, is the central city of the French Riviera with beautiful beaches and scenery. While in Cannes, I went on a tour to Montreux, Switzerland. Our bus trip took us through Grenoble, France, and Geneva, Switzerland. We had a short stop in Grenoble for a meal and sightseeing. We passed over the Alps, just like Hannibal and his elephants. We passed through Geneva and Lausanne on the north shore of Lake Geneva to Montreux on the eastern shore of Lake Geneva. I visited the Chateau Chillon, where Lord Bryon was inspired to write "The Prisoner of Chillon."

We rented skis and took a small commuter train up a small hill for about five minutes, disembarked from the train and skied down the hill. Most of us had never skied before; the short five-minute trip down a gradual slope was about all we could handle. The train ran every 30 minutes, so we had to wait a bit for the train. We had a bottle or glass of French biere to soften the wait time. We enjoyed the skiing and skied until it was dark. I made about six trips, which must have been five beers. Oh well, we were getting a lot of exercise. We stayed in Montreux two nights, so we got to know the town pretty well.

I was assigned another disbursing duty while we were in Cannes. Villafranche-sur-Mer was another port of call for US Navy ships, and there was a small ship with a crew of about 100 in port. I was assigned to pay the crew. There was a disbursing clerk on the ship, and he had computed the pay due per person. I, along with two clerks from the **Randolph**, traveled by Navy car to Villafranche-sur-Mer with the necessary US dollars. It was a magnificent drive, mostly along the beautiful Côte d'Azur, near Nice, France. The duties were successfully performed, the crew was happy, and we returned to the **Randolph**.

A visit to southern France would not be complete without a visit to Monte Carlo. It was a short train trip from Cannes. As usual, I wore a coat and tie, but I must have looked like a poor foreigner amidst all the glitter of the casino. I gambled small amounts on Baccarat (I barely understood the game.) and Roulette — not enough to become addicted. On second thought, how could I become addicted with the small amount of money I had? I kept a couple of chips as souvenirs, so I guess you could say that "I left as a winner" and I had been to the casino at Monte Carlo.

Aircraft landing on the
USS Randolph, 1954

While at sea we conducted air operations in coordination with other ships of our task force and with foreign ships. My position in the leadership on the **Randolph** was low on the totem pole, and I was not aware of specific missions of our aircraft. However, I did glean a little information from my 15 roommates in the forward junior officers' bunkroom on the main deck where we had hatches that opened to the open bow under the flight deck. I did know enough to realize that the pilots were very skilled and had great courage to safely take-off and land their aircraft, particularly at night. On one occasion, a Douglas Skyraider took some shell fire, probably near or over East Germany. The damage was not severe, and the pilot safely returned to the **Randolph**.

During one of our Sundays at sea, our captain allowed a swim call. An elevator was lowered to the level of the hangar deck, about 30 feet above the water line. An accommodation ladder was also lowered for the faint of heart, who did not want to jump 30 feet into a sea of unknown depth. We also had lines to climb down and to grab while we were in the sea. The average depth of the Mediterranean Sea is 4,900 feet, and the deepest part is over three miles. Now, that's damn deep, as the mathematician would say about Kansas being damn flat. While I realized that I

Swimming, Mediterranean Sea, 1954

would swim only in the top six feet, I was concerned about the depth. I made sure, when I let go of something, I always visualized another grab-onto point. Anyway, it was great fun, and I treasure the experience.

The passage through the Straits of Messina between Sicily and Italy was exciting. The narrowest part of the straits is at the toe of the Italian boot, a distance of two miles, so you can easily see both shores. Also, from this vantage point, Mt. Etna, with a height of over 10,000 feet, dominates Sicily. We traversed the straits in the daytime, and we could see clouds of smoke coming from the world's oldest active volcano.

After transiting the straits, we turned west and called at the port of Palermo, Sicily. It was like going back in time with streets congested with colorful horse-drawn carts carrying all sorts of goods and passengers.

Vegetable cart, Palermo, Sicily, 1954

Our softball team played a game in Palermo against a team from another US Navy ship. The ball field was bordered by hedge lines of cacti. When balls went into the cactus area, and they often did, they were retrieved by some local boys who attached themselves to our team. I have no idea why I was not wearing a shirt in the picture below — I do know that it was not to display my modest torso. Although I was the team manager, I managed by consensus because the team had veteran ball players who had been with the **Randolph** for two or three years. Perhaps I was assigned as manager so I would be the person named responsible for any misbehavior by the team. None of us got into trouble.

USS Randolph softball team (Darrell standing on right), 1954

The next stop was Valencia, Spain, an old and historic city with crowded neighborhoods where people clustered on the streets around their houses in the evening to do their visiting and do some drinking, probably sangria. The main attraction that I was looking forward to was bull fighting. The day was warm and sunny — what you would expect for this spectacle. I was, of course, unfamiliar with the ritual of bull fighting, but gradually gained some understanding.

Bull fight, Valencia, Spain, 1954

The day starts with a parade of participants, arrayed in bright and colorful traditional attire passed down through many generations. The main participants are the matador, banderilleeros and picadors, the latter two had the responsibility to weaken the bull before the final blow by the matador. Of course, it is a dangerous "sport," and there are often injuries. It was a great spectacle, but you could say it was not my "cup of tea." Earlier in our deployment, I had seen a “minor league” bull fight in a small ring in La Linea, Spain, perhaps good for the tourist, but not in any way in the same league as Valencia. Valencia was founded by the Romans in the second century BC and, of course, I saw all the sights of this historic city.

The evidence of a Roman presence was everywhere, just like “Kilroy was Here.” During World War II, American soldiers would mark a new place they had been, generally in a war zone, with the graffiti “Kilroy was here.” It was also used by persons on the home front.

Taranto, Italy, on the instep of the Italian boot, is the main port of the Italian navy. It is a large port, and we saw ships and sailors from the Italian, British, and French navies. We played a couple of softball games there. It would have been nice if we could have played against teams from ships from other countries, but softball was not a game that they played.

Genoa, Italy, has a nice port and is a large and pleasurable city to visit. I took a day trip down the coast to the small seaside villages of Rapallo and Portofino. The villages were quaint, with many fishing boats and fishermen repairing their nets — a far cry from the yachts and small cruise ships that call on these tourist places today.

We made one last stop at Gibraltar, and then left the Med in August 1954 and headed home. It was a good deployment. I learned a lot about the duties of a junior officer, and at the same time, I saw some of the wonders of the world. Was it a deployment in defense of our country or a paid vacation? It was both. After all, wasn’t my desire to “see the world” one of the reasons I joined the Navy? I had been in the Navy for six years and eight months, including my time at the Naval Academy, and I had been on three continents and in 12 countries. What a life! I came to a fork in the road, and I took it.

I went home to Kansas on leave in September 1954. Soon after departing on leave, Hurricane Edna swept up the East Coast, leaving a path of destruction. The **Randolph** was put to sea to ride out the hurricane, only to catch the wrath of the storm. The **Randolph's** open flight deck was curled up at the bow, and many other parts of the ship were damaged. **Randolph** was in the Portsmouth Naval Shipyard when I returned. Many of the Supply Department storerooms were in disarray, particularly the small-parts storeroom, where parts were all mixed up and a foot deep on the deck.

In December, a friend and I caught a US Navy seaplane flight to Bermuda. We rented motor scooters and toured the island. Bermuda was decorated for Christmas, and the citizens had everything except snow. When we were ready to leave, we waited and waited at the Air Force Base for a return flight to Norfolk, and then decided we would be better off going to anyplace in the US — it was the Little Rock Air Force Base in Arkansas. We take our chances when we fly space available. Arkansas was close to Kansas, so when I arrived in Little Rock, I caught a bus to Wichita to visit my parents and then made my way back to Norfolk.

I caught a very unusual flight from Wichita to Washington, D.C. I flew in a bomber aircraft. My seat was near the rear of the aircraft in the bombardier's seat. There was a door to access this area, but I was separated from the pilot, co-pilot, and other personnel in the cockpit. The flight was lonely and cold. There were two small port holes for light and sight. I had headphone communications with the radio officer forward, but was reluctant to bother him. As we made the long flight of about seven hours, I tried to identify the landscape to see where I was. Of course, there is a lot of flat land, but I identified the Mississippi River and the West Virginia mountains. I was very pleased to complete that flight. Would I do it again? I think not, but on second thought, it depends on the destination. I traveled a long way and some of the roads were not paved. Maybe it was time for me to grow up and settle down.

Darrell, Pisa, Italy,
Leaning Tower of Pisa,
1954

Rock of Gibralter from Spanish border,
1954

Darrell, Funicular, Mt. Vesuvius,
Italy, 1954

Darrell, Rome, Italy, Vatican St.
Peter's Cathedral, 1954

Marseille, France, Bastille Day,
1954

Algerian children, 1954

CHAPTER 10: USS BARTON (DD-722)

In early 1955, I was transferred to the destroyer **USS Barton**, the second Navy ship to bear this name, to serve as supply officer. The **Barton** had just returned from the Far East in August 1954. On a previous deployment to Korea in 1952, the **Barton** was hit by a 105 mm shell from an enemy shore battery, and one sailor was killed. Also, in September 1952, the **Barton** hit a floating mine off the coast of Korea, and five sailors were killed. The **Barton** hit the mine on the starboard side, destroying the number one boiler room, allowing water to enter the ship. Repair crews went to work shoring bulkheads and stabilizing the ship. The boiler room hatch was closed to maintain water-tight integrity.

Andy Anderson, a **Barton** storekeeper and valued long-time friend related to me the part he played in the mine blast. Andy and many of the crew were watching a movie in the crew's mess hall below the main deck when the **Barton** hit the mine. The **Barton** rolled to the port side and Andy, who was standing, was thrown against the bulkhead and then, being dazed, fell to the deck. Sailors ran over him as they escaped to the main deck. Andy was the last to climb the ladder, and when he reached the main deck, there was a second explosion caused by the rupture of the engine room boilers. Steam pipes burst causing release of 800 degree steam known as liquid knife because it could cut the skin like a knife. Andy was trapped in darkness in a 4 x 8-foot area. He later learned that after a muster he was listed as missing. A search party found him and applied ointment to his burns, and he was guided to sick bay for treatment. When he approached sick bay, he saw shipmates with much more serious injuries than his, and he became ill. The injuries included puffed faces, skin hanging from face and arms, and one sailor with a protruding bone. Andy declined to be treated, and in despair, he went to the relative calm of the fantail and waited there in the dark until they found him again.

When I served on the **Barton,** about half the crew had served on the **Barton** during the 1952 deployment, and I had many conversations with them about the disasters they encountered. However, I did not know of the gruesome recovery details until 2014, when Andy sent me a detailed story of the incident. The story was written by Don Banks, a sailor in the repair department of the **USS Bryce Canyon**, a destroyer tender that was based in Sasebo, Japan. With only one operational boiler, it took five days for the **Barton** to limp to Sasebo. The **Barton** was placed in dry dock, and Don Banks was one of the **Bryce Canyon** crew to open the hatch and descend into the boiler room. The ladder was bent and broken and care had to be taken in descending through twisted metal and debris. The smell from decaying bodies was overwhelming, and it was with supreme effort that the repair crew, assisted by hospital corpsmen, recovered the five bodies.

Andy told me that after the **Barton** arrived in Sasebo and the **Bryce Canyon** personnel had opened the boiler room, Captain Seim asked for volunteers to assist the **Bryce Canyon** in recovering bodies. After the first volunteer from the **Barton** supply department got sick from the difficult work in the boiler room, Andy volunteered to assist. Among the many body parts that Andy recovered was an eyeball. Since Andy assisted in paying the crew and saw all the sailors in the payday line many times, he knew immediately to whom the eyeball belonged.

In the aftermath of this ordeal, Andy suffered various ailments including claustrophobia, bad dreams, and nightmares. Andy lived through these ailments and said, "I just had to get this out of my head, as it has been inside me for all these years, and back in my Navy days, we had nobody to talk to and explain our pent-up feelings."

Wartime brings the crew together. All crew members must be trained to perform their assigned duties to the best of their abilities. This is critical to their assigned mission and the survival of the ship. The **Barton** crew performed heroically. I now understood the **Barton** camaraderie I observed when I attended some of the annual **Barton** reunions. Most of the **Barton** crew were not career personnel. They served four years, and left the Navy to pursue other careers. Their time on the **Barton** was their only Navy experience, and they had seen and experienced the tragedies of war. The captain of the **Barton,** at the time of the mine blast, Commander Seim (later Captain Seim), made a very emotional speech at one of the reunions that kept the crew and their guests spellbound. It was an honor to serve with this heroic crew and on the heroic ship **Barton.**

The first **USS Barton (DD-599)** was commissioned in May 1942 and soon deployed to the Pacific. Her first action was the first Battle of Guadalcanal in November 1942, where she was hit by two Japanese torpedoes. She sank within minutes with the loss of 164 of her crew of 206 — 80 per cent of her crew. The first **Barton** had a life of six months. When you look at this picture, just imagine that four of the five men you see on deck will perish at Guadalcanal. You can also imagine that this loss of life occurred many times in many battles on land, on the sea, and in the air during World War II.

First **USS Barton** in Pacific, 1942

However, my time on the **Barton** was not to be like that. I guess for the **Barton**, you could call it catch up or to get well. We were at sea a lot, but we did not deploy to the Mediterranean or to the Pacific. During our time at sea, we had training exercises with other ships, conducted gunnery exercises, and had drills where we activated all our weapons and equipment.

The **Barton** had a crew of about 275, with about 18 officers. I was the supply officer with a crew of about 20. My senior enlisted man was a chief hospital corpsman. We had a small ship's store, a wardroom staff, a disbursing clerk, storekeepers, a barber, who also ran the ship's store, laundry men, a galley crew of cooks and bakers, and a small sick bay. Sailors from other departments were assigned as mess cooks on a rotating basis to assist the cooks and perform clean-up chores. It was a small homogeneous group — easy to manage and work together. I was also the wardroom officer/mess caterer, responsible for providing the weekly menu and managing the wardroom staff and wardroom finances. Officers received a monthly allowance for meals. It was my responsibility to serve top quality meals while keeping the cost of meals within this allowance.

Moderate seas for **USS Barton** in Atlantic Ocean, 1954

We had several at-sea periods while we were in Norfolk. How did the **Barton** handle rough seas? You can see that in moderate seas, we had water over the deck. It was not uncommon to have 20-degree rolls and severe pitching fore and aft. Did I get seasick? Yes, during my first at-sea periods, I often felt that I was going to get sick, and I resorted to the lessons that I had learned as a midshipman on the **Putnam** when we crossed the Atlantic — eating saltines. I gradually got used to rough seas.

We had a small wardroom amidships that we used as a rest area. There was a table placed fore and aft and anchored to the deck that would seat five. During our infrequent spare time, we played card games. We sat on the sides of the table and when the ship rolled, the metal chairs would either slide against the bulkhead or against the table. We played our cards when the chair slammed against the table. Our meals during rough weather were generally soup or something else easy to prepare, as the cooks also had trouble keeping their pots and pans in place.

We made a port call at Washington, D.C., where we tied up at the historic Washington Navy Yard. We had a few days to see the Washington sights, many of them within walking distance of the Navy Yard. It was quite an experience to go out during the day, knowing that we had berthing back on the ship. Our captain maintained his home in the Washington suburbs, and he invited the wardroom officers to a dinner at his home.

Early in the summer, we transited to the Naval Shipyard, Charleston, South Carolina for a five-month repair availability. Since our berthing and mess spaces were being repaired, we had living spaces off the ship. A group of officers rented a seaside vacation home on the Isle of Palms. It was an easy commute, and we settled in for the summer. Each of us was responsible for overseeing the repair of our spaces on the ship, but we had time in the evenings and on weekends for sightseeing in the Charleston area.

Scene of old South

Charleston is an historic and charming southern city with many byways to explore. Going into the country around Charleston, and taking an unpaved road, we found scenes of the Old South on each side of the road. Also, there are many plantations around Charleston, as well as Atlantic beaches, both north and south of Charleston.

On October 1, a group of us went to Columbia to see Navy beat the University of South Carolina, 26 to 0. Our repairs were completed in the late fall, and the **Bar-**

ton returned to Norfolk. Early in the new year of 1956, I bid farewell to my **Barton** shipmates, and I was transferred to the Naval Air Station, Patuxent River, Maryland.

CHAPTER 11: NAVAL AIR STATION, PATUXENT RIVER, MARYLAND

The Naval Air Station, Patuxent River, is located in rural St. Mary's County, about 65 miles south of Washington, D.C. I was assigned to the Fleet Logistics Air Wing staff. I accounted for the maintenance and fuel expenditures of air wing aircraft. As the name implies, our mission was to provide logistics support by providing transport for personnel and cargo. Of course, being the junior officer on the staff, I was assigned many other tasks.

I quickly adapted to shore duty at Patuxent River. I had quarters in the Bachelor Officers' Quarters and also had my meals there. I bought a 16-foot lapstreak boat with a 25-horsepower motor and some water skis. I stored my boat at the Patuxent River small-boat facility and took to the water quite often. I was involved in several sports activities: softball, tennis, handball, and golf. These kept me busy during the week, and on weekends, I went sightseeing in the local area and to Washington, D.C.

My main leisure activity was flying to distant points. Our squadron, in Norfolk, flew regular routes to Europe and Africa. We also had a squadron in Port Lyautey, Morocco, which had a regular route to Spain, England, and Italy. I observed this activity for a while and soon planned a vacation to the places our aircraft flew. I met an officer from another aircraft squadron who was going to marry a French girl in Rabat, Morocco, and I agreed to be an usher in his wedding. But first, I had to visit some new places.

I flew to Cannes, France, on an aircraft that was taking Naval Academy midshipmen to the Mediterranean to board ships for their summer training. After a couple days in Cannes, I took a train to Milan, Italy, where I rented a small Fiat car and commenced a 15-day tour of Europe and Africa.

Swiss countryside, 1956

I stopped the first night at Lake Como in Northern Italy and obtained a hotel room at a grand hotel on the lake. After a sightseeing tour of the lake, I departed for Switzerland. On the way, I picked up two German boys who were hitchhiking through Europe. They stayed with me about three days. I dropped them off each evening at a campsite near a town and picked them up each morning. One of them spoke a little English, and we got along just fine, although we were cramped in the small car. They were great

Swiss village square, 1956

companions and were just as excited as I was to venture into new and exciting surroundings. The drive from Lugano, Italy, to St. Moritz, Switzerland, and on to Chur, Switzerland, with two passengers and our luggage, involved some serious mountain driving. The drive certainly tested the endurance of the small Fiat 500, and we were rewarded with the rural, pastoral beauty of the countryside and the scenic and breathtaking views.

I had nice accommodations in Chur, Switzerland, and drove north to the Principality of Liechtenstein, then to Lake Constance in Germany and on to Munich, Germany. My German passengers departed my company en route to Munich. I obtained accommodations at a US Army Base on the outskirts of Munich. I went to the Hofbrauhaus beer garden and toured Munich. I was struck by the World War II damage still remaining in the city. I also drove a short distance outside of Munich to visit the Dachau Concentration Camp that was in operation from 1933 to the end of the war.

World War II destruction, Munich, Germany, 1956

I left Munich late in the afternoon in a driving rain storm and was on my way to the not-too-distant Austria. As I cleared Austrian customs, a lady came to the window of my car and offered me accommodations at her home. She was with her father. I had no desire to drive to Salzburg in the heavy rain, so I accepted her offer. They were soaking wet, as they got into my car, and we drove to their home near the border. It was a nice, but sparsely furnished, home. My room was small, but very nice with a big comforter on the bed. I had dinner with the family and retired for the night. The cost of the room was not much, about $10. I had to wonder about the plight of this family, relying on sporadic room rentals to help make a living. The woman spoke excellent English, as she had worked with both the British and the Americans after the war. I learned a lot about the effect of World War II and the Allied occupation on the Austrian people. It was through the experiences of this woman and her father that I would view Europe for many years. In general, the Austrian and German people had been railroaded by Hitler's diabolic view of the future and had suffered immeasurably. The occupation of Austria by the Allied American, British, French, and Russian forces lasted from 1945 to 1955, so I was there within a year of the end of the occupation. Salzburg had been in the American sector, and the local people had a favorable view of America.

After my stay in the beautiful city of Salzburg, I departed on a trip over the Austrian Alps to Venice. I did a lot of planning for this trip, but I did not plan or anticipate the difficulty of driving on this mountain road. I just knew that it was the most direct route to Venice. When I left Salzburg, I started climbing and did not stop climbing until I reached the Franz Josef Hotel at the foot of Gross Glockner.

I reached this hotel in a spectacular manner. I had been climbing this mountain road for about two hours with a few stops at viewpoints. As I crested the mountain road, my little car lost momentum, and I coasted into the parking lot of the hotel. I will not say that my life flashed before me, but I certainly wondered what I was going to do — I was stranded at the top of Austria, thousands of miles from home. So, I went into the hotel and asked for help. The hotel manager and I took a look at my car, and we observed that the transmission rod had broken. He called a mechanic in Lienz, Austria, about an hour south of Gross Glockner, and explained the condition of the car. We were advised that a mechanic would come to the hotel the next day.

I could not have picked a better place to have a catastrophic failure. Gross Glockner is the highest mountain in Austria and one of the highest in the Alps — a height of 12,460 feet. The Franz Josef Hotel is at the 8,200-foot level. If the failure had occurred before I got to the hotel, I would have been stranded alongside an inclined road, perhaps on one of the many switchbacks, and it would have been a real problem getting the car to a safe place, to say nothing about how I could get help. Remember, there were no cell phones then and where would I have found shelter? But, that was not a problem, was it? My car failure happened in the hotel parking lot, and I was all set — a warm fire, nice bed, good meals, and very friendly and helpful people. I was there because I was there, not on purpose, but by happenstance.

My situation was unlike the famous British mountaineer, George Mallory, when, in 1923, he was asked, "Why do you want to climb Mount Everest?" He answered, "Because it's there." (**New York Times**, March 18, 1923, "Climbing Mount Everest is Work for Supermen") George Mallory was at Mount Everest because that is where he wanted to go.

Pasterze Glazier with Gross Glockner in background, Switzerland, 1956

Gross Glockner is now one of the most famous tourist destinations in Austria. I spent some time viewing Gross Glockner and taking short walks near the Pasterze Glazier. People travel half way around the world to see Gross Glockner, and I was there because my car broke down while traveling from Salzburg to Venice.

This is a life lesson — take what life deals you and make the best of it. You never know what lies around the next corner. The mechanic from Lienz came the next morning and fortunately, he had the correct parts. He repaired the car and by noon I was on my way to Venice.

Darrell's Fiat 500 being repaired, Gross Glockner, Switzerland, 1956

The first 25 miles downhill were just as difficult as going uphill, with hairpin turns one after the other. I stopped at Cortina d'ampezzo, Italy, the site of the just completed 1956 Winter Olympics, to see the Olympic venue and then continued on to Venice. I drove until I could not drive any further, or I would have been in a Venice canal. I obtained lodging within walking distance of all the sights of Venice. Of course, I enjoyed Venice and saw everything that I could see in a single day. I then departed for Milan, where I would return my rental car.

Prior to the car breaking down, I expected to be in Morocco for my friend's wedding by Thursday. It was now Wednesday morning. I planned to get an overnight train from Milan to Naples, and hoped that I could get a flight to Morocco mid-morning on Thursday.

The police stopped me on the way to Milan for some sort of a headlight or blinker infraction. The policeman spoke rapid Italian and explained my infraction, but I could not understand what he was talking about. I answered, "No capish," or "No comprende," or whatever, and he answered, "NO, no comprende." This meant, "No, you must understand." After several rounds of this, he gave up and sent me on my way.

I made it safely to Milan and was pleased to return the rental car with no damage. I was now on my way by train to Naples. I arrived in Naples before noon, only to find that I had missed an early morning flight. However, I could get on another flight scheduled to leave Friday afternoon. I would miss the Friday rehearsal dinner in Rabat, Morocco, but if things went well, I could be at the wedding Saturday afternoon.

I had a day in Naples, so I went about seeing the city. I had been in Naples three times, when I was on the **Randolph**. A young Italian man asked me if I wanted to buy a Beretta pistol. By this time, I had enough experience to be wary of street vendors. After some discussion and haggling, I decided I could trust him. I rode on the back of his scooter for a few blocks. He went into a building and came back with a 22-caliber pistol. He took me back to the commercial area, and we completed the transaction. Now, I had no idea whether it was legal to carry this pistol on a Navy aircraft, so I put it in my luggage and kept quiet. I recently gave the berretta to one of my sons. It was something I never really needed, but it seemed like a good idea at the time. I learned to be a little more careful with these "good ideas."

I caught a flight on Friday afternoon and was in Port Lyautey late evening. I met other people at Port Lyautey who were in the wedding, and I made arrangements to travel with them to Rabat on Saturday. I had carried my dress white uniform and sword in my luggage through many countries, but they came through in fine shape, and I was ready for the wedding. It went well and I enjoyed meeting many prominent French citizens (the father of the bride was the Minister of Tourism) who provided me with guided tours of Rabat. Morocco gained its independence from France on April 7, 1956, and the French gradually left Morocco. On Sunday, the day after the wedding, I caught a flight to Norfolk and then back to Patuxent River. My odyssey was completed.

Before I left on my odyssey, I had asked the wife of a classmate if she knew of any interesting women from her time at the University of Maryland. She gave me the name, Sally Strott, who had been her roommate, and had just graduated with a Bachelor of Science Degree in Nursing. I wrote this young lady to introduce myself, but I did not hear from her before I departed on my trip. I had a letter from her when I returned. I invited her to attend the homecoming football game at the Naval Academy in September 1956. I picked her up at her parents' home in Catonsville, a suburb of Baltimore, and we had a great time at the game, dinner with friends, and at a dance club on the way back to Baltimore.

We continued to date both in Baltimore and at Patuxent River. I went to Baltimore on weekends when I wasn't traveling, and Sally came to Patuxent River about every third weekend, where she had lodging in the Women's Bachelor Officers' Quarters. Patuxent River was a great place for a holiday. We played golf, went swimming and boating, went to the movies, and had nice meals at the famous Roos Roost Restaurant, a favorite of the aviators stationed at Patuxent River. When I was in Baltimore, my quarters were on the Strott's living room couch. We also had great weekend experiences in Baltimore: the Preakness horse race, Kutztown Pennsylvania Dutch festival, and, of course, Sunday church services at Christ Lutheran Church on Light Street at the Baltimore Harbor. Baltimore Inner Harbor is now a well-known entertainment and tourist area, but in the 1950s, Light Street was a warehouse and shipping area dominated by McCormick spice warehouses, with the aroma of a Moroccan souk. Ships from around the world were at the Light Street docks. Christ Church is now known as Christ Church, Inner Harbor.

I made another trip to Europe early in 1957. I flew to Norfolk on one of our airplanes, then to Port Lyautey, Morocco, via Argentia, Newfoundland, and The Azores. I was in Newfoundland in the middle of the night, and it was very cold. We deplaned and had a meal in the Officers' Club. When we arrived in Port Lyautey, I caught a flight to England via Spain and stayed there three days.

Since it was my first time in London, I was very busy seeing the sights. I was there on a Sunday and had heard about the political activism displayed on a Sunday in Hyde Park. I spent most of the day there. The speeches were mostly nonsense, and the speakers were constantly heckled. Both the speakers and the hecklers were regulars. It was their Sunday pastime. I noticed one particular heckler who was constantly on the move. His name was Desmond, and he also noticed me. He asked me how I liked his performance. I told him he was quite good and a real character. We went to a pub for a cup of coffee and chatted about the problems of the world. We did not have solutions for anything. I stayed in an apartment that was rented by the air crews that laid over in London. It was near Trafalgar Square with plenty of excitement in all directions.

Sunday at Hyde Park, London, England, 1956

I wanted to stay in London longer, but would have had to wait three days for the next flight, so I left London for Naples and then back to Port Lyautey via Malta. I didn't have time to leave the Malta airport terminal, but I did get some flavor of that small island nation. On landing and take-off, I sat behind the pilot in the engineer's seat, and had a view of farmlands and towns. The approach was over high cliffs to the airfield on a plateau. How many Allied aircraft pilots had that view of this strategic island in World War II? We left Malta and flew over the North African coast of Tunisia, Algeria, and Morocco. I had a view of the World War II battlefields of the North African Campaign of 1940 to 1943. I left Port Lyautey on the next flight and returned to Patuxent River.

It was good to return home and to see Sally. I took a giant leap for myself around Valentine's Day and asked Sally's father for her hand in marriage. He said yes, and I asked Sally, and she said yes, so we were engaged to be married. Sally set a date of July 13, 1957, and we went about our business of getting ready to get married. Sally was in graduate school and scheduled to graduate in 1958. Life was great!

I went about my daily business at the office and was asked by my boss to accompany our Commodore on an inspection trip of our squadron at Port Lyautey. I was assigned the normal junior officer duty of being custodian of classified material, in this case 17 large canvas bags. I signed for this material at Patuxent and would sign the material over to a receiving officer at Port Lyautey. We made the usual stops at Argentia and The Azores. We arrived in The Azores about 3 AM and deplaned for a meal. I had been sleeping most of the way from Argentia and was still dozing, when it was announced that we would get off the plane for a meal. I woke up, got off the plane, got on the bus, and went to the club to eat. I had ordered breakfast, when I realized that I had left the classified material unattended. I rushed out of the club and returned to our plane. The pilot, a Commander, who was waiting at the top of the ramp, proceeded to chew me out. He told me he was going to submit a report on my dereliction of duty. What could I say? I had left the classified material unattended. All I could do was wait until we returned to Patuxent River.

We performed reviews of the operational procedures of the Port Lyautey squadron for two days. The Commodore then scheduled us to go to Marrakech, Morocco. Our flight to Marrakech took us over Humphrey Bogart's World War II city of Casablanca. Today, Marrakech is a must-see tourist destination. In 1957, Marrakech was not crowded with Europeans.

Marrakech was definitely a Muslim city, but it was not an Arab city, as many Moroccans are not Arabs. I would just call it an exciting and mysterious city, with all the sights and smells imaginable. I rented a horse-drawn buggy and explored every nook and cranny of Marrakech. I had heard of all the excitement in the Marrakech town square. There were snake charmers, the Barbary apes that I had seen in Gibraltar, storytellers, magicians, and all the merchandise that you never wanted. I soon had enough of all the antics on the square, and it was time to venture into the souks (bazaars) on the side of the square, where everything imaginable was sold. I had some experience with the chaos of the Arab marketplace, but nothing like this — it was intimidating. Vendors stalked me and it was hard to say, no. I had to get out, but I had a mission.

Moroccan camel saddle

I wanted to buy a camel saddle. I found one I liked, after pretending I was not interested. Did I think I could fool a Moroccan merchant? No way. I paid a just price and was now burdened with toting a camel saddle the rest of my time in Marrakech. At least, I didn't lose my camera or have my pockets picked. How would you like to be a camel with one of these things on your back?

I had heard that the leather for the camel saddle was cured in camel urine. This camel saddle was with us, as we traveled the world for 30 years, through nine moves. I suspected that I could smell the camel urine. During later research, I learned that another curing process uses bird excrement. I guess both smells would be about the same. Anyway, I escaped the wildness of the souks and got another buggy ride down streets with orange trees on both sides — the aroma was a bit more pleasurable. I departed Marrakesh for Port Lyautey, and had a safe trip back to Patuxent River.

I should mention that I had enough time in Port Lyautey to go to the Navy Exchange and buy an engagement ring for Sally. I saw Sally the next weekend, gave her the ring, and our engagement was now official. There was no turning back. I had one more trip from Patuxent River to Bermuda and had completed all my travel missions for awhile.

In May 1957, I was transferred from Patuxent River to the US Naval Academy. I packed all my earthly goods in my car and reported for duty at the Naval Academy.

Oh, I forgot to report the conclusion of my classified material escapade. Well, a few days after I returned to Patuxent River, the administration officer called me to his office. He was holding the report in his hands. I thought, this is it — this is the end. It was not the end. The administration officer explained how critical it was to safeguard classified material and told me he was sure I would be more careful in the future. That was it. Case dismissed!

CHAPTER 12: US NAVAL ACADEMY AGAIN

In May of 1957, I reported to the US Naval Academy to serve as assistant-in-charge of the Midshipmen's Store and Service Activities. My quarters were on the **Reina Mercedes (Reina)**. The **Reina** was berthed in the Severn River at the end of a pier where the Crown Sailing Club is now located. My stateroom, on the **Reina,** was very small. It had a small roll-top desk and a small wooden bunk — not much had changed since 1887.

The **Reina** was a Spanish cruiser launched at Cartagena, Spain, in 1887. She fought in the Spanish American War in Cuba and was captured by the United States when Spain surrendered on July 17, 1898. Since the **Reina** had been scuttled by Spain, she had to be raised and towed to Norfolk where repairs were made. The **Reina** was transferred to Annapolis in 1912 and was used as a station ship. Midshipmen served their punishments by being restricted on board the **Reina** until this practice was discontinued in1940. The **Reina** was also used as quarters for enlisted personnel stationed at the Naval Academy. During the time I was berthed on the **Reina,** she was being evaluated to see if needed repairs were economical. It was determined that repairs would be too costly, and the

Reina was decommissioned and scrapped later in 1957. I was on the **Reina** for about two weeks before I was assigned quarters in the Bachelor Officers' Quarters. I continued to eat meals on the **Reina** until Sally and I were married.

Sally and Darrell wedding, Baltimore, Maryland, 1957

Sally and I were married July 13, 1957, at Christ English Lutheran Church at Baltimore Inner Harbor. Six of my Naval Academy classmates served as ushers and saluted us with an arch of swords, as we exited the church. We went to Nova Scotia on our honeymoon and settled in a rented house in Edgewater, Maryland. Our house was an old farm house and was fine in the summer, but very cold and drafty in the winter. We settled in and commenced to enjoy the rest of the summer.

I was busy at the Naval Academy, as the plebes, the new first-year midshipmen, were receiving their uniforms. One of my duties was to manage the uniform contract and to ensure quality and fit of uniforms. The fit was a bit of a problem, as some of the midshipmen would shed 20 to 30 pounds, and more, during the rigorous summer training. A uniform would fit perfectly, and, two to three weeks later, it would have to be adjusted by two or three inches.

Other activities under my cognizance were the tailor shop, dry cleaning shop, four barber shops, cobbler shop, and gedunk (soda fountain). There were about 65 civilians employed in these activities. The tailors were mostly European, many of them first generation. The barbers were all black, and most of them were Annapolitans, whose families lived in Annapolis for generations. The head barber was employed by the Navy for over 50 years, starting as a teenager as a mess boy (kitchen helper) on ships that took the midshipmen to sea for summer training. Many of these employees had a story to tell, and I enjoyed hearing about their lives. I also had the periodic duty of Officer of the Watch. I monitored midshipmen activities and inspected them at various formations. It was only four years earlier that I had been on the other end of this gauntlet, and I knew very well what tricks the midshipmen might employ. I liked to consider myself a "good guy." I enforced discipline, but I did not nitpick the behavior of the midshipmen.

The midshipmen had compulsory chapel attendance. When I had the Sunday "watch," I stood in a formation with the superintendent or commandant of midshipmen on the chapel steps. We reviewed the midshipmen, as they marched to the chapel. The Naval Academy band was in the bandstand in front of the chapel, playing marching music. My favorite was "Onward Christian Soldiers."

Darrell (on right), chapel formation, 1958

On a cold winter day, I was standing behind the commandant, in this case, a commander, who was standing in for the commandant. Vice Admiral Holloway, the Naval Academy superintendent, was also there. On an occasion such as this, Admiral Holloway wore a cape, dark blue on the outside and crimson on the inside. The midshipmen wore dress blues with overcoats. Since it was really cold and windy, the midshipmen were told to turn up their overcoat collars. Uniform means uniform — they had to all look the same. But, they did not all look the same. One quarter of the midshipmen, the plebes, had a black button instead of a brass button under their collar that was now exposed because their collars were turned up. The commander saw the problem about the same time I saw it. He turned and looked at me, and I knew I was in trouble. I quietly told the commander that I would take care of the problem. It turns out that the uniform contractor had tried to save a little money by replacing the top brass button with a black button. The contractor readily agreed to correct the problem, and 1,100 plebes brought their overcoats to the contract tailor to replace the buttons — another case of unintended consequences.

When I was a Midshipman, just before we left on Christmas leave in 1952, we went to the chapel steps to listen to a Christmas message from Admiral Holloway. It was cold and snowing. As Admiral Holloway spoke and led us in Christmas carols, he opened his cloak and spread it wide several times, displaying a sea of crimson against the white of the snow — a display for the Christmas season.

Sally took a position as a public health nurse in the county department of health in Annapolis. The Anne Arundel County Department of Health provided excellent services. Other health departments, from across the US and foreign countries, often came to Annapolis, as they wanted to base their operations on the Anne Arundel model. Sally held weekly clinics and visited homes. The home visits highlighted problems of sanitation, housekeeping, and poor dietary habits that contributed to diseases, such as tuberculosis, which was on a rampage. Sally loved her work, particularly the smiles on patients' faces, as she listened to their problems and helped them.

Sally often encountered a patient who needed medical help and she usually took the patient to the office of Dr. Aris Allen or his wife who was also a doctor. Both doctors were always very kind to Sally and the patient and were helpful to Sally by counseling her of various actions to take. Doctor Aris Allen died from a self-inflicted gunshot wound in 1991 after suffering from prostate cancer. A freeway, Aris T. Allen Boulevard, connecting Route 50 to Annapolis from the west is named for him.

Sally remembers a 17-year-old boy, who, although sick, was collecting funds to assist others with similar illnesses.

The boy later died. His mother gave Sally the money he collected to use for other patients. Sally says that she had many down moments, but she loved what she was doing. Her listening skills, compassion, and dedication held her in good stead as a public health nurse. These attributes were important to the nurturing she has provided to our family.

Our first winter in Annapolis was very cold with lots of snow, and it was hard to keep warm in our old farm house. The water lines froze often, and many times I had to crawl under the house on the frozen earth and use a blow torch to thaw the lines. We resolved to move to another location the next summer.

Sally with Randy skating on creek, Annapolis, Maryland, 1958

Sally wanted a pet, and we got a small dog from the SPCA to keep us company. We named him Randy after the aircraft carrier **Randolph**. The creek near our house froze, as did the South River, so we got plenty of ice skating exercise. During one particularly bad weather spell, we lost our electricity and relocated to a classmate's house for two days. He lived in Navy quarters at the North Severn Naval Station across from the Naval Academy. There was no room at the inn for Randy, so he stayed in a kennel.

Randy was an outdoor dog — he came into the house to eat and sleep. We took him to Catonsville on a visit to Sally's parents. Randy escaped from the house, and we paced the streets for about two hours looking for him, to no avail. We came home very disappointed and regretted letting him get out of the house. We put an advertisement in the **Baltimore Sun,** and after about two weeks, we received a postcard telling us that Randy was in a Baltimore kennel. We were happily reunited.

In addition to her work as a public health nurse, Sally was busy during the winter writing her master's thesis. The house was so cold that we spent most of our time on the second floor, where it was warmer. We used one of the bedrooms for Sally's office and that is where I typed a rough draft of Sally's thesis. Her thesis was approved and Sally was awarded a Master of Science Degree in Nursing by the University of Maryland in June 1958.

Sally, Master's Degree, 1958

We took a summer vacation to the Shenandoah Mountains where we stayed in a small log cabin. We hiked, rode horses, and saw the Natural Bridge of Virginia, as well as many other sights. We also took short trips to Virginia Beach, Virginia, and Ocean City, Maryland, where we rode the waves and soaked up the sun. One day in Virginia Beach after swimming, we returned to our spot on the beach, and I discovered that my billfold had been stolen. Here I was in Virginia, an experienced world traveler, and my billfold was stolen, when I carelessly left my possessions unattended. I had visited some dangerous places, both in the US and abroad, without incident, and it happened on a quiet beach in Virginia. Are there crooks around every corner? I don't think so, but given the opportunity, a regular person can become a crook. Was someone observing our activities? Probably so. I took some comfort in the fact that I had a beautiful wife, and someone observed our activities, probably gawking at Sally. I was an incidental bystander and became the victim. Since we had only enough money left to buy gas for the trip home, we terminated our short vacation and drove back to Annapolis.

In the summer of 1958, we moved from the old farm house in Edgewater to a town house in the community of Dream's Landing, north of the Naval Academy on the Severn River. It was a two-story home with a large basement, more than adequate for our needs, and Randy still had the run of our quiet neighborhood.

We relocated our small boat to a spot north of what is now the Naval Academy Bridge on the property of Arundel Estates, a housing community consisting mainly of Naval Academy professors and officers. I didn't get anyone's permission to do this — I just did it. There was no pier — the boat was tied to the shore. Most of the time, I removed the motor, but it was a real chore to carry the heavy motor through the marshy beach to our car. It was risky to leave the motor in the boat, but nothing bad ever happened.

We had a sad event in the fall. One day when I came home, Sally met me with the news that Randy had been hit by a car and died. By coincidence, he was hit in the street by Glen Hatch, one of my classmates. Glen, of course, didn't know it was our dog. When he stopped and inquired, he was told it belonged to us. Glen was grief-stricken, as we were. Glen took Randy to a vet and took care of all arrangements before I got home. I saw Glen many times over the years, and he always mentioned and apologized for the event. Of course, it was not Glen's fault. Randy was a friendly pet and was always loved by our neighbors. He loved the outdoors, especially romping in the snow and ice skating with us.

My official duties at the Academy continued to be interesting. Most of the officers were career naval officers, many of them later achieving flag rank. My closest interaction was with the officers in charge of the 36 companies of midshipmen. One of them was Captain George Patton, US Army, son of General George Patton. We were in the Executive Department, and he played on our softball team. We played against teams from the academic departments that included civilian professors. Some things remain forever in our memory, and one of my memories is the line drive I dropped while playing the outfield. Why should I remember this error? After all, I am a mere human, but at that time, I thought I was bullet-proof and error-proof. It took me a long time to learn not to take unnecessary chances, to concentrate on the task at hand, and to accept that I would make mistakes. On second thought, I am still learning.

Our son, Charles Edwin (Eddie) was born at the Naval Hospital, Annapolis on Monday, April 27, 1959. Sunday, the previous day, was the day of the Naval Academy Golf Club annual banquet. Again, being one of the junior officers, I was assigned several duties for the banquet. I left home in the late afternoon for the banquet, a distance of about three miles from our home. Sally decided that she had better not attend the banquet. Just before dinner was served, I received a call from Sally that she was ready to go to the hospital. I left the club immediately, rushed home, and took Sally to the hospital, also a short distance from our home. The doctor told me it would be awhile before the baby arrived, so I went to downtown Annapolis to the La Rosa Restaurant to have dinner. I returned to the hospital about 10 PM. Eddie was born the next morning. We had decided that if the baby was a boy, he would be named after our fathers, John Charles Strott and Edwin Laib Dempster. I don't remember what a girl's name would have been — maybe Sally knows.

Sally, Darrell, and Eddie,
Annapolis, Maryland, 1959

About the time Eddie was born, I received orders to the Navy Purchasing Office, London, England. Our scheduled departure date was mid-June 1959. We began preparations for our departure. About two weeks later, these orders were cancelled, and I received new orders for the Naval Supply Depot in Yokosuka, Japan. Now we were faced with an entirely different situation. This would be the first time Sally would be a long distance from her parents, and the trip to Japan would be a lot more arduous than a flight to England. Of more concern was Eddie's hernia. It pained him so much that he cried a lot at night. Although he was only two months old, the doctor agreed to repair his hernia rather than have us wait until we arrived in Japan. We took some time for Eddie to recover and then departed Annapolis for Japan.

We left most of our household goods in storage and packed the rest into the back seat and trunk of our Plymouth sedan. There was barely enough room for the three of us. When Eddie was not in Sally's arms, he slept on a fold-out chair on top of the pile of "stuff" in the back seat. At that time, there were no car seat or seatbelt laws. People kept their children safe without the benefit of government regulations.

We were on our first cross-country trip, one of many that we would take in the next 20 years. We stopped in Wichita for a short visit with my parents and to show off our newborn son. We traveled the northern route, from Kansas through Colorado and Salt Lake City, and through Nevada to San Francisco. We had enough time to see some of the sights of the Great Plains, the Rocky Mountains, the Great Salt Lake, and the Bonneville Salt Flats, where we watched the high-speed-racing cars. We went over the Donner Pass, where the Donner party, traveling to California in the winter of 1845-1846, became snowbound. Many of them died, and some resorted to cannibalism. It was one of the most tragic episodes in the migration of immigrants to the western United States.

We turned in our car in San Francisco for shipment to Japan. We left Travis Air Force Base, California, on a propeller-driven Air Force plane for Hawaii for a refueling stop and then to Wake Island. We arrived at Wake just as the sun was rising. Wake is a small spot in the vast Pacific Ocean. Wake Island, an unincorporated territory of the United States, was attacked by the Japanese on the same day Pearl Harbor was attacked. The marines, sailors, and civilians put up the good fight, but surrendered to the Japanese on December 23, 1941. Wake Island remained under control of Japan until the Japanese surrender.

We deplaned at Wake and had breakfast in a Quonset hut. I had time to take a short walk to the beach where the bow of a Japanese ship lay stranded — look closely and you will see a Japanese Rising Sun. This ship is testimony to the brave fight put up by the American defenders 18 years earlier.

World War II Japanese ship off
Wake Island, 1959

In about eight hours, we would be in the land of the Rising Sun, our former enemy. We left Wake and arrived in Japan in the afternoon. Each of our three flights took about eight hours. Eddie was a real trooper — he handled the trip well and had no trouble with his recent surgery. He slept a lot, but when he was awake, he was a big hit with other passengers, and he was now in Japan.

CHAPTER 13: THE LAND OF THE RISING SUN

We were met at the Tachikawa Air Force Base in Japan by our sponsor from the Naval Supply Depot Yokosuka. The traffic drives on the left side of the road in Japan, as it does in England. The drive to our lodgings at the Hakkien, near Yokosuka, took about two hours on crowded and narrow roads. The drive was almost all alongside houses and rice paddies. We went alongside a canal that was full of debris. The drive connected with the Tokyo-Yokosuka Road. We turned south toward Yokosuka and our lodgings at the Hakkien. The Hakkien catered to military personnel waiting for quarters or private rentals. We were assigned a room with a double bed and a baby bed. We bought our own food, stored it in the kitchen refrigerators, and cooked our own meals in a large kitchen. We settled into the Hakkien, and I reported for duty at the Yokosuka Supply Depot, where I was assigned to duty as the assistant stock control officer. There were about 30 officers, 50 enlisted personnel, 20 American civilians, and 500 Japanese civilians assigned to the depot. It was a large operation that served all Navy ships and shore activities in the Far East.

We had been in Japan for less than two weeks when one of the worst typhoons in history hit Japan. The worst damage centered on Nagoya and the Ise Peninsula, about 200 miles west of Yokosuka. There were over 4,000 deaths and about 34,000 homes destroyed. The government was severely criticized for the lack of warning and preparation for the typhoon. This was our introduction to the destruction that can be caused by violent storms on an island nation with many homes built on hilly and mountainous ground. The destruction was compounded when one considers that Japan was still recovering from World War II bombings. We had very heavy rain and high winds at the Hakkien but not much damage.

We had a great time introducing ourselves to Japan around the Hakkien. The Hakkien was not on a main road — it was in the middle of the Japanese community. We encountered a different aspect of Japanese life with every step we took. We took walks, with Eddie in a stroller, every evening. Japanese children would stop and gaze at Eddie and want to touch him. We never had a problem with animosity — everyone was friendly.

We had not studied Japanese, but we really did not have a problem with communication. We got along by pointing at things we wanted to buy. The shopkeepers would write the price in English numerals on paper. In the rare case the Japanese did not know how to write numerals, we did have a small problem, so we quickly learned a modicum of Japanese to solve this difficulty. To me, the most important thing in learning a foreign language is to not be afraid to make mistakes. The Japanese never made fun of my torture of their language. At the same time, we sometimes struggled to understand their English. Some of them must have thought that we did not speak English. If there was a communication problem, it was most often the pronunciation of a word. We learned to not ask a negative question. For example, we ordered a piece of furniture in Yokohama and were told that it would be ready in two weeks. We returned later to pick up the item, and we asked, "Isn't it ready?" The shopkeeper answered, "Yes." When he did not give us the item, we realized he meant yes, it is not ready.

We stayed at the Hakkien for two months and then moved to a private rental on the beach in the Shinjuku area of Zushi. Our landlady, Eto San, had a large compound consisting of her large Japanese-style house, a large gardener's house, and three almost western-style houses. Ours was a duplex with two bedrooms. The back of the house was on the sea wall above Zushi beach with a view across Sagami Bay of Mt. Fuji-yama (Mt. Fuji). The compound was separated from the street by a large wooden fence. The entrance to the compound was through a large black gate, known in Japanese as kuroi seki.

Eddie and Darrell, compound yard

Eddie with Japanese friends, Zushi, Japan, 1960

The compound had a large yard that was perfectly manicured by the gardener and his wife. The gardener and his wife had two young girls, and Eddie played with these girls almost every day.

Very few houses in Japan had street numbers. A typical direction was to "go to a certain named street, turn right at the candy store, go up the hill nine houses, turn left, and we are the fifth house on the left."

Mt. Fuji, Sally, and our old Chevrolet coupe, 1961

Our house was a 30-minute drive from Yokosuka. For additional transportation, we bought an old roadster. I found a picture of the car, and I hit a trifecta, my beautiful wife, Sally, the car, and ever present Mt. Fuji. This car had been in Japan a long time. Once a car got this old, it remained in Japan — one military person selling it to another. We sold our new Plymouth to a Japanese man, who wanted to use it for a chauffeur-driven car. We bought a 1954 US Army excess Chevrolet sedan at an Army auction. We paid $200 for this car. We drove both of these cars until we left Japan in 1963.

One of the great benefits of living in Japan, at the time we were there, was the value of the Japanese currency — the yen value was 360 yen to the dollar. Most families employed a Japanese maid at a cost of about $35 per month. Our first maid was Toku-San. She was young and experienced and became a member of our family. Since Toku-San lived some distance from our house, she stayed with us during the week. Her bedroom was very small — a three-tatami-mat room. A tatami mat has a standard size of three feet by six feet, so her room was 54 square feet. Most Japanese houses, at the time, had tatami mats in almost every room. Today it is common to have only one or no rooms with tatami mats. All the other rooms in our house had wood floors. Toku-San slept on a futon, a mattress stuffed with cotton and wool. Toku-San also had a small 12-inch high table and a zabuton, a cushion for sitting. Toku-San was not married, so her work schedule was flexible. If we had a special event on the weekend, Toku-San would stay at our house and have other days off.

Our commanding officer had the interest of all of us at heart, when he established a mandatory Japanese language class, taught by Mrs. Murakami. Murakami-San was born to Japanese parents in Ketchikan, Alaska. She visited Japan in 1940, as a young girl, and was trapped in Japan, when the Japanese attacked Pearl Harbor. Her first language was English, and she learned Japanese in a Japanese school. By coincidence, she lived near us in Zushi, and I took her to and from work. She insisted that I speak Japanese when we were in my car. She was an excellent teacher, and I soon spoke enough Japanese to get by in most situations. Sally also learned to speak Japanese from our maid, Toku-San, and from our Japanese friends and neighbors. At the time, not many Japanese spoke English, and it was a necessity to communicate in Japanese in many situations, such as with merchants and neighbors and when asking for directions.

In December 1959, we learned that the Fuji New Grand, one of the Japanese hotels run by the Military Welfare and Recreation Center, was to be returned to the Japanese government on January 1, 1960. We quickly scheduled a three-day stay there just before Christmas. The Fuji New Grand was near Mt. Fuji, about a three-hour drive from our house. It was a European-style hotel that you would expect to see in the Alps. There was a lot of snow on the ground. We had western-style meals and took food to supplement Eddie's meals. They had a skating rink, sledding, and a small ski slope, but no tow line or chair lift. We had to walk uphill in order to ski downhill.

Eddie sledding at Fuji New Grand Hotel, Japan, 1959

This was the first of many grand adventures that we would have in Japan. However, we really did not have to leave the comfort of our Japanese house on the Zushi beach to enjoy one of the greatest views in Japan. All we had to do was stand by our bedroom window and look across the Zushi

Winter view of Mt. Fuji from Zushi beach, Japan, 1960

Hokusai Mt. Fuji woodblock print

Hokusai Mt. Fuji woodblock print

beach and Sagami Bay to see the magnificent Mt. Fuji. The island under the snow of Mt. Fuji is Enoshima Island.

The famous Japanese wood block artist, Hokusai, made 46 woodblock prints of different views of Mt. Fuji. One of them was a view from Kamakura and another with Enoshima in the foreground. My picture is not a woodblock, but like the woodblocks by Hokusai, it captures the majesty of Mt. Fuji. You can see that the slope of Mt. Fuji, as drawn by Hokusai, is much steeper than in my photo. Sally and I both know that the actual slope is not as steep as depicted by Hokusai, because we climbed Mt. Fuji. It was there and was something we had to do. But, more about that later.

Beach at Zushi, Japan, 1960

We enjoyed the beach during all seasons, but we had an unexpected surprise when it turned warm in the summer. Japanese vendors constructed stalls on the beach next to our house where they sold food and souvenirs and rented beach items. The beach was very crowded and noisy during the daylight hours, but there were no nighttime activities, so the crowded beach was not a bother to us. As a matter of fact, we enjoyed watching the Japanese families frolic on the beach and in the shallow water. On many days, Japanese school children came to the beach to exercise. Exercise was important to the Japanese. Of course, since most of the Japanese did not have cars, walking and bicycling provided a lot of exercise.

Japanese school children, exercise class, 1961

School children had daily exercise classes. These classes were not like a recess period in the States, where the children were free to do things on their own. The exercise class in Japan was like a military drill, with all the children flexing their limbs and jumping in unison. On special days, parents and guests would be invited, and large school yards would be filled with children exercising. It was more like a dance — a recital at the end of the year. They were demonstrating their skill in working together and performing in perfect harmony.

A big problem surfaced late in the summer. In many cases, the left-over food from the vendors and their patrons was simply tossed onto the sand or into the water. The Japanese played a game where they placed a watermelon on the sand and one person was blindfolded. The blindfolded person was then spun in a circle until he became dizzy and then given a big stick. He then whacked away until he hit the watermelon. It was then eaten, with no real attempt to thoroughly clean up the rind. It was left to the rats to clean up the beach. Every rat has its day

Feasting on watermelon, Zushi beach, 1960

in the sun, but, at our house, they were especially active at night. Rats began to appear, and early one morning, I discovered a rat on our kitchen counter. I obtained a rat trap from the Health Department at the Yokosuka Base and trapped the rat. The recommended disposal method was to drown the rat in the bathtub. We were warned by the Yokosuka Base Health Department that the water at Zushi beach was contaminated, and we should not go into the water. The only contact we had with the water was to wade along the shore.

During storms, the windows would rattle and the waves would whip the shoreline. In the morning after a storm, glass floats, the largest being about 16 inches in diameter, would drift onto our beach. They were used to hold fishermen's nets near the surface. They broke away from the heavy nets and drifted onto the beach. I would always look at the beach early in the morning to see if any glass balls had drifted ashore. If so, I would pick them up. They were wonderful garden decorations. I did have competition from an elderly Japanese gentleman, who regularly patrolled the Zushi beach, using a bicycle to cart his morning treasures. I retrieved only a few glass balls as he was a very early riser.

Eddie in garden with glass ball

One day, we noticed a small puppy wandering on the street in front of our compound. He seemed to be lost or abandoned. We asked Eto-San and Toku-San to check with the neighbors, and all agreed that the puppy was a stray, so we adopted him. We named him Hachiko, after a legendary Japanese Akita dog. The original

Eddie and Hachiko,
Zushi, Japan, 1960

Hachiko was owned by a professor at Tokyo University. Hachiko's habit was to meet the professor at the Shibuya Rail Station at the end of each work day. One day, the professor did not return — he had died at the university. Each day for the next nine years, the loyal Hachiko went to Shibuya Station at the time the train was to arrive. Other riders and station personnel observed Hachiko's loyalty and fed him meals and treats. Hachiko died on the street in Tokyo after a long and loyal life. A bronze statue was erected on the spot where Hachiko waited for his master. If we were to meet someone in Tokyo, we would meet them at the statue of Hachiko. Our Hachiko was a great pet. He had the run of the compound and was Eddie's best friend.

Unfortunately, Hachiko did not live a long life. He was a member of our household for only about three months, when he was hit by a noodle delivery man. Noodles were delivered in boxes piled high on the back of a motorcycle, and the driver was probably afraid to swerve for fear that his stack of noodles would topple to the street. Toku-San was notified that Hachiko was injured. She picked him up and brought him into the house. Toku-San called the veterinarian. The veterinarian told Sally that Hachiko had internal injuries and would not survive. Sally asked the veterinarian to take Hachiko to his office and put him to sleep. Sally gave the veterinarian our name and address and 500 yen, about one dollar and forty cents. She was assured that Hachiko would receive a proper burial. And that was true. We received a postcard indicating where Hachiko was buried, and we were given the visiting hours. We mourned our loss — it was our joy and pleasure to have had Hachiko as a member of our household.

There were several beaches near Zushi. On one excursion, we went to a rocky beach. While we were climbing over the rocks, we came across a large group of photographers. There was a photo shoot of some Japanese bathing beauties. The girls posed on the rocks, on the sand, and in the water. I joined the photographers to take some pictures. When I turned my head, I saw most of the photographers taking pictures of Sally and Eddie. I was not in the picture. Sally was blonde and taller than most of the Japanese people, and with adorable Eddie in her arms, I didn't blame the Japanese for taking pictures of them. We were the subjects of many pictures — on the Ginza in Tokyo, in department stores, and at tourist sites.

I took a lot of photos of fishermen. We enjoyed watching their activities: tending and repairing nets, repairing and maintaining their boats, and, of course, bringing in their catch. They worked on the beach and, in most cases, it was a family affair.

Families assist in retrieving fish from net, Zushi, Japan, 1960

There were a lot of small fishing ports along the beach road going south from Zushi to Hayama. Most of the time, we would see an old man, probably a retired fisherman, standing on a rock at Hayama. He looked out to sea, as if he were waiting for the return of his family of fishermen. He didn't pose for pictures — his stature and gaze were a part of his normal self-assurance. He was at peace by the sea. We took an unposed picture of Eddie that is remarkably similar to that of the fisherman.

Retired fisherman looks out to sea, Hayama, Japan, 1960

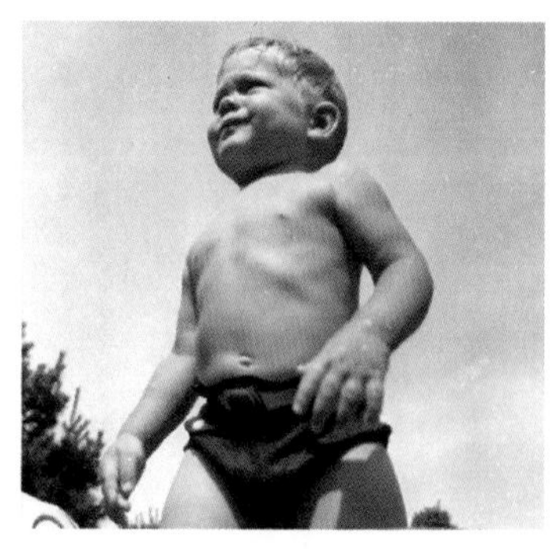

Eddie, in pose of retired fisherman, 1960

Sally and her parents visit Mt. Fuji, 1960

Sally's parents came to visit us in the summer of 1960. We took them to see the highlights of Japan, the first being a journey to Hakone for a close-up view of Mt. Fuji. We encountered many Japanese school children. They were not bashful about staring at us and giggling. Sally's parents found this disconcerting, but it was only natural to the children. They were from rural areas and had seen very few, if any, gaijiin (foreigners) in their young lives. Sometimes, they asked us for autographs. It was great fun and a great day to savor the beauty, people, and mystery of Japan.

Japanese school children visit with Sally and her parents, 1960

We took a train to Tokyo to see the Imperial Palace and walk on the Ginza. We were having a meal in a restaurant on the top floor of a Japanese department store, and we were placed at a table with some Japanese. When Sally's parents joined the conversation, they, of course, spoke English. They thought if they just spoke really loudly, the Japanese would understand them. They were amazed at the way the Japanese held a bowl of noodles up to their mouths and scooped the noodles into their mouths with chopsticks. This was their first time to travel outside the US, but they were good troopers; willing to travel with us on crowded roads, teaming with traffic and people, as well as over mountain roads with steep drops on the sides.

We took Sally's parents to Nikko, also our first trip to this mountainous region about 60 miles north of Tokyo. Nikko was known for its many Shinto shrines, especially the Toshogu Shrine, known as the most colorful in Japan. Toshogu had about 30 separate buildings. It was overwhelming in its grandeur, with expansive gardens filled with tori and statues

Toshogu Shrine, Nikko, Japan, 1960

"Hear no evil, speak no evil, see no evil."

and, of course, the ubiquitous "hear no evil, speak no evil, see no evil" monkey carvings seen at many Japanese shrines. We stayed in a Japanese Ryokan (guest house). Sally and I had a tatami mat room with futons, but her parents had beds in their room. They could have slept on futons, but did not object when we suggested they have a room with beds. We could not have possibly seen all of Nikko in two days, but we made the most of the two days. After a lot of walking, we rested com-

Dinner party for Sally's parents, Kamakura, Japan, 1960

fortably in our Ryokan and enjoyed traditional Japanese meals. We had a farewell party for them with some of our Japanese and American friends.

We made many trips by train to Tokyo. The trains were often very crowded, so if they were, we would upgrade to first class for about a dollar. We walked the famous Ginza, Tokyo's main street. We saw shows like the Nichigeki, with dancing girls similar to the Rockefeller Center Rockettes, Kabuki Theater, and Noh Theater. Kabuki and Noh have centuries-old traditions. They are highly stylized with singing, dancing, and elaborate costumes and stage settings. At the time we were in Japan, all actors were male; female roles were played by male actors. They are difficult to understand without the devotion of time to study the plays in detail. We were satisfied to stop when we had seen one Kabuki and one Noh play. You could say that we did not become devotees.

We also attended a puppet (Bunraku) theater. All but the most elemental characters have three puppeteers. The main puppeteer controls the head and right hand of the puppet. The second puppeteer controls the left hand. The third puppeteer controls the feet and legs. After sufficient training, the third puppeteer can move to second puppeteer and then to main puppeteer. The puppeteers perform in full view of the audience, wearing black robes with faces either covered or uncovered. By tradition, they are treated as being invisible. The puppeteer's learning process can take 30 years. Many of the Bunraku themes are lover-suicide plays.

Burial ground of 47 ronin

The story of the 47 ronin, probably the most popular story in Japan, is portrayed in both Kabuki and Bunraku. The story displays the attributes of honor, loyalty, and persistency, but it seems to me that revenge was also involved.

The daimyo (feudal lord), Asano, assaulted a court official named Kira. Asano was forced to commit seppuku (ritual suicide). A group of samurai in his service didn't have a Daimyo now, and becoming leaderless, they were now known as ronin. The 47 ronin vowed to avenge their master, and after a long planning period, killed Kira. Since the 47 ronin committed murder, they were now also required to commit seppuku. They were all buried in the Sengakuji cemetery near Tokyo with their Daimyo and his family.

The story of the 47 ronin is a story of honor. The ronin were convinced that their master's honor was besmirched, and they wanted vengeance. They were willing to sacrifice their lives to recover their master's honor. Those who followed the way of the Samurai followed the seven virtues of Bushido described in the book, **The Soul of Japan,** by Japanese Professor Inazo Nitobe: righteousness, courage, benevolence, respect, sincerity, honor, and loyalty. A failure to adhere to any of these virtues could result in disgrace and the resultant seppuku, sometimes called hara-kiri. **The Soul of Japan,** written in English in 1889 (later translated into Japanese), was widely read by important people, such as President Theodore Roosevelt and Robert Baden Powell, founder of the Boy Scouts. It is well known that President Roosevelt was very interested in all aspects of Japanese culture. As for Baden Powell, when I reviewed the Samurai code, I saw a similarity to the twelve points of the Boy Scout Law. A scout is trustworthy, loyal, helpful, friendly, courteous, kind, obedient, cheerful, thrifty, brave, clean, and reverent. Since Baden Powell had a copy of Professor Nitobe's book, it is entirely possible that he got some ideas for the Boy Scout Law from the Samurai code. Why reinvent the wheel?

Of course, the scouts are not a militant organization, but they live by a code of honor as the Samurai did. One might also surmise that Baden Powell also was aware of the code of chivalry of the ancient British knights; after all, he was Knight of the British Empire. These qualities are generally courage, honor, courtesy, justice, and helping the weak. And, of course, every schoolboy knows, or maybe I should say, used to know, the story of Sir Walter Raleigh, laying his cloak over a mud puddle, so Queen Elizabeth would not get her feet dirty. This is most likely not a true story, but it is a chivalrous story. It is in the category of George Washington and the cherry tree. When he was asked by his father if he had cut down a cherry tree, the young George Washington admitted that he had, adding, "I cannot tell a lie." This is also, perhaps, not a true story, but it is a lesson in integrity.

As I write this, I can't help but remember trips from Kinsley to Hutchinson that my sister Wilma and I took during the summer. We went to spend some time with our Grandma and Grandpa Dempster and our Aunts Opal and Geraldine. When Opal and Geraldine took us for a walk, they told me that as a young man, I was to walk on the side nearest the street. They told me that this was what a gentleman did, because if it was raining and a car came by, the mud would splash on me and not on the women. I guess they were trying to make me into a little Sir Walter Raleigh. I think of this learning moment frequently today, as this custom is often violated.

This Samurai code drove military training in Japan, and most certainly, played a part in the Japanese soldiers fighting to the end against immense odds during the last stages of World War II. When defeat was imminent, they chose to continue to fight, rather than surrender. Even though the end of the war was near, Japan launched thousands of aircraft kamikaze (suicide) attacks on Navy ships. Over 3,800 Japanese pilots were killed when they piloted their bomb-laden aircraft into Navy ships. When their units were near surrender, many Japanese senior officers committed hara-kiri. Notable among them were these: Generals Ushijima and Cho, when the Battle of Okinawa was lost; General Anami, who was War Minister and signed the surrender document; General Nakagawa, when the Battle of Peleliu was lost; and Admiral Onishi, who organized the deployment of kamikaze attacks. Admiral Onishi apologized to the families of the Japanese pilots that he had sent to their deaths. He committed seppuku the day after the surrender of Japan.

When Sally and I went to Japan, we were, of course, somewhat familiar with the Japanese military code of honor. - We really did not know what to expect when we encountered Japanese who were of an age to have fought in the war.

During our time in Japan, the Japanese did not have an offensive armed force. They had defensive forces known as the Japanese Self-Defense Forces. I had interaction with the Maritime Self-Defense Force. Some of their senior officers had been in World War II, but we never talked about the war. Neither did we talk to our Japanese civilian friends about the war. That's just the way it was. I guess we had better things to do.

In 1961, in accordance with our responsibility of supporting US Armed Forces in the Far East, my commanding officer asked for volunteers for a purchasing assignment in Vietnam. The US had just escalated its support of Vietnam in the Vietnam War. The Vietnam government was fighting against Communist forces of North Vietnam assisted by Russia, China, and other Communist forces. The US became involved to stop the spread of communism. I welcomed this assignment, but the commanding officer did not select me.

Tokyo fish market,
Tokyo, Japan, 1961

We had heard about the fish market in Tokyo where there was an auction early in the morning. We went to Tokyo for a weekend, and early on Saturday morning, we found our way to the dock where the auction was held. We could smell it well before we saw the thousands of large fish lying in row after row. Somehow, Sally maneuvered herself (actually I did some prodding) to an open spot among the fish. The auction was completed before we arrived, and the fish were being claimed by the new owners. I can only surmise that the reason the fish were un-

Sally and Japanese dancing
teacher, Zushi, Japan, 1960

loaded during the night, and the auction held at daybreak, was to avoid the fish being cooked by the sun. We had a rare look at one of Japan's largest industries.

Sally was involved in many activities in Japan, such as Japanese dancing, flower arranging, teaching English, and lifesaving. One of her English students invited us to her wedding in Tokyo. We were the only foreigners at the wedding. Of course, it was a traditional Japanese wedding and our first Japanese wedding, so in addition to our limited ability to understand the language, we did not understand the Buddhist ceremony. We followed the actions of other guests and acted as if we knew what we were doing. After the wedding, we danced traditional Japanese dances, including one where we danced in columns. Again, we did not know the dance, but not wanting to be wallflowers; we joined the group and followed the lead of the person ahead of us. The Japanese appreciated our participation. The other guests did not have the temerity to initiate a conversation with us, so it was up to us to make comments and ask questions in our halting Japanese. A grand time was had by all.

Sally with Japanese bride,
Tokyo, Japan, 1960

Eto-San, our land lady, was the widow of a prominent Japanese land owner who had been educated at the University of Pennsylvania. His properties included the Zushi compound and a compound of over 50 rooms in Niigata, Japan. Most of the Niigata property had been turned into the Northern Cultural Museum. Bunchiko (Bun-

Eto compound, Niigata, Japan, 1960

ny) Eto, the eldest son of Eto-san, managed the Niigata compound and lived in a multi-room apartment in the compound. Bunny visited Zushi often, and on one visit, Bunny invited Sally and me to Niigata for an annual tea ceremony on his property. The celebrant for the tea ceremony would be Sen Soshitsu of the Urasenke School of Japanese Tea Ceremony. The ceremony was to be held in the fall of 1960. Sally was pregnant with Diane and felt that she should not make the five-hour train trip to Niigata, so I went alone. I stayed in Bunny's spacious apartment. On the day of the tea ceremony, I did not know what to expect, but I knew it would be a big deal. Bunny knew I would enjoy it, and I did. The day dawned bright and warm — a beautiful day for a tea ceremony. The compound had several tea rooms in the main house and an outside tea house on the side of a lake.

Lake Tea House, Eto compound, Niigata, Japan, 1960

There were several ceremonies scheduled throughout the day. Bunny didn't give me much of a heads up as he was busy acting as host and attending to the comfort and hospitality of the throng of guests. The attendees were almost all women, both young and old, most of them dressed in colorful kimonos with exquisite hairdos. I was walking in the gardens and crossing a knoll when I saw a crowd of women surrounding Sen Soshitsu. He was a tall man, about a head taller than the women, and he spotted me on the knoll. I was

Urasenke Tea Ceremony Master Sen Soshitsu and followers, Eto compound, Niigata, Japan, 1960

easily identified, as I was the only gaijiin (outside person or foreigner) there. He sent a devotee to me to invite me to his tea ceremony. When I arrived, all seats were taken, and he asked each person to move one seat to the right. I would be on his right, the kamiza, or the seat of honor. I was red from embarrassment, as an elderly lady was at the seat of honor, and all those seated moved one seat to the right. The last person lost their seat, but I would not say or do anything further to disturb the solemnity of the tea ceremony. Sen Soshitsu greeted me and quietly explained what was about to happen. He further advised me as the ceremony proceeded. If I had not been there, the ceremony would have been conducted without any talking. It might have disturbed the prayerful attitude of the guests, but Sen Soshitsu was Sen Soshitsu. Even in those days, when I was much younger, I had trouble sitting graciously on a tatami mat, but I did my best. The tea ceremony is composed of many solemn, scripted steps that occur in a precise manner in a precise order.

It was an extreme honor for me to have the pleasure of attending a tea ceremony led by Sen Soshitsu, who was the 15th generation of the Urasenke family line dating to 1522. He was a revered master of tea ceremony. It was almost like meeting the Emperor of Japan. When Japanese people learned that I had been a guest of Sen Soshitsu, they were flabbergasted, or maybe I should say, amazed. To the American, it would be like meeting a famous sports figure, movie star, or war hero. I also met Sen Soshitsu's social secretary, Mr. Hayasaki. We corresponded with Mr. Hayasaki and exchanged Christmas cards with Sen Soshitsu for many years.

Sally and Wedded Rocks,
Tokaido Road, Japan, 1962

Later in 1962, we made an automobile trip to Kyoto. The trip from Yokosuka to Kyoto was about 300 miles. We made many stops at scenic points, temples and shrines, and even though it was only about an eight-hour trip, we made one overnight stop. We were essentially traveling the Tokaido Road made famous by the artist Hiroshige's **The Fifty-three Stations of the Tokaido.** The Tokaido was the ancient coastal road connecting Tokyo and Kyoto.

Our friends, who had been to Kyoto, recommended that we stay at the Sawabon Inn. The Sawabon was a traditional Japanese inn and very appropriate for immersion into Japanese culture that we would experience in Kyoto. Mr. Hayasaki was our guide during the time we stayed in Kyoto. Kyoto probably has at least 30 temples and shrines, some of them having 20 or more buildings. Hayasaki-San selected the most elegant and important of the temples and shrines and expertly guided us through them.

Kofukuji Temple, five-story pagoda, Nara, Japan, 1962

Nara, a nearby city, is also full of temples and shrines. After two days, you might say that we had seen enough Buddhas, toris, rows of lanterns, rock gardens, lily ponds, monks, and priests to last us a lifetime. We also talked to priests and monks and found them to be devoted to their calling and eager to share with us something about their daily lives and the hidden secrets of the vast complexes. For example, the Kofukuji Temple complex in Nara is one of the most impressive in Japan. Founded in the year 710, the complex once consisted of over 150 buildings. The centerpiece is the five-story pagoda, the second tallest in Japan. It was constructed in 730 and was rebuilt in 1426 — now that was before Columbus "discovered" America. It is OLD and still looks great. There are now less than 25 buildings in the complex. The Kofukuji Temple also has many famous Japanese art treasures, including the three-faced Buddha with six arms. We had time to get a good look at five other shrine and temple complexes in Kyoto and Nara, thus gaining some understanding of the practices of Buddhism and Shintoism in Japan.

Kyoto is the home base of the Urasenke School of Tea Ceremony. Mr. Hayasaki invited us to meet Sen Soshitsu. We met at a geisha house, YES, a geisha house. When we arrived at the geisha house, we were met by Mr. Hayasaki, who escorted us to a large room where we met several geisha. The geisha were excited to meet Sally and wanted to touch her hair and skin. Sen Soshitsu came into the room and graciously greeted us. We had tea, sake, and other drinks, as well as Japanese bon bons. The geisha were just as excited as we were to be in the company of Sen Soshitsu. Sometimes we called him Soko Sen.

Sally with Tea Ceremony Master Sen Soshitsu and geisha, Kyoto, Japan, 1962

After our visit to the Geisha House, we had our first sight of the sand and rock garden at the Ryoan-ji Zen Temple in Kyoto. We had seen photographs of this garden many times, as it was usually the centerpiece of Japanese coffee-table art books. This type of dry-landscape garden serves as a place of contemplation and meditation. Fortunately, there were few people there, so we could look at the garden in the quiet time it deserves. There is a wall around the garden to reduce outside distractions. Despite the years of effort by the Zen architects of the garden, I found myself distracted by a puzzle — how did the novice monks rake the garden with circles around the rocks complemented by straight lines? How did they do this and not paint themselves into a corner? Were they suspended by a rope above the garden? Of course, with

Ryoan-ji Zen Temple sand and rock garden, Kyoto, Japan, 1960

hundreds of years of experience in their history, the answer was easy. They just did it.

There was a waiting list of about 18 months for base quarters. Some families opted to move into quarters in a housing complex in Yokohama, where there was a short waiting list, but it would have entailed an hour commute to Yokosuka. Some families preferred to remain in Japanese housing, but we were looking forward to moving to the Yokosuka Base. We were notified in December 1960 that quarters were available for us, and we moved to the base in early January 1961. The move was very welcomed, as Sally was eight-months pregnant with twins; we would be very near the Yokosuka Naval Hospital. There had never been twins on either side of our families, and the Dempster/Strott families were looking forward to the miracle in Japan. Our new house had two bedrooms and a small fenced back yard. Eddie was used to meandering in a large yard, but this would be just fine for him, and he would have more playmates.

About the same time as our move, I received orders to report on January 19 to the Navy Nuclear Reactor Program in Washington, D.C., for an interview by Admiral Rickover for entrance into the Navy nuclear program. Due to the expected birth of our twins, I requested, and was granted, a one-week delay and was due to report on January 26. On Thursday morning, January 19, I received a call from Sally — she needed an immediate ride to the hospital. We arrived at the hospital before noon, and Sally was admitted. I was in a small cafeteria and heard, over the loudspeaker, a summons for a doctor. I saw him leave the cafeteria in a hurry. Shortly after that, the doctor informed me that one of the twins, Deborah, was stillborn. The other twin, Diane, was fine. Sally was very upset with the doctor. He apologized to her. The head doctor at the hospital was also upset that the death occurred "on his watch."

The feelings that Sally had were those that can only be felt by a mother who had been with Diane and Deborah for nine months, and now Deborah was with her no more. This was a terrible tragedy for us, and it didn't have to happen — it should not have happened, but it happened. Sally asked the doctor to see Deborah. Deborah had rosy cheeks and she looked just like Diane except that she was not breathing. The doctor told Sally that Deborah died from lack of oxygen — **LACK OF OXYGEN! WHY LACK OF OXYGEN? Why! Why! Why!** We had the comfort of our many friends in Yokosuka, and we had a new family member, our beautiful and healthy daughter, Diane.

We informed our parents in the US and prepared to face life, happy that Diane was fine, but grieving over the loss of her twin. We decided that I would report for the nuclear program interview as rescheduled, and that Deborah's body would be transported to Baltimore to be buried in the Baltimore National Cemetery in Catonsville, Maryland. The service would be on Monday, January 31 after the Rickover interview. President John F. Kennedy was inaugurated as President of the United States amid snowy and cold conditions on January 20, 1961 —the day after Diane was born.

I reported to the Naval Reactors Office on January 26 to be briefed on the interview process. I was told to report at an exact time, such as 0743, on the next day, to the World War II temporary buildings behind Main Navy near the Tidal Basin and near the location of the current World War II Memorial. Both the Main Navy building and the temporary World War II buildings were demolished in the late 1960s, and the area was made into a park in honor of Lady Bird Johnson, wife of President Lyndon B. Johnson. I was well aware of the reputation of Admiral Rickover and the tenacity of his leadership style and interviews. He more than lived up to my expectations.

On Friday, I was interviewed by various assistants to Admiral Rickover. It snowed all day Friday, and there was no way I could get to Baltimore where I was staying with Sally's parents and return to Washington the next day. So, I stayed with my classmate, Dietrich Kuhlman, who was also being interviewed by Admiral Rickover, and was staying with his mother-in-law in Washington. On Saturday, I was interviewed twice by Admiral Rickover. These interviews and waiting time took most of the morning. The only question that I remember the Admiral asking me was: "Do you think you can climb Mt. Everest?" I said, "Yes." He screamed at me, "Who do you think you are — Jesus Christ? You are the first person in two thousand years who thought he could do everything." At least, I was in good company. Since Admiral Rickover neither dismissed me nor told me to get out, I sat there until an officer sitting behind me told me the interview was over. Of course, you could still be called back, but after the second interview and after a long wait, I was told that I was not accepted for the program. I really was not disappointed. I had tried, but now I had more important things to do — handling the funeral service of our daughter, Deborah, in Catonsville, Maryland.

Baltimore National Cemetery, 1961

The gravesite service was held in clear weather on snowy and frozen ground near the cemetery flag pole on January 31, 1961. My mother came from Wichita, Kansas, and Sally's parents and relatives were there. I stayed in Baltimore another day and returned to Japan on February 2 to be with Sally and Diane and her older brother, Eddie.

Toku-San, our maid, decided that she did not want to commute from her home to Yokosuka and departed from our household. Sally got some recommendations from other Navy wives, and she interviewed and accepted Tora-San. Tora-San went home most nights, but when she stayed overnight, she slept on a futon in Eddie's room. Diane slept in a crib in our room, and later she slept behind a shoji screen in the living room. A shoji is a door, window, or room divider made of a wooden frame and a lattice of wood covered by a translucent paper. Tora, as in Tora-San, means tiger. Tora-San was an outstanding maid and a good friend. She loved Eddie and Diane and they were happy to be with her.

In 1962, my commanding officer asked Sally and me to participate in the Sister City Program, in particular, the program between the sister cities of Mishima, Japan, and Pasadena, California. Of course, we were not from Pasadena, but Pasadena was not sending representation. Mishima was having a festival and we, along with some other families from Yokosuka, would be representing Pasadena. The Sister City Program was established by President Eisenhower in 1956 to advance peace and prosperity through cultural, educational, humanitarian, and economic development exchanges. We would support this mission by doing what came naturally — simply being ourselves and enjoying the company of our new Japanese friends.

Since Diane was just a baby, we thought it best that Eddie and Diane not go. We would be accompanied by two teenage daughters of a fellow officer. We were assigned a host family that had teenage and older children. We did not know what to expect during our visit, but we were satisfied that whatever happened, the four of us could handle any situation. Mishima is 77 miles from Yokosuka, about a four-hour drive for us with rest stops, shopping, and sightseeing. Mishima was the 12th station on the old Tokaido Road, 83 miles from Tokyo. Traveling by foot or on horseback in 1825, from one station to the next station, would have required a pace of seven and a half miles per day — a pretty good pace for walkers, many with all their belongings on their backs.

Auto trips, such as this, were always a pleasure for us with so much to see, do, and learn. When we arrived in Mishima, we went directly to the home of our host family. Our hosts were about 60 years of age, with married children, grandchildren, and a teenage son. They had a large house, and we were assigned to comfortable Japanese rooms. We didn't have long to rest though, as the schedule called for us to be in an automobile parade through the city.

Welcome parade, Mishima, Japan, 1962

We hadn't been told we would be in a parade, but, fortunately, we drove our black four-door sedan, and not the old green coupe that now had holes in the floorboards. The black sedan was a bit old, but it was stylish enough to not be an embarrassment to America and the good citizens of Pasadena. It was a long parade route, flanked by many citizens and school children waving American and Japanese flags. We attended a large welcome dinner, Japanese theatre, and met with Japanese dignitaries. There were not many English speakers, so conversations stretched our limited capability to communicate. However, as usual, this limitation did not bother us or the Japanese hosts. Nods and smiles were sufficient to us and the Japanese in getting by — humor was enough to get us out of tight situations. Despite the generally stoic Japanese nature, they liked a good laugh. It was an honor and a delight for us to be in the presence of the fine people of Mishima. Sally and the two Smith girls had more association with the women of Mishima than I had with the men. It seemed that there was always a group of women surrounding them. Maybe our hostess was more interested in the contact than was her husband. Sally and the girls had no problem answering and asking questions. We had a grand time at Mishima. Our hosts wanted to see our children, so a couple months later we took Eddie and Diane to Mishima.

Sally and the Smith girls with our hosts in Mishima, Japan, 1962

Eddie, Diane and Japanese children, Mishima, Japan, 1062

We had an opportunity to join the Yokosuka Ski Club on an excursion to Zao in north central Japan. We jumped at the chance. The ski group consisted of 500 Japanese and three Americans. We rented some primitive ski equipment from the Yokosuka Recreation Department and off we went. We took an overnight train from Yokosuka to Zao. The Japanese celebrated most of the night, and we didn't get much sleep. We were a bit worried about our overnight accommodations in Zao since there would be several persons to one room, but the Japanese took care of us. We had a small room to ourselves with two futons for sleeping and a charcoal fire in a pit under a small table — all the comforts of home. We slept with our feet near the charcoal fire. Of course, we had Japanese food. Our first breakfast consisted of rice, raw eggs, bread, and some juice. When the maid brought the raw eggs, I asked her to have the cook fry the eggs. I asked by pantomime and after about three minutes, the maid understood, and we had fried eggs.

There were some easy ski slopes and that is where we stayed. Sally easily learned to ski, and we skied until we were hungry or exhausted. Since it was a beautiful weekend, the resort was very crowded with long lines. We soon learned a new Japanese custom. When we reached the bottom, some of our 500 new Japanese friends called to us to join them at the head of the line. We declined, but they almost pulled us into line with them. Nobody complained. At first, we thought they were just being helpful to two helpless Americans, but soon more Japanese were jumping ahead of us to be with their friends.

Sally, ski lift, Zao, Japan, 1961

The cold weather and exercise called for a long spell in the hot bath known to us as the "hotsi" bath. The bath area was dimly lit, and after we found our way to the water, Sally felt some cold drops on her shoulders — it was snow. The bath was out in the open air. The next morning, after some skiing, our hosts herded us back on the train for our return to Yokosuka.

I participated in many sports in Japan. We had an active golf group, but golfing was restricted to infrequent weekends, as it was a two-hour trip to the Atsugi Naval Air Station. Atsugi was only 35 miles from Yokosuka, but there were no major highways then, and the travel was though populated areas with many small villages. We also had a couple golf outings each year, when we traveled to outstanding Japanese golf courses. We always had caddies (all female) with a cost of about three dollars per round.

Arnold Palmer golf exhibition, Japan, 1962

Arnold Palmer came to Japan in 1962. Palmer had won 22 tournaments, including two US Open and two Masters Championships. He was an international celebrity. Of course, Arnold was as big a hit to the Japanese as he was to us. You can see the action in the photograph. The spectators are looking at the flight of the ball, while Arnold has already given his club to the female caddy, has picked up his cigarette, and is looking at where the ball has landed. Golf was a new sport to the Japanese, and their courses were excellent with well-manicured grounds.

I also played handball, volleyball, softball, and badminton at the Yokosuka Base. There were several competitive leagues. After we moved to the base, I was able to participate more often. We generally had a good volleyball team, and we formed an all Yokosuka team and participated in the Army/Navy/Air Force tournament at the Tachikawa Air Force Base. We beat the Army team, but the Air Force team whacked us badly. It seemed as if we were playing "playground" volleyball at Yokosuka, and the tournament referees held us to the high standards of collegiate, or maybe I should say, "Air Force volleyball." With no further need to conform to all the rules of volleyball and no need to keep score, we played a friendly game against the Japanese Maritime Self-Defense Force

We took many weekend drives around the Miura Peninsula to small seaports, beaches, festivals, and Japanese shrines.

We always visited with the Japanese in the countryside: farmers, fishermen, wood carvers, shopkeepers, doll makers, Buddhist monks, and Shinto priests. Most of the time, we took picnic lunches, but we often sampled the local fare. All menus were written in kanji (Japanese characters), but we could not read kanji. We went to restaurants with a display in the window with pictures of each menu item. It was easy enough to go with the shop owner to the window and point out the desired menu item. We did have one bad experience in a small restaurant in Yokosuka. I went to the counter to talk to the cook and saw a rat running on a shelf. I said in Japanese to the cook, "There is a rat up there." He said "No, that is a badger." A badger would have been bad enough, but I know that I saw a rat, or did I smell a rat? We finished our meal.

Darrell, Eddie, and Diane with farmer and family, Japan, 1961

On one stop in the countryside, we took pictures of a farmer and his family. He wrote his name and address for me, and I said I would send him the pictures. I sent him the pictures, and he wrote and thanked me in English and said many gracious things about America. I showed the letter to a Japanese friend at the Depot, and he assured me that a farmer could not write this prose, not even in Japanese. He surmised that the letter was written by a Buddhist monk. That was fine with me. We had a wonderful time and made some new friends, and our picture was probably shown to many other people. When traveling in the countryside, one of our favorite snacks to buy was mikan (Japanese oranges about the size of mandarin oranges). Mikan, eaten with cheese that we bought in a country store, was delicious. We bought the mikan from Japanese farmers for about 100 yen for 30 mikan — about one cent each.

Giant Buddha, Kamakura, Japan

There were a lot of Japanese shrines, temples, and historic sites around Zushi and Yokosuka, the most famous being the giant Buddha in Kamakura, known as Diabutsu. Kamakura was only a 20-minute drive from Zushi and about 40 minutes from Yokosuka, so we often went there. The Buddha was cast in 1252 and is 44 feet in height. The Buddha was originally in a temple hall, but the hall was destroyed many times by typhoons and tidal waves. It has been in the open air for 500 years. Another spectacular event that we saw each year in Kamakura was Yabusame, where archers on horseback, riding at a fast gallop, shoot arrows at a target. Yabusame originated as an exercise to sharpen the skills of samurai. Kamakura was full of activity on the Yabusame weekend with street vendors, dancers, musicians, and many Japanese dressed in traditional attire. We never missed this Kamakura festival.

Each week, the Yokosuka Base newspaper highlighted a festival or site that was worthy of a visit. One such festival was the Star Festival held in Hiratsuka on July 7 each year. Here is a description of the Tanabata (Star) Festival, by Jessica Korteman, a school teacher in Japan, dated July 9, 2012:

> This weekend in Japan, we've been busy celebrating Tanabata or the Star Festival. Celebrated annually on July 7th, this festival commemorates true love overcoming adversity and wishes coming true.
>
> The Tanabata story is one for all you hopeless romantics out there. While there are many versions, this is one of the most popular and also my favorite.

So legend has it Orihime, a weaving princess represented by the star Vega, worked diligently making beautiful cloth. While her work pleased her father, the Sky King, she felt empty in her heart. One day she met Hikoboshi, a cow herder represented by the star Altair. The two fell madly in love and quickly married.

Everything was perfect until the love-struck couple began abandoning their work duties to spend ever-more time together. Orihime's father, the King, became angry and banished Hikoboshi to the other side of the Milky Way. Heart-broken, the two reluctantly carried on with their work on their respective sides of the galaxy.

Touched by his daughter's deep sorrow, the King decided to allow the couple to meet, but only on one day of the year (the 7th day of the 7th month). The condition was that Orihime had to complete all her tasks by this date. Of course, she threw herself back into her work with renewed passion and completed all her tasks ahead of time.

It is said that on the first reunion date, the couple was still blocked by the Milky Way's river. While the King had given them the time off to meet, he hadn't given them the means to do so. Orihime cried and cried with such sorrow that a flock of magpies took pity on her and made a bridge out of their wings, allowing her to cross to the other side and be reunited with her husband.

As magpies don't fly when it is raining, if it rains on Tanabata, the couple cannot meet and have to wait until the following year. That's why the Japanese hope for clear skies on this day.

Unfortunately this July 7th was one of the dreariest days we had had in while. Let's hope that the rain stopped long enough for the magpies to help Orihime cross the river or that the Sky King goes by the lunar calendar which sees the date fall a month later on our August 7, like celebrations in Sendai.

One popular Tanabata custom is to write a wish on a strip of paper known as tanzaku and then tie it to a bamboo tree in the hope that the wish will come true. The wishes are often related to study/work ethics or ability in the same spirit as the industrious Orihime. I have been making tanzaku with my young students all week. Their wishes have ranged from long-term aspirations and goals such as "I want to be a school teacher" to more immediate desires like "I want to eat lots of watermelon."

The tradition of holding the Star Festival on July 7 in Hiratsuka was a commercial venture started in 1950. From all that we saw, it was a commercial success. The streets and shops were crowded, and everyone was having a great time. I guess, when there is a festival highlighting star-crossed lovers and making a wish, it will be successful. I must add that this story does not really fit the narrative of true star-crossed lovers, as they always have a sad ending, whereas Orihime and Hikoboshi can, at least, get together once a year, unless it rains.

1962 Star Festival, Hiratsuka, Japan

We liked Hiratsuka so much that we went there again with Eddie and Diane. We had a meal on the top floor of a department store, and Diane had a chance to ride a mechanical pony with some Japanese friends.

Once we settled on the base, both Sally and I took trips on military aircraft and on American President Line's (APL) ships. I went to Taiwan on a military aircraft with a friend. We played golf, shopped, and saw the sights of Taipei. With so much unemployment, it was almost mandatory to use caddies when playing golf. After about four holes, I hit a ball into the woods, and, surprisingly, I had a straight shot to the green. After a couple more holes, I realized that the caddies had sized up our golf game, and had placed bets on the outcome. The caddies moved our golf balls to give us an advantage and enhance their chances of winning their bets.

By this time, I was accustomed to using Japanese when I encountered a person who did not speak English. Of course, most of the Taiwanese did not speak Japanese, but some of them did. Those people born before 1940 would have been of an age during WWII that they would have learned Japanese during the Japanese occupation of Taiwan. When I encountered anyone over the age of about 25 to 30, they generally spoke Japanese. I had to be careful about speaking Japanese in Taiwan, as the Taiwanese were not friendly towards Japan, due to the harsh treatment they received from the Japanese during the Japanese occupation of Taiwan in World War II. I had a great time in Taiwan and departed on an APL ship and returned to Japan.

Sally traveled with a group of women on an APL ship to Taiwan and Hong Kong. They stayed a few days in each place and had plenty of time for tours and shopping. Sally had a bad experience in Taiwan when money from her purse was stolen while waiting in line to pay for items. The money was not recovered, but the other ladies helped her with funds for expenses. Sally was the first in our family to go to Hong Kong. Hong Kong is composed of three entities, the main island of Hong Kong, Kowloon, and the New Territories. The New Territories were mostly rural, as opposed to the high-density living conditions in Hong Kong and Kowloon. The most interesting sight in the New Territories was the ancient walled village of Kat Hing Wai, dating back about 500 years.

Darrell, sampan housing

I went to Hong Kong on a military aircraft in 1962. I was there five days and had sufficient time to enjoy this international city. The waterways were filled with Chinese junks (small ships) and small Chinese boats called sampans. The sampans were crowded together in small harbors, and, as you can see, they weren't going to sea anytime soon. You might call them "land-locked" — they were stationary homes. When I saw small children on the sampans, I always wondered how the children could be restrained from falling into the water. The parents must have had a way to maintain safety for the children. It looked to me as if the parents went about their daily chores, while the children went about their business of playing.

Sampan children

Floating restaurant

Absolutely everything was for sale in Hong Kong: birds, live chickens, spices, cuts of meat that I had never seen, butchered right on the street, large fish, also cut to size on the street, fruits, vegetables, and used items of every possible description. You name it — you could buy it in Hong Kong. If you lived on a boat, many of the necessities of life were available to you at your door, or should I say shipside.

Next to these Chinese striving to eke out a living were opulent floating restaurants, a must go for all tourists. Although I didn't see it, I am sure that these restaurants had no problem with garbage disposal, as there would certainly have been small scows willing to remove the leftovers to see if there was something to be eaten or sold. Were these folks **dead broke**? I didn't ask them, but I am sure they did not have savings accounts. With all these commercial activities taking place on the street and on the water, sanitation was not at a high standard. Do you think that these small sampans with four and more people living aboard worried about their toilet facilities and disposal of waste? I would not want to take a swim in Hong Kong Harbor.

Japanese friends join us for Christmas, 1962

We had Japanese friends over to our house many times, particularly when our house was decorated for Christmas. Our Japanese friends enjoyed their visits. They were always joyous and grateful and brought unique Japanese items as gifts. Their dress was festive. We always invited our guests as families, but the men, most often, did not bring their wives or children, and many of the women were single. The Japanese often stayed quite late at our house, and since none of them had cars, I drove all of them to the Yokosuka train station and sometimes I drove them home which was a real challenge as they lived some distance away and in different directions. It was worth all the effort, as it was a great experience for them, but especially for us. Our guest book is full of Japanese entries. We received a touching thank-you letter from our friend, Terishima-San, who was a bit of a prankster. He said that he was very upset because our young son, Eddie, could speak English and all he had to do to learn was eat and sleep. I must admit that I also had these thoughts when traveling in a foreign country and hearing young children conversing in a foreign language I did not understand.

Merry Christmas and a Happy New Year

Japan 1961

We dressed in kimonos for our 1961 Christmas card, and it looks as if we also had a cup of tea.

When we went to Japanese houses, we also took gifts. These gifts were not handed to the hostess. They were discreetly placed on the Tokonoma, a raised portion of a traditional Japanese room. The Tokonoma generally has a Kakemona (hanging scroll) and a flower arrangement. The Tokonoma is the focal point of the room, similar to a mantel in an American living room, where a picture hanging above the mantel serves as the focal point. However, unlike the mantel picture that often remains in place for many years, the Tokonoma art is changed with the seasons.

Having been in Japan for two years, we decided to climb Mt. Fuji. We planned our trip by seeking advice from others who had climbed Mt. Fuji and by reading literature. We compared our physical condition to others who had made the climb, and we both felt that we could do it. We selected the evening and nighttime climb, so we could see the sunrise from the summit (12,388 feet). There are ten stations on the climb, and there is bus transportation to the fifth station, at an altitude of 7,874 feet. Our actual climb would be 4,514 feet. We made the climb in early July to avoid the school holiday season. The downside was that we had to start our actual climb in the late afternoon to avoid the July heat. We drove our car to the Fujinomiya Rail Station and caught the Mt. Fuji bus at about 3 PM. The bus was very crowded, and we had to stand and hold onto a strap for the two-hour ride. None of the normally very courteous young Japanese hikers offered us a seat. We started our hike at about 5 PM. We bought Fuji hiking sticks that we would have stamped at about 20 different rest stops on the climb.

There were sleeping accommodations at the seventh and eighth stations. We planned to get some sleep in a hut at the eighth station, a climb of 2,789 feet. We had packed enough food and water for two days, so we carried some extra weight at the start. The climb over volcanic ash and rocks was gradual for about the first two hours and then got steeper. The climb became more difficult when it got dark at about 9 PM. We reached our "sleeping accommodations" at about 11PM. We wanted to be up and climbing by 3 AM. You can see that Sally looks quite comfortable on the bottom bunk with her backpack and coat on the floor. I wasn't quite as comfortable

Sally in sleeping quarters,
Mt. Fuji, Japan, 1962

Sally has early morning tea,
Mt. Fuji, Japan, 1962

on the upper bunk, as I had less headroom. It was a bit cold, and we didn't sleep much, as there were people arriving and departing throughout the short night. We awoke, had a cup of tea with our hosts, and we were up, up, and away.

We had 1,725 feet to climb. This was the steepest part of the climb, mostly over a path of rocks. Sally led the way and set the pace. That was fine with me — one step at a time as we slowly climbed. Not many people passed us. We arrived at the summit in time to see the sunrise. The visibility was great, and as we walked around the rim with the crater on one side and all of Japan on the other, we were satisfied and grateful. A few Japanese climb Mt. Fuji every year, but most Japanese just want to do it once — we did it once, because it was there. This achievement did not give us seats of honor, but our Japanese friends appreciated and accepted our willingness to explore their country and learn their history and culture. This acceptance was not due to any great effort on our part; it came naturally as a part of our everyday life.

We descended Mt. Fuji by the Gotemba Trail. This trail was mostly a sand-like lava slide interspersed with rocks. We bought some shoe coverings at the summit. They looked like straw snow shoes. We watched some other people descending and soon got the hang of it. Imagine people running down a sand dune — that was the way we descended Mt. Fuji. We jumped about six feet, dug in one heel and took another leap. We had to dodge rocks, as we swerved down. It took us about three hours to descend to the Gotemba Station, a drop of 7,795 feet — almost one and a half miles. We had a meal in Gotemba and boarded a bus for our return to the Fujinomiya Rail Station to get our car and return to Yokosuka. We were tired, but didn't have much soreness except in our calves caused by the descent. We had a great two days.

We made several more trips to the Mt. Fuji foothills, and on one occasion, we took Eddie, Diane, and Tora-San to the fifth station. It was a foggy day with little visibility. Tora-San was seeing Mt. Fuji close up for the first time, and we wanted Eddie and Diane to know they had been there. We bought Fuji climbing poles for Eddie and Diane and Eddie rode a horse. You can see in the picture to the right that Diane is clutching her stick. She didn't want her mother to help her.

Commander Klofkorn from the Yokosuka Supply Depot and I were asked to go to the Japanese Self-Defense Force Maritime Academy at Etajima, Japan, to make a presentation on logistics in the United States Navy. Etajima is south of Yokosuka and near Kure, Japan. Etajima is the site of the former Japanese Imperial Naval Academy that was disbanded after the Japanese defeat in World War II. In addition to the Maritime Academy, it is also the site of several other Maritime schools. We gave our presentations in English that were translated into Japanese for the students. My quarters at Etajima were in the bachelor officers' quarters on a hill with a nice view of the academy and the sea. I slept on a futon under a mosquito net. My room had a Japanese-style toilet. We had Japanese-style meals in the mess hall. Etajima had a museum that honored kamikaze pilots, as well as a Japanese two-man submarine.

Maritime Academy exercise exhibition, Etajima, Japan, 1962

During our stay, Japanese Navy officers and men, as well as local associations and schools, had what I would call a "Field Day," consisting of marching, dancing, and shows of agility and strength. There were hundreds of spectators, and it was an honor for us to be there. We also saw a military review attended by high ranking officers and dignitaries from Tokyo, some of them wearing formal attire of tailcoats and top hats — like those seen on Japanese officials on board the **Missouri** during the Japanese surrender in World War II.

Maritime Academy Review of Troops, Etajima, Japan, 1962

Hiroshima

During our trip back to Yokosuka, we made a stop at Hiroshima. We didn't have to ask questions or have a guide to witness the horrible scenes of destruction caused by the first atomic bomb.

The Yokosuka Naval Base had a motor yacht called **Miss FAY** (Fleet Activities Yokosuka). Sally and I and four other couples chartered **Miss FAY** for a weekend trip on Sagami Bay to Oshima Island and Shimoda, on the opposite side of Sagami Bay from Zushi. Oshima Island was about the halfway point across Sagami Bay from Yokosuka. It is a volcanic island with an active volcano that last erupted in 1990. We rode horses and played nine holes of golf. A volcanic cliff was on the side of one of the holes, so if the ball strayed towards the cliff, it would bounce back in the fairway — my kind of a hole. The horseback ride took us up to the side of the volcano where we could see the volcanic caldera. It was foggy at the top of Mt. Mihara, so we could not see Mt. Fuji on the Japanese mainland.

Sally (right) and fellow Miss Fay passengers with two Japanese movie stars, Mishima Island, Japan, 1962

We had a little excitement when we were docked at Port Habu. Two Japanese movie stars joined our group.

After a day at Oshima, we departed Port Habu for Shimoda. Shimoda is famous in history as the port where Admiral Perry established diplomatic relations with Japan in 1854. The entry of Perry's "black ships" into the port was a disgraceful event in Japan at the time, as Japan had enforced its policy as an insular nation with no contact with the outside world. Perry forced this door open, and now the celebration of Perry's arrival in Japan is considered an historic event in Shimoda. The Black Ship Festival is celebrated annually, with US Navy and diplomatic attendees, and the Japanese dressed in Perry-period formal diplomatic and priestly attire.

In 1962, Shimoda was nothing more than a fishing village, barely creeping into modernity. Now it is a thriving metropolis with impressive avenues and modern buildings. Its port is filled with magnificent yachts. When we docked at Shimoda, we were one of the few boats at the pier. The streets near the port were like the streets in other Japanese villages, packed with small wooden houses. We were in the Japan that had existed for hundreds of years.

Sumo is a very popular sport in Japan. The wrestling ring is on a raised platform about 15 feet in diameter. There are two white lines in the center where the wrestlers stand when they start the match. There is a rope around the ring circumference, at platform level, that the wrestlers use to help locate the edge of the ring and arrest their steps backward as they are being pushed by their opponent. The bout is decided by the first wrestler to push his opponent out of the ring or by the first wrestler to force his opponent to touch the ground with any part of his body, other than his feet. The match begins with a ritual face-off. The wrestlers glower at each other with intimidating stares, then raise their legs and stomp their feet in precision. Some of the ritual is based on the purification rites of the Shinto religion, such as throwing salt into the ring and drinking water.

Introduction of sumo wrestlers, Tokyo, Japan

The life of a Sumo wrestler is extremely regimented. At the beginning of their career, every minute of their day is controlled. The junior wrestlers are up at 5 AM and ready for training sessions. They generally do not eat breakfast. They have a large lunch followed by sleep that helps them to gain weight. Their activities, dress, and hair style are dictated by the Sumo Association.

Purification of sumo ring

There are six championships each year with each championship lasting 15 days, from Sunday to Sunday. The sumo tournaments were televised, and I watched my first sumo tournament in November 1959. The daily matches were scheduled to end about 6 PM, with the top wrestlers having their matches towards the end of the day. The wrestler, Taiho, immediately caught my attention. He was tall and handsome, with less belly fat than most of the wrestlers. The average weight of sumo wrestlers, in 2014, was 326 pounds. These guys are big, but not much bigger than the National Football League offensive linemen who have an average weight of about 300 pounds. At the start of his career, Taiho was almost 6 feet 2 inches tall and weighed 220 pounds. He weighed about 273 pounds during most of his career, a lightweight, indeed, for Sumo, winning his bouts on skill rather than weight.

Taiho had his first sumo match in 1957. He won three championships at the lower levels before being promoted to the top-level, makuuchi division of sumo, in January 1960. Taiho won his first championship in the makuuchi division in November 1960. After winning his third championship in September 1961, he was promoted to yokozuna, the top rank in the top division, and won his first championship at this level in November 1961. Taiho retired from Sumo in May 1971, having been at the top-level of sumo for nearly ten years. Taiho had a record 32 championships. One might have thought that this was like Cal Ripken's record of consecutive games — it will never be broken. But on January 25, 2015, Hahuko, a Mongolian, won his 33rd championship and beat Taiho's record.

We went to our first and only sumo match in Tokyo in September 1962. We had what you might call box seats that were close to the ring. We sat on the floor. I sat in the back of the box, so I could lean against the side of the box that was about one-foot high. We were there for the opening ceremony and had a great time. I had a fair understanding of the Sumo tradition, but was continually surprised by nuances that I had not noticed when watching on TV, such as the ritual prelude and the audience reaction to winners and losers. We tried our Japanese, but understanding an explanation of a sumo tradition is much more complex than getting directions, ordering food, or conversing with friends. We understood most of what happened that afternoon, and we enjoyed the things we didn't understand just as much. AND, I saw my sumo hero, Taiho, win his sumo match. He ultimately won the championship, his fourth overall.

Taiho died January 27, 2013, at the age of 72. His obituary described his birth and early years: "The son of a Japanese mother and a Ukrainian father, Taiho was born Ivan Boryshko on May 29, 1940, on Sakhalin Island, off the east coast of Siberia. Sakhalin had been colonized by both the Soviet Union and Japan. At the end of World War II, the Soviets gained control of the island and Ivan and his mother were repatriated to Hokkaido, the northernmost of Japan's major islands. His father, an anti-communist who fled his homeland for Sakhalin after the Bolshevik Revolution of 1917, was apparently arrested. The family never learned his fate. Years later, touring the Soviet Union as a sumo star, Taiho reportedly sought his father's whereabouts to no avail."

In 1993, the Hawaiian-born Chad Rowan became the first Sumo wrestler, not born in Japan, to reach the rank of yokozuna. Chad Rowan, wrestling under the name of Akebono, won 11 championships before retiring in 2001. At six feet eight inches and weighing over 500 pounds, Akebono was one of the tallest and heaviest of Sumo wrestlers. After Akebono, many foreign-born wrestlers have entered the Japanese Sumo Association. As of November 2014, the last 38 sumo tournaments have been won by foreign-born wrestlers from Mongolia, Estonia, and Bulgaria. To the Japanese, the dearth of Japan-born champions could be considered a disgrace. Does this look a bit like the entry of foreign-born athletes into the American pastimes of baseball, basketball and the Professional Golf Association of America tournaments, and particularly, women's golf? Globalization of Japanese sumo is a problem with fewer Japanese sumo recruits and decreasing attendance at tournaments. Sumo, founded in Shinto traditions, has existed in Japan for about 2,000 years and in the current format for about 300 years, but the future of sumo, at the highest level, is in doubt.

Why did I spend so much time on Sumo? It was the Japanese national sport. When tournaments were held, it was the talk of the town. Most Japanese and a few Americans watched the daily matches for 15 days. The sports page of the **Japan Times** English newspaper covered the tournament, including the traditional nuances of matches and predictions for the next day. It was a conversation starter to discuss the bouts with my Japanese friends. It gave them satisfaction that I was interested in their culture.

In late 1962, I received orders to the US Navy Aviation Supply Office in Philadelphia, Pennsylvania. This was good news, as it was a large activity with many opportunities for the future. The transfer would allow us to travel cross-country with a stop in Wichita to see my family, and we would be near Sally's family in Baltimore. We had been in Japan so long that one would think that we had done everything we wanted to do, but not so. We were certainly ready to return home, but we had been so immersed in the Japanese culture that we were going to miss travel in Japan, friendships, and the excitement of knowing that there was a new adventure around every corner. However, time was short, and we went about selling our two cars, readying our household goods for shipment, celebrating one last Christmas in Japan, and saying sayonara to our friends.

CHAPTER 14: RETURN FROM JAPAN

We departed Yokohama, Japan, aboard the **US Navy Ship Patrick** on January 14, 1963, for our next duty station at the US Navy Aviation Supply Office in Philadelphia, Pennsylvania. Our maid, Tora-San, and many of our Navy and Japanese friends, came to Yokohama to bid us farewell. Sally and Eddie had been away from the United States for 41 months — four Thanksgiving days and four Christmas seasons. Since I had made one trip from Japan to Washington, D.C., I could not claim this lengthy absence. Diane had never been in the US. We were assigned a stateroom with two double bunks. Sally and I had the upper bunks, and the kids had the lower bunks. The ship had a civilian crew with a mili-

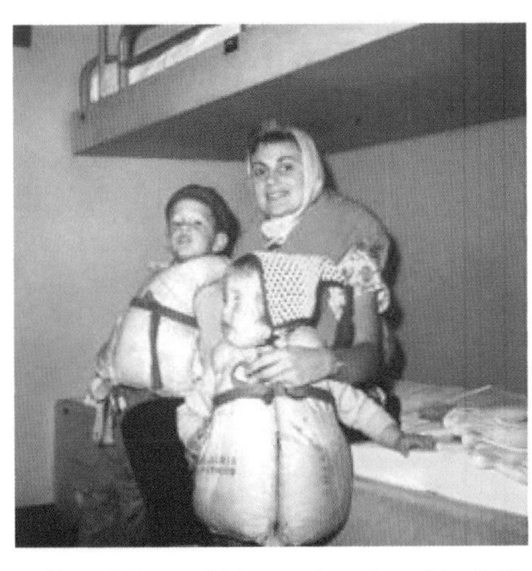

Sally, Eddie, and Diane, abandon ship drill, **USNS Patrick**, Pacific Ocean, 1963

tary detachment of an officer-in-charge, an Army chaplain, and a small enlisted crew. We had shipboard drills to be prepared for at-sea accidents. We had a couple days of rough seas when we left Japan. Eddie and Diane got seasick the first day, but after that, they were super sailors. We had very nice meals in the dining area that were served by civilian stewards. We had the choice of three menu items for each meal — we ate quite well. A snack buffet was also available each evening. Diane was almost two years old and had an independent streak — she wanted to do her own thing — she didn't want help. She would say "I do," and we called her "Little Miss I do."

When the stewards set a table, they put six tablecloths on the table and removed one after each meal. During our first three or four meals, Diane spilled something. The steward then had to change all six tablecloths. About our fifth meal, we found ourselves eating off an oil skin table cloth. This procedure continued throughout the rest of our voyage.

Diane plays on slide on top deck of **USNS Patrick**, 1963

The ship had a playroom for the children, and there was also a playground on the top deck. During the first three or four days, it was too cold to spend much time on deck, but as we neared Hawaii, it was much warmer. It was more enjoyable when we could spend more time on deck.

We crossed the International Date Line about January 18. Since the date is one day earlier to the east of the date line, we had two January eighteenths.

Chaplain, Diane, and Eddie, Diane's birthday party, **USNS Patrick**, 1963

Diane's birthday is January 19, so she almost had two birthdays in the same year. The Chaplain organized a birthday party for all children who had birthdays during the voyage. All the children on the ship and their parents attended the birthday party. It was a festive occasion with party hats, presents, and cake and ice cream. This was just one of the many activities to keep the children occupied — there was never a dull moment.

We reached Hawaii after being at sea for about eight days. We were all presented with the customary Hawaiian lei when we arrived in Hawaii. We had a full day in Hawaii, and we took a bus tour of the island. Most of the road was covered by a tree canopy with greenery and flowers in every direction. We broke out of the canopy as we climbed a mountain with beautiful views of the coastline and sea. There were many Samoan women selling beads and other items at the mountain top. Eddie and Diane were intrigued by the women in their colorful dresses and by the items they were selling. We also had time to walk on the beach at Waikiki and to explore the tourist shops along the beach.

Sally with Eddie and Diane at viewpoint, Hawaii, 1963

We departed Hawaii in the late afternoon and proceeded around Diamondhead to the open sea to continue our sail to Oakland, California. The weather was much warmer, and we spent lots of time on the top deck playground and walking on the main deck. The meals were not like those on a present-day cruise ship, but we had more varieties than we were accustomed to, so we had to get plenty of exercise.

Sally, Diane, and Eddie brave the rolling seas on the deck of **USNS Patrick**

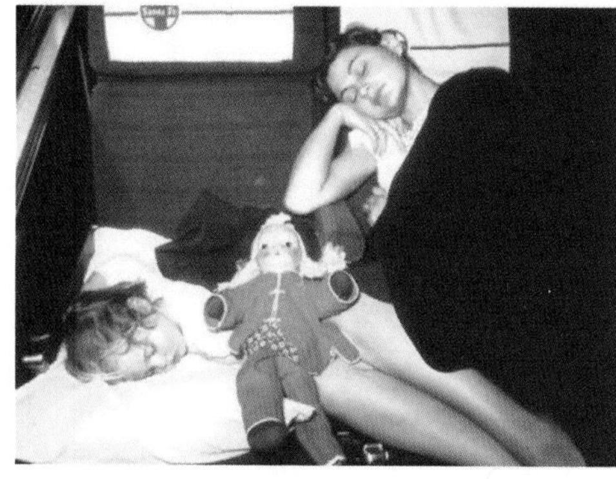

Sally and Diane sleep on train trip from Los Angeles, California, to Wichita, Kansas, 1963

We passed under the Golden Gate Bridge and the San Francisco Oakland Bay Bridge and were welcomed at the Port of Oakland by a United States Army Band. We were back in the good old USA. We traveled by train from Oakland to Los Angeles to visit my father's sister, Opal Dempster King and her husband Kollis, and my sister, Phyllis and her family. We made the mandatory trip to Disneyland and then proceeded by train on our cross-country trip to Pennsylvania via Wichita, Kansas.

We left Los Angeles, midday, for an overnight trip to Wichita. Aunt Opal and Phyllis had prepared sandwiches and snacks for our trip, and we also had two meals in the dining car. Eddie and Diane were good travelers, and we had a good night's sleep on the train. We spent a lot of time in the observation car, especially when we passed through Offerle, Kansas. We had alerted my grandparents, John and Luella Boehme, of the time that we would pass through Offerle. They were standing on the sidewalk of the Offerle main street when we passed. We could see them waving their arms. I am sure they could not see us. They only saw the train, but it was joyful to see their enthusiasm. An hour and a half later, we were in Newton, Kansas, the end of our rail journey.

We were met by the entire Dempster clan. It was a splendid reunion after an absence of three and a half years. We had Christmas in February in Wichita. Eddie and Diane were thrilled to have a second Christmas. We took a day trip west to Offerle to see my grandparents, John and Luella Boehme. Grandpa was 84 at the time — he lived to the age of 100 years. The kids always had fun when they visited Offerle, especially on the Boehme farm that was now being farmed by Uncle Elmer Boehme and his wife, Joyce. Fun on the farm hadn't changed since I was a kid: climbing on farm machinery, playing in the barn, petting the animals, and chasing barnyard cats — now that's what I call fun.

Dempster family welcome home, 1963

A stop at Grandma and Grandpa Boehme's house
in Offerle, Kansas, 1963

I had ordered a 1963 automobile, and we picked it up in Wichita. We again had our own transportation, and we were on our way to Philadelphia. We stopped in New Albany, Indiana, to see my grandmother's sister, Aunt Virginia Laib. Aunt Virginia, who never married, lived in a large house that had been built by her father, Elias Laib.

We visited in Baltimore, the home of Sally's parents. We arrived late in the evening and celebrated another Christmas with Sally's parents and her brother, Bud, and his family. We arrived in Philadelphia in February 1963, and rented a house in Montgomery County, north of Philadelphia.

CHAPTER 15: PHILADELPHIA, PENNSYLVANIA

Our small community of about 20 houses was located in Bucks Count adjacent to Montgomery County. We had a nice-sized house; the disadvantage was the 10-mile distance to the Aviation Supply Office in Philadelphia. I quickly joined a car pool, so Sally would have transportation during the day. The Navy commissary and Naval hospital were even farther away — a distance of about 12 miles. Eddie and Diane had lots of playmates, and our neighborhood, with no thoroughfares, was a safe playground.

We were in our new house about two weeks when our commanding officer asked us to host a visiting Japanese Admiral for dinner. Some of our household goods, including most of our china and silverware, were still in storage, so we were a bit reluctant to accept. Now you understand that this was neither a request, nor an order — maybe it was somewhere in between. Whatever it was, I thought it was something we had to do, and Sally agreed. We had about three days to get ready, so Sally called her parents. After Sally explained our dilemma, her parents agreed to supplement our meager dinnerware. So, with their help, we prepared a feast suitable for Admiral Segawa. He spoke adequate English, and all of us enjoyed the evening. Admiral Segawa appreciated being in our home with Sally's parents and two young children. Admiral Segawa was a junior officer on a destroyer that accompanied the aircraft carriers that struck Pearl Harbor on December 7, 1941. He corresponded with us a few times after he returned to Japan.

Our job at the Aviation Supply Office was to provide repair parts for all Navy aircraft. We were in the initial stages of the computer age, and most of our data was processed by accounting machines. My job was to maintain the quality of the data used to order repair parts, to account for their receipt, storage, and issue, and to schedule the repair of parts that were, in themselves, repairable. There were about 50 civilians in my section. We had an important function, as incorrect data could result in both part shortages and excess purchase when sufficient quantities were already on the shelf.

There were a lot of historic sites to see in Philadelphia and the surrounding countryside. Washington's Crossing, where George Washington crossed the Delaware River on Christmas night 1776, was nearby. The Revolutionary Army surprised the Hessian forces at Trenton, New Jersey, and decisively won the Battle of Trenton.

Philadelphia, of course, is one of our major American cities. We made many visits there to see the living history of the founding of our great country. One of my major disappointments was that, at the time we were in Philadelphia, I did not know the importance of Philadelphia to the history of my family. My Lightcap ancestors were among the first German immigrants to Philadelphia in 1683. They settled in the Germantown area. My grandmother, Luella Boehme, was a Lightcap. I started my genealogy research in 1985 and regret that I did not pay more attention to family history in my earlier years.

On a visit to the Philadelphia Art Museum, I recalled a name from my past. One of the large rooms held some of the art collection of Edgar and Evelyn Chrysler Garbisch. One of my friends at Patuxent River in 1956-1957 was Ed Garbisch, Jr. We played a lot of golf together. Ed invited me to his home in Cambridge, Maryland, for a weekend, but I was dating Sally, and we were spending all our weekends together. Ed was very modest and sometimes wore trousers that might have needed minor repairs. He had a portable chemistry laboratory in his room that had a bit of a smell from his experiments. I never made it to Ed's Cambridge home, even with the enticement of a home bowling alley. After seeing a small part of his parents' art collection, I did some research and found that, not only did his father marry a Chrysler, but he had many accomplishments. He was a graduate of both Washington and Jefferson College and West Point, where he was captain of both the football and tennis teams. In 1922, he kicked a field goal to beat Navy 17-14. In 1923, he kicked four goals to beat Navy 12-0. He received All-American football honors while at West Point, playing the "roving center" position and place kicking. He played in the Wimbledon Tennis Tournament in 1925. Commissioned as a 2nd Lieutenant in 1925, Garbisch served in the Army only six months before resigning in December 1925 to pursue a business career. Garbisch again served as a Colonel in the Army Corps of Engineers in World War II from 1942-1945. Colonel Garbisch died in 1979, and his wife, Evelyn Chrysler Garbisch, died hours later. The Garbisch art collection consisted of over 2,600 pieces and, at their death, was considered the largest art collection ever assembled, A Picasso from their collection was sold in 1980 for $14.8 million.

My friend Ed Garbisch left the Navy in 1956, received his Ph.D. in chemistry from Northwestern University, and was a professor at the University of Minnesota. Leaving Minnesota in 1971, Ed returned to the eastern shore of Maryland and became involved in environmental control of wetlands. I missed visiting the Garbisch home, meeting Ed's parents, and seeing their art collection, but what can I say — I can say that I emerged the winner. I spent my time courting Sally, and it paid off for me.

Sally, Diane, David, and Eddie, Philadelphia, Pennsylvania, 1965

The Philadelphia Art Museum was made famous by the 1976 movie **Rocky,** where Sylvester Stallone runs up the 77 steps leading to the museum entrance. This uphill climb depicts the courage and stamina of the underdog who will never quit. This photo of Sally, Eddie, Diane, and David was taken in1965 on the plaza in front of the art museum. You would think they are looking at Rocky running up the steps, but this was 11 years before the movie.

President Kennedy's car, Arlington National Cemetery, Memorial Day, 1963

During a visit to Baltimore to see Sally's parents in 1963, we went to Arlington Cemetery on Memorial Day to see the memorial activities. When President Kennedy left the amphitheater, we were at the bottom of the hill, and I took this picture of John Junior looking out of the President's limousine and waving to the people on the side of the road. Six months later, President Kennedy was assassinated in Dallas, Texas.

I was at work at the Aviation Supply Office when I was told that Kennedy had died. We were all told that we should go home for the rest of the day. When I got home, of course, I watched TV and learned that Lee Harvey Oswald was accused of the crime and arrested. There was wall-to-wall TV coverage on Saturday, and then on Sunday, Jack Ruby killed Oswald while Oswald was in police custody. My memory to this day is of the policeman in a light colored suit, wearing a Stetson hat — there is shock on his face as Ruby sticks his gun in Oswald's stomach and pulls the trigger.

The funeral of JFK was the next day, Monday, November 25, 1963. The funeral was preceded by an all-day vigil at the Capitol Rotunda on Sunday, lasting through the night. Two hundred and fifty thousand people passed his casket. There was all-day TV coverage on Monday of the funeral procession, from the Capitol Rotunda, down Constitution Avenue, past the Lincoln Memorial, over the Memorial Bridge, and into Arlington Cemetery. Everyone knows where they were the day Kennedy was assassinated.

Eddie and Diane at German Club pool, Southhampton, Pennsylvania, 1964

We looked for a swimming pool in our area. The closest was the German Club, an old club very near our house. However, we did not meet the membership requirements of being German immigrants or descendants of German immigrants. Our German ancestors came from Germany more than 100 years too early. If I knew then, what I learned 25 years later, I could have easily presented proof of our German heritage on both sides of our family. I heard that they made some exceptions for military personnel, and we ultimately were permitted membership. It was a nice club located in a wooded area, and we had a great time there. Both Eddie and Diane learned to swim. Sally was qualified as a water safety instructor and taught swimming at the club. You might say that both Eddie and Diane had an excellent instructor.

Eddie in Philadelphia Municipal Stadium, 1964

We were visiting South Philadelphia in 1964, and I took Eddie to Municipal Stadium where the Army/Navy football game was played. Municipal Stadium was built in 1926 for the 1926 Sesquicentennial Exposition. The stadium seated 102,000. You can see in the picture that Eddie is the only spectator — there are 101,999 empty seats. Municipal Stadium was renamed John F. Kennedy Stadium in 1964 in memory of the president.

Snow day in Southampton, Pennsylvania, 1965

As you would expect, we had some cold and snowy winters in Southampton. In the picture, Sally, pregnant with David, preferred to stay inside.

A world's fair was held in New York in 1964. We went to the New York World's Fair in May, when Sally was eight-months pregnant. We left Eddie and Diane with the Klatt family, friends from Japan. They lived in New Jersey, across the Hudson River from New York. Before going to the fair, we stopped in New York City to see our Japanese friend, Soko Sen, who was making a tea ceremony presentation at the Buddhist Temple in New York. When we entered the Temple, we were told that the venue was full, and no other people were allowed to enter. We both needed bathroom breaks, so we went down the steps to the restroom. While I was in the restroom, I encountered Soko Sen, and we had a conversation. He later spoke to Sally. It was an honor to us that he took this time to spend with us.

The theme of the fair was "Peace through Understanding." The General Motors exhibit was the most popular. We were seated in moving chairs, as we were transported through exhibits of what the future held for us. The IBM exhibit was the most fascinating to me, as it ushered us into the computer age. As I look back on the evolution of computers, the vision of IBM, at that time, took us only into the infancy of the computer age. In one of the hands-on exhibits, the visitor could enter a date and find out what happened in the world on that date. That capability existed for many years in accounting machines, through the use of punched cards. The Japanese exhibit, which included the tea ceremony and women dressed in kimonos, was a must see for us. Soko Sen was scheduled to make an appearance, but we had to return to New Jersey to pick up Eddie and Diane and could not stay to see his appearance. The Maryland exhibit featured crab cakes and a Baltimore TV celebrity dressed as a clown.

Our son, David was born in Abington, Pennsylvania, in 1964. Since we lived about 15 miles from the Naval Hospital, we received permission to use the nearby Abington Hospital. David was born the day before Father's Day and was named David Andrew Dempster (DAD). David was a happy baby from the beginning. Eddie and Diane were pleased at this addition to our household and were very helpful in caring for him.

Sally loved to ice skate. The next winter, we found a frozen shallow pond near our home. On a nice sunny, but cold day, we bundled up and went skating. David had to stay in the car, so Sally and I alternated between skating and watching David. Sally was skating and we traded places. As Sally was climbing up the hill to the car, her left foot slipped on ice under the snow. Her right leg went down and her ankle snapped. I was in the car and saw her waving to me. At first, I waved back, but then realized she wanted help. She told me her ankle was broken, and I helped her to the car. Sally tells me that I then asked her if I could skate a little more. This is a true statement because Sally said so.

We drove to the Naval Air Warfare Development Center, Johnsville, near our home, but the small staff did not have the capability to treat a broken ankle, so we returned to our neighborhood and deposited Eddie, Diane, and David with our neighbor. We then drove to the Valley Forge Army Dispensary. Yes, the Valley Forge where George Washington and his Revolutionary War troops constructed their camp and lived in horrible conditions in the winter of 1777-1778.

The doctor at Valley Forge set Sally's ankle and put on a plaster cast with her toes sticking out in the cold. Sally's trousers were removed so the cast could be put on her ankle. She left the hospital wearing a hospital gown. When we returned to pick up Eddie, Diane, and David, our Italian neighbors insisted we join them for a spaghetti dinner, so Sally sat elegantly at their dinner table, wearing a hospital gown securely tied at the back. Isn't that what neighbors are for? How grateful we were to those wonderful people!

Sally and David, Atlantic City, New Jersey, 1965

It was only about a two-hour drive from Southampton to Atlantic City, New Jersey, and we went there several times. Eddie and Diane took readily to the ocean surf, and David demonstrated that he would soon take to the water.

In 1965, we attended the Mummers' parade, an annual event on New Year's Day. The Mummers' tradition has its roots in European folk festivals. The Philadelphia roots come from Irish and Italian immigrants who once heavily populated South Philadelphia. The parade is said to be the largest folk festival in the world. The costumes and movable scenery take months to complete and cost thousands of dollars. It was a cold and windy winter morning, as we trekked to downtown Philadelphia to take our viewing post on the east side of Broad Street, about 10 blocks north of City Hall. We were all bundled up in winter coats to fend against the cold. David was only six months old, so one of us had to stay in the warm car, while the other watched the parade. Sally was in the car with David, and I was watching and filming the parade with Eddie and Diane. I glanced around and could not see Diane. I went back to the

Mummers' parade, Philadelphia, Pennsylvania, 1965

car to see if she had gone back to get warm — she wasn't there. We frantically looked around, but could not find Diane. We notified a policeman, and he called City Hall. Diane was at City Hall, enjoying herself, talking to the policemen, and telling them she was about to have her fourth birthday. Now, it was not easy to get across the street to make our way to City Hall — we needed a police escort to cross the Broad Street parade route. We retrieved Diane and returned to the warm confines of our home in Southampton.

I joined Toastmasters International. We had monthly speaking meetings at the Aviation Supply Office. It was a great learning experience when my fellow club members critiqued my speeches. Of course, expressing yourself effectively in front of an audience is absolutely necessary to perform the duties of a naval officer. It also served me well when I was an instructor for many years after retiring from the Navy.

A fellow officer, who had his college degree in mathematics, developed a course on understanding the basics of computer operations. I studied with him for a few months; the main thing I remember learning was the elements of Boolean algebra. The values of variables in Boolean algebra are true and false, or the numerals 1 and 0. Boolean algebra is basic in the development of digital electronics and is used in all modern computer programming languages. I didn't quite understand what I had learned, but this knowledge was to become important, as I was selected to attend the Naval Postgraduate School in Monterey, California, in the Management/Data Processing Program. This meant that we would pack up our belongings and travel cross-country to Monterey, California. We had a notice of about three months, and after many family discussions, we decided to buy a small camping trailer and enjoy our cross-country trip.

The trip did not start out well though, as after our household goods had been packed in a moving van, we had lots of "stuff" left to load into our car and small trailer. After they were loaded, I observed that the trailer hitch was almost touching the ground. The trailer was repacked, and some of our treasures were left behind. Our "extra" treasures were distributed to neighbors who were observing this fiasco. Refer to the photo on page 200 and you can see that even after we unloaded about 250 pounds, our rig still dipped in the middle, but at least, the hitch didn't touch the ground and throw sparks. We then got a "running" start on our cross-country trip at 10 PM, and we were on our way to our first stop in Baltimore. And you know what — I never missed any of those treasures.

Eddie, Sally (with cast on broken ankle), David and Diane, Southampton, Pennsylvania, 1964

CHAPTER 16: DISCOVERY OF AMERICA

After a short stay in Baltimore, we headed west towing our little trailer. We commenced our 1965 voyage of discovery of America. We made our first stop before we really got started, when we stopped to visit the Baltimore National Cemetery in Catonsville, near Sally's parents' house. We were there to pay our respects to our dear daughter, Deborah, who died at childbirth in Japan in 1961. It looks like Eddie is saluting, but maybe he is just shielding his eyes from the sun.

Sally, Eddie, and David, Baltimore National Cemetery, 1965

We stopped in New Albany, Indiana, to see Aunt Virginia and were on our way to Wichita to visit with the Dempster family. The trailer was small and easy to tow. I had a close call in Missouri when I was braking to avoid a car that darted across the highway. I was afraid the trailer would jackknife, but it held steady, and we rolled on. After a nice reunion in Wichita, we stopped to see Grandpa and Grandma Boehme in Offerle, Kansas, and now we were really on our way west.

We had traveled half-way across the US through the mountains of western Maryland, western Pennsylvania, and the mid-western flatlands. Now, we were ready to explore the beautiful western USA. Crossing the Kansas-Colorado border, we were still in flat country, when we arrived in Lamar, Colorado, on Highway 50, where we posed by the Pioneer Woman Statue. There are 12 of these monuments across the US, from Maryland to California, along the Old Trails Road that the pioneer families used to travel west. The construction and location of these monuments were sponsored by the Daughters of the American Revolution to honor the bravery of the pioneer women. The monument depicts a pioneer woman with a baby in her arms, a gun by her side, and a boy clinging to her skirt. Sally, David, and Eddie embody this pioneer spirit. Diane adds an additional touch as she stands resolutely against all perils to be encountered on the trail west.

Pioneer woman statue, Lamar, Colorado, 1966

Eddie and Diane with Grand Tetons, Wyoming, 1966

Diane's peanut butter and rock sandwich, 1966

We visited the Garden of the Gods and Pikes Peak, then headed north. After entering Wyoming, we passed through the Grand Tetons. We stopped at a viewpoint to have our noon meal. Eddie and Diane requested peanut butter sandwiches, as kids are accustomed to do. Diane dropped her sandwich on the asphalt and added a few pebbles to her delicacy — she now had a peanut butter and pebble sandwich. We continued on to Yellowstone National Park, where we found a nice camping spot. It was a chore to ready the camper for eating and sleeping, as the trailer was packed with many of our earthly possessions. Some had to be transferred to the car to make room for our overnight accommodations. It was a cold night in Yellowstone with some overnight snow. We had a sumptuous meal, a good night's sleep, and we were now ready to tour Yellowstone, but first we had to transfer

Eddie and Diane,
Yellowstone National Park snow, 1966

Sally, David, Eddie, and Diane, Old Faithful, Yellowstone, Wyoming, 1966

many items back to the trailer to make room for our family in the car.

Yellowstone National Park, the first national park in the United States, was established in 1872. Our first priority was to see the geyser "Old Faithful" that erupts an average of every 63 minutes. Sure enough, it erupted when we were within sight, but we wanted to see another eruption, so we spent some time walking on a boardwalk around the sulfur pools. There were awesome sights everywhere: waterfalls, lakes, mountain ranges, grizzly bears, and bison. We walked down wooden steps to the Yellowstone River at the bottom of the Yellowstone Grand Canyon. Although not nearly as mighty as the Colorado River that carved the Grand Canyon, the Yellowstone packed plenty of punch. None of us wanted to take a swim in those swift and cold waters.

Sally, Eddie, Diane, and David at Lander, Wyoming, campsite, 1966

Having seen a good bit of this magnificent national park, we headed south for Salt Lake City, Utah, to visit Aunt Donna Boehme Hammontree, my mother's sister. Even though Donna was my aunt, she was three years younger, and we grew up together. We made an overnight stop at Lander in central Wyoming. Our campsite in Lander was by the middle fork of the Popo Agie River. You can see that we still had our small sailfish boat and a messy campsite. In many of our campsites, I don't remember signing in or paying. We just staked a claim and set up housekeeping. We got an early start from Lander, as we had high expectations of our stay in Salt Lake City and wanted to spend as much time there as possible.

There was much to see in Salt Lake City, especially the Mormon Tabernacle. We made a day trip to the Great Salt Lake. We knew that the lake was very salty, but it was not until I rubbed my eye with my hand, which had just been in the water, that I knew how really salty it was. My eye stung so much that I had to go back to the beach to rub my eye with a towel. We would not let David, at 13 months old, go into the water, but he had just as much fun playing in the sand. It was

David, Great Salt Lake, Utah, 1966

Darrell, Great Salt Lake, Utah, 1966

easy to float as you can see. The water was very shallow. I can assure you that my rear was not touching the lake bottom.

The next part of our western odyssey was to cross the Bonneville Salt Flats, west of the Great Salt Lake. Bonneville is famous for automobiles and other vehicles setting land-speed records. We saw automobiles racing when we were there. It was hot, but only a prelude to what we encountered as we continued across the desert. You can see that Eddie and Diane, after a walk into the desert, are asking for water.

Diane and Eddie, Bonneville Salt Flats, Utah, 1966

We crossed into Nevada and started looking for a campsite. We found a camping spot at Rye Patch Dam. Rye Patch is now a well-known Nevada recreation area, but it was not developed when we were there. Our camping spot was under a lone tree, surrounded by sage brush and populated by jackrabbits.

Rye Patch Dam, Nevada campsite and jackrabbit, 1966

We were all alone except for the rabbits. We felt like pioneers on a western migration, who might be attacked by Indians at any time, although I didn't relate this to the kids. They didn't need a scary story to disturb their sleep. Our little trailer was nice and comfortable, and we slept well before continuing our journey in the wild-wild west.

After leaving Wyoming, we followed the western portion of the old Lincoln Highway. The Lincoln Highway, the idea of entrepreneur Carl Fisher, was dedicated in 1913. It was the first cross-country highway for automobiles and opened all areas of the US to tourism and transportation of goods. Fisher's original intent was to build the Lincoln Highway as straight as possible across the US. The original travel distance from the point of origin, Times Square, New York, to the terminus, Lincoln Park, San Francisco, was 3,389 miles. The original route passed through New York, New Jersey, Pennsylvania, Ohio, Indiana, Illinois, Iowa, Nebraska, Colorado, Wyoming, Utah, Nevada, and California. By 1928, realignments eliminated Colorado and added West Virginia. The western part of the Lincoln Highway includes Highway 50, the Kansas highway where I rode my bicycle in the early 1940s.

In 1955, when Eisenhower was president, the interstate highway system began to replace older roads, such as the Lincoln Highway. "Ike" was influenced by a cross-country trip he made in an army convoy in 1919. He recognized that interstate highways would facilitate the movement of troops in time of war. The interstate highway system would increase the speed of travel, but would also change the economy of small-town America by bypassing many small towns. This led to businesses in city centers closing or moving to shopping centers on the bypasses. Downtown areas became ghost towns at night. As we traveled this great country, we saw a way of life disappearing in many small towns. Some cities reacted by innovative downtown designs, such as river walks, entertainment areas, and traffic-free streets. However, there was not much that could be done in small towns. Small businesses and mom and pop stores closed, putting people out of work and causing them to move to larger towns and cities. Our travel west often took us off the main roads, and we saw many examples of this adverse effect on rural America. I was saddened by the loss of this way of life: a closed "Billy the Kid Saloon" on a rural road, closed service stations, grocery stores, and movie theaters. I put myself in the shoes of these business owners who had invested their blood, sweat, and tears into their ventures. Their fate was similar to the farmers who had lost their land and livelihood during the Great Depression and Dust Bowl. Many of these former business owners were now **dead broke** and had to pack up their families and move on. Where did they go? That is a question for another day.

Having had enough sightseeing, we continued over the Donner Pass into California and on to Monterey, south of San Francisco. Having completed our "Discovery of America" odyssey, we were now ready to spend a year on the beautiful Monterey Peninsula.

CHAPTER 17: NAVAL POSTGRADUATE SCHOOL

The Naval Postgraduate School was established at the Naval Academy in Annapolis, Maryland, in 1909. In 1945, Congress passed legislation making the school a fully-accredited, degree-granting, graduate school. In 1947, due to lack of space at the Naval Academy, Congress authorized the purchase of the Hotel Del Monte and surrounding property in Monterey, California, for use as the Naval Postgraduate School. The Naval Postgraduate School moved to Monterey in 1951.

The first Hotel Del Monte and Resort opened in 1880. The resort area included the famous 17-mile drive along a rocky beach and through forests with beautiful views of the seascape. That hotel was destroyed by fire in 1887 and rebuilt in 1888. This hotel was also destroyed by fire in 1924 and rebuilt 1926. The Victorian design of the first two hotels was replaced by the current Spanish revival architecture. In its heyday, the Del Monte Resort was known as the largest and most elegant seaside resort of its kind in the world — quite a statement, and from my point of view, very true.

We were assigned Navy quarters in a housing complex across a valley from the school. It was a nice duplex house with two bedrooms and a small room where Eddie could sleep. The complex had an elementary school where Eddie started first grade. I purchased a bicycle to commute to school, so Sally would have a car during the day. The ride to the school was downhill and then up a slight hill. The ride home was more difficult with a rigorous-uphill ride to our quarters. I often walked some of the last part, as I almost always had a heavy book bag on my bike.

My course of study was management and data processing. Management is clear and understandable, but data processing requires an explanation. The year 1965 was the beginning of a rapid computer evolution. The purpose of the computer was to collect and store data, perform computations and evaluations of data, and make this information available to users as quickly as possible. The information needed to be in a form that users could easily understand, thus enabling them to perform their assigned responsibilities more efficiently. As I progressed through the course of studies, I gradually understood that I was learning how to manage computers.

But first, we started with the basics — learning how to write computer programs that provided instructions to the computer on how to manipulate the data input. We developed computer operating instructions (computer code) in the Formula Translating System (FORTRAN) language, developed in the 1950s for scientific applications. Updated versions are still in use today.

The computer we had at Monterey was designed by Seymour Cray of the Computer Data Corporation (CDC). Seymour Cray later designed the world's first super computer. The Naval Postgraduate School acquired the first commercial CDC-1604 in 1960. The floor area for the computer and working space was about 20 feet by 60 feet (1,200 square feet) — the floor area of a small house. The total capability of a CDC-1604, and more, is available today in the palm of your hand and at a much greater speed.

Program instructions and data were developed on a handwritten transcript. These transcripts were then entered on 80-column punched cards (known as IBM cards) by a key punch operator on a machine similar to a typewriter. These cards were then converted to magnetic tape for computer entry and processing. The customer was then provided computer results by a printed output. Computer programs and data were stored on 10.5-inch magnetic tape reels. In large computer facilities, hundreds of these reels would be accessed to retrieve programs and data. This was very time-consuming and reliance was placed on the tape librarian to file and retrieve the correct reel. These tape reels were also used for back-up of the computer system. The back-up interval was set by management based on the risk of system failure, generally about once a week.

We quickly learned how to write simple programs. After writing a program and input data on a transcript, we placed the transcript in a queue for the key punch operators. The punched cards were then entered into the computer, and we received the results on a computer printout, along with the punched cards. If the results were what we expected, the job was complete. If there were errors, we revised our input program to correct the errors. Errors were either key punch errors or programming errors. If the errors were minor, we would key punch new cards ourselves, then place them in the correct order in the card deck, and enter our new program in the queue. If the program required significant change, we would prepare correction transcripts for key punching or dump the program and start anew. It all depended on when the assignment was due and the complexity of the program. The computer system operated from 8 AM to midnight, and sometimes, we could get program turnaround three times a day.

We also studied machine language programming; the language interface that allows programs such as FORTRAN to work. Machine language programming, or assembly programming, was done in binary coding and required knowledge of the computer registers and all the internal workings of the computer. I was paired with my classmate, Joe Fidd. Sometimes, as we were working on our assembler, I was willing to accept a work-around, but Joe was meticulous. He wanted to know exactly what was happening. Joe was a great helpmate and I am forever grateful to him. Joe and I would sometimes schedule a time that we would have the computer to ourselves, generally on Saturday night. We would enter our deck of punched cards into the computer and wait for the results to be printed. If we had programming errors, we would make corrections, key punch new cards, collate them, and enter them into the computer again. We treated the CDC-1604 as our personal computer (PC) — you could call that my first time operating a PC. Our personal programs were not stored in the computer. Our storage medium was the deck of punched cards. At one time, I probably had 50 programs (about 2,500 cards). Sometimes, I would repackage an old program by adding and subtracting lines of code to create a new program.

I have gone through these details of computer technology to illustrate the use of computers in the 1960s, compared to 21st century computer use. We were at the forefront of the computer age, and I was pleased to be a part of this evolution. When I see what we can do with computing devices today, I must say that in 1965, I was in the computer Stone Age.

I kept up to date with the rapidly advancing computer evolution for about 30 years through positions I held in the Navy and in civilian life. I obtained my first personal computer in 1979. At first, I wrote my own programs, I guess to show that I could do it. I soon accepted that if I were to be more efficient, I would need to use available "canned" programs such as word processing, accounting, spread sheet, and more. The use of a canned program is like making a meal by taking it out of the can and heating it, rather than starting from scratch. As to storage of data, my Zenith computer had very little internal memory. The storage medium was a removable 5.25-inch floppy disk. The Zenith was advertised as a portable computer, but it was a heck of a load to carry on an airplane. I was retired from the Navy and commuting frequently from Falls Church, Virginia, to Pensacola, Florida, where I taught a course in logistics to foreign officers. I used my computer to illustrate risk versus reward in stocking repair parts. I took my computer to Florida a couple of times, but decided to find another way to teach this aspect of the course.

When I went to my second computer about four years later, I didn't gain much in portability, but I gained a lot in computational speed and storage capability. I converted all data storage to the 3.5-inch floppy disk. Storage evolved over the years to much higher internal memory, compact discs, removable hard drives, thumb disks, and other memory cards. Now, all my data can be stored on my computer, and removable devices are only used to back up or transfer data. Of course, there is other "stuff" available, but I'm satisfied with what I have. I will note that I am probably using about ten percent of what I have. That's enough progress for me.

We made plans to go to Los Angeles to see my sister for our Christmas vacation. We also wanted to go to the Rose Parade. About three days before our departure, Diane came down with the chicken pox. Eddie was next and we delayed our trip for two days. Eddie still had some spots on his face, but he felt OK, and we left for Los Angeles with our camper in tow. We drove the coastal road and stopped at a camping site about half way to Los Angeles. It was a cold and rainy night, comfortable in the trailer, but not too pleasant when we went outside to the restroom. We survived the night and were on our way to Los Angeles bright and early. We celebrated Christmas Day with my sister Phyllis and her family and my Aunt Opal Dempster King and her husband Kollis. We had a great time at the Rose Parade, until a policeman looked at Eddie and told Sally that Eddie must have chicken pox. I thought he was about to arrest us for child endangerment, but his

Rose Bowl parade floats, 1966

children also had chicken pox, and he just wanted to have a friendly chat. We also had a great time in Disneyland, where we celebrated the Christmas season with all the Disney pageantry — parades, cartoon characters, and splendid Christmas decorations.

Bing Crosby watches play from eighteenth green, Pebble Beach, 1967

The Bing Crosby Professional Amateur (ProAm) Golf Tournament was held in February at the nearby Pebble Beach Golf Course, and I was able to attend in 1966. It was a bright and sunny day on this beautiful course with magnificent views of the Pacific shore line. Bing Crosby started this tournament in 1937 in southern California and moved it to the Monterey Peninsula in 1947. It became one of the most popular tournaments on the Professional Golfers Association (PGA) tour. The Monterey Peninsula was subject to wild swings in weather, from bright and sunny days to high winds and driving rain. In any kind of weather, Pebble Beach was a challenge for the players. Its popularity was due to the star power of Bing Crosby and the beautiful Pebble Beach site. Bing Crosby convinced many of his Hollywood friends to start other PGA tournaments. Bing Crosby died of a heart attack after finishing a round of golf in Spain in 1977.

On a chilly day in January, I decided to use our fireplace. I gathered wood from a hillside, and we had a nice, cozy fire. Little did I know that the wood was covered with poison ivy; identification of plants in the woods was one of the Boy Scout merit badges that I missed. None of us got poison ivy on our bodies, but WOW, did it affect my face and eyes. My face swelled as if air had been pumped under my skin. My eyes were almost swollen shut — I looked like a balloon. I could not see looking down. I could see only by looking straight ahead. I went to class, but could see books and papers on my desk only by bending my neck to the point that my chin was pressed hard against my chest. It took about five days for the swelling to subside. I didn't forego the pleasure of the fireside in future years, but I was a lot more careful in the selection of fire-wood.

Darrell with poison ivy, Monterey, California, 1966

Eddie and Diane took swimming lessons, and I still have vivid images to this day of them shivering as they were standing on the side of the Monterey pool, waiting to plunge into the cool water. With all the water surrounding us at Monterey, we did very little swimming. Our water exposure usually consisted of wading along the seashore. However, since we had hauled our little sailfish from the East Coast, we did feel compelled to do some sailing in Monterey Bay. Sally went with me a couple times, but generally, I was the lone sailor. It was a bit of a chore to haul the boat to the beach and to rig the sail. I had to wade in the water up to my waist, before I jumped on the boat and sailed away. When we had a good wind, about half the deck of the boat would be awash (covered by water), with little chance to get on the high side and stay dry. With the exhilaration of sailing, I really did not notice the cold water, but when I approached the shore, I had to jump into three feet of water, lift the rudder and centerboard, and beach the boat. Again, I was in cold water and ready to sit by a warm fireside.

We had 22 students in our class, consisting of 18 Navy and four Marine officers. Our course of study was heavily math and statistics-oriented. Mathematical statistics is the collection and analysis of data by techniques such as linear algebra, differential equations, and probability theory to provide information for decision making. Sometime in the 1970s, when I read of the process used by Federal Express (FedEx) to deliver packages overnight, I thought back to a study project I worked on in 1966.

Basically, the FedEx model uses a central hub to collect all packages and then flies these packages to all distribution points, as opposed to flying all packages from the originating city to the destination city. This concept came from an idea concerning overnight delivery in the age of computers that Fred Smith, FedEx founder, developed in an economics class, while he was a student at Harvard University in the mid-1960s.

Our project objective was to find the most economical method to purchase, store, and supply repair parts to world-wide customers at the least cost with a given level of parts provided on time, such as 95 percent of orders being available when ordered. The cost of the parts, storage locations, and quantity of parts to purchase were some of the many considerations. We developed a statistical model, developed a computer program for data analysis and optimization, and came up with the best solution.

Our model was based on the same idea that formed the FedEx model. But Fred Smith did more than develop a model — he put his model to work and is now a multi-billionaire with a company that has a world-wide delivery system with 650 aircraft and 160,000 employees. Fred Smith served in the Marine Corps from 1966 to 1969 with two tours in Vietnam. His observations of the Navy logistics system helped him to develop the FedEx model.

I had many of the opportunities that Fred Smith had. I was not only an observer of the Navy logistics system, I was also directly involved at the retail, regional, and world-wide levels. I was educated in management, computer sciences, and statistics to understand and improve the Navy logistics system. I was always trying to get a "better bang for the buck," but I lacked something that Fred Smith and my Naval Academy classmate, Ross Perot had. It was entrepreneurship. I was satisfied to be an innovator. I was comfortable and made a nice living, despite the hardship of regular household relocation, but, as a matter of fact, our family looked at relocation as something of an advantage. So, that's the way it was and is. I am just where I should be. HEY, whom am I kidding? Of course, I would like to have some of the money that Fred Smith and Ross Perot have, say about one percent.

The Monterey Peninsula was a great place for daytime and overnight trips. We frequently went weekend camping with Joe Fidd, my project teammate, and his wife, Harriett, and their two boys. Our camping spots were all within a one-day drive of Monterey. We took our small trailer and the Fidd family camped in tents. We went to mountain ridges, redwood forests, and Pacific beaches. Our favorite was the Pinnacles National Monument, mentioned earlier in Chapter 2, in a discussion about the CCC.

After one year of studies, I graduated with a Master's Degree of Science in Management/Data Processing, and we prepared for our east coast trek to an assignment in Washington, D.C., at the Naval Supply System headquarters, later named the Naval Supply Systems Command.

Chapter 18: Monterey, California, to Washington, D.C.

Our new road trip from west to east was south of the course we took one year earlier. In 1965, we traveled across the northern United States. Our interest points on the southern route were Yosemite National Park, the Ancient Bristlecone Pine Forest, Grand Canyon, Mesa Verde, Four Corners (the point where four states meet), my grandparents' home in Offerle, Kansas, my parents' home in Wichita, Kansas, and Perry, Missouri, to visit my Naval Academy classmate, Roy Fishback, and his wife, Shirley, who introduced Sally to me in 1956.

Grizzly Giant redwood tree, Yosemite National Park, 1967

We had seen many redwood trees in California and were always astonished at the majesty and age of these gigantic trees, but the bristlecone pines were older, and we were anxious to make a comparison. Yosemite, as we expected, was magnificent — there was so much to see, and we could only see the highlights. David was only two years old. I carried him on my back in a Japanese sling on hiking trips. Of course, I was young then, and the extra weight was no problem, but we limited our hikes to about one mile. The principal attraction in Yosemite was the Grizzly Giant, at a height of 209 feet and an age of 1,800 years. It was an awe-inspiring sight. Although not the tallest or oldest of redwoods, it was over 1300 years old when Columbus discovered America in 1492.

Now, we wanted to see the bristlecone pines a bit farther south and east in California. The Navy fight song "The goat is old and gnarly and he's never been to school, but he can take the bacon from the worn-out Army mule" must have been written with the bristlecone pine in mind, for this is the exact description of these venerable trees — old and gnarly. We approached these trees with reverence; as you can see we were very close to them. We saw several groves of bristlecone trees on this very hot and dry day. The oldest, in this ancient forest in 1966, was Methuselah, at an age of 4,797 years. In 2013, a bristlecone pine was discovered that is 218 years older than Methuselah, 5,064 years old. This tree ger-germinated in 3,051 BC. I'll leave it to the reader

Sally, Eddie, Diane, and David, Bristlecone Pine, California, 1967

to investigate the Bible to see what was happening when this tree was born and how many generations of our ancestors lived during the life span of this tree.

Our road trip from the Bristlecone Pine Forest to the Grand Canyon took us through Las Vegas, where we obtained lodging for the night. The next day, we were ready for a scenic tour of Las Vegas — not much to see except the "strip." We parked our car and started a walking tour. The casinos were all open at this early hour, but since we were accompanied by three minors, the doormen would not let us enter the casinos. We satisfied our curiosity by taking a few pictures. Unlike today, the casinos were not in large hotels. They were on the street and you walked right in from the sidewalk. We completed our tour in about 30 minutes and we were on our way to the Grand Canyon.

Darrell, Eddie, Diane, and David,
Las Vegas, Nevada, 1967

The road to Flagstaff, Arizona, and the Grand Canyon passed the Colorado River (the Nevada/Arizona border) near Boulder Dam. We couldn't pass up the opportunity to see this great engineering marvel. Boulder Dam was constructed between 1931 and 1936 during the Great Depression. It was a

Canyon where Boulder Dam was to be built

Boulder/Hoover Dam

significant public works project, employing thousands of workers, including many CCC members. In addition to generating electricity, Lake Mead, created by the dam, serves as a popular recreation area. The flow of water from Lake Mead through the dam and into the Colorado River provides irrigation for hundreds of thousands of acres in the southwest United States.

Low water level at Lake Mead, 1967

We descended into the heart of the dam, a drop of about 700 feet. We saw some of the 17 turbines that generate electricity, as well as the control systems that regulate the flow of water through the turbines. The entire work area was as clean as a whistle. Boulder Dam was officially renamed Hoover Dam (for President Herbert Hoover) in 1947.

USA Today reported on June 24, 2015, that Lake Mead had reached a record low water level. With a normal water level, the maximum depth of Lake Mead is 532 feet. The southwest United States, especially southern California, has experienced serious water shortages, affecting farmers and home owners, even causing water rationing. I don't think the Southwest will experience a tragedy anything like the dust storms and drought of the Great Depression, but the drought will cause rethinking of the normal usages of water, especially for farmers. If the real costs of water were allocated to farmers, they would alter crops for more efficient use. Recreational boat use on Lake Mead has been seriously affected by the low water level. Some marinas have closed — many of these owners were now **dead broke** — and others faced costly relocation expenses.

Having completed a fascinating and educational visit to Hoover Dam, we headed to Flagstaff for an overnight stay and then on to the Grand Canyon. The travel east from Hoover Dam seemed to be over fairly-flat farm land, but, in fact, we were gradually climbing from an elevation of 1,200 feet at Hoover Dan to 7,000 feet at Flagstaff. There were high mountain ranges to the north. As we neared Flagstaff, we could see Mt. Humphreys. At a height of 12,633 feet, it is the highest point in Arizona. We were essentially following the route that I had traveled twice by train in 1948 — from San Diego to Wichita and from San Francisco to Maryland. After a night in Flagstaff, we headed north through a ponderosa pine forest on the Colorado Plateau and to the Grand Canyon. This fairly level terrain belies the rugged features of the Grand Canyon just ahead of us. Our first sight of the Grand Canyon was as awesome as we expected. This was before the days of National Park crowd control and parking restrictions, and we could drive our car and trailer and find parking at all the overlooks. We were worried about the curiosity of Eddie and Diane and watched them carefully, as we neared deep canyon drops. We had to walk a few trails to get to the best views, and, as usual, I carried David in the Japanese sling. We took our time, had lunch, and enjoyed the beauty of this American natural wonder.

Eddie, Grand Canyon, 1967

As we gazed at the Colorado River and the small canyons and peaks below us, I remembered an aircraft accident that occurred over the Grand Canyon. On June 30, 1956, almost exactly ten years before our visit, a United Airlines Douglas aircraft and a Trans World Airlines Lockheed aircraft collided over the Grand Canyon, killing all 128 people on board. At that time, it was the world's worst commercial aircraft crash. As we gazed at the vast expanse of this famous sight, I questioned how these two aircraft could meet with all this space — a case of someone being in the wrong place at the wrong time.

Leaving the Grand Canyon visitors' center, we drove east 25 miles to the exit. There were several overlooks along the way. Just past the east entrance is the Desert View Tower with a beautiful view of the Painted Desert. The Painted Desert continues for about 60 miles east past the Grand Canyon. To the south are the Petrified Forest and Canyon de Shelley, but visits to these sites would have to wait for another time.

The remaining 200 miles to Four Corners were almost entirely within the Navajo Nation. The Navajo Nation consists of over 27 thousand square miles — about the size of West Virginia, with a population of 250,000. It is an immense area with mesas and beautiful rock formations on both sides of the road. We saw a large mesa and a town with hundreds of automobiles. Something was going on, and we were going to find out. It was a pow-wow — a gathering of Indian tribes. As we approached a building, some Indian men came to our car. They had been drinking and didn't seem to be in a mood to welcome us to their pow-wow. We took the opportunity to "get out of Dodge" on the double. We were not pursued; maybe we overreacted. It would have been nice to see some native dances and experience their culture, but it was not to be. As Shakespeare's Falstaff said, "Discretion is the better part of valor."

We started looking for a place to set up camp for the night. We spotted a picnic table on a small rocky hill — not a mesa. We surveyed the site and certified it as OK — not great, but OK. Who knows what we might find in the next 100 miles — perhaps nothing? There was not a tree in sight, so we maneuvered the car and trailer to provide shade for the table. There were no toilet facilities, so we made do with our small porta potty. We saw a beautiful sunset in this soundless and barren landscape. We were up bright and early for our voyage to Four Corners, Mesa Verde, and on to see my grandparents in Offerle, Kansas.

Four Corners

Four Corners is a destination without much to see. But, you

could say that you have been there. It is the point where the states of Arizona, Colorado, New Mexico and Utah converge. Stand on that spot, and you are in four states.

Mesa Verde is famous for its cliff dwellings. The largest of these dwellings could house as many as 100 people. These large structures had granaries for food storage and all the comforts of home, so to speak. They have been described as some of the world's greatest archaeological treasures. They always had sources of water, that is, until there was no water. Long periods of drought led to the decline, and ultimately the end, of this culture at Mesa Verde. The last inhabitants left in 1285, after 700 years of habitation.

Sally, Eddie, Diane, and David
Mesa Verde, Colorado, 1967

We completed the sightseeing part of our cross-country voyage, and our plan now was to drive to Offerle and Wichita, Kansas, and then on to Baltimore, Maryland, but first we had to negotiate the most difficult part of our road trip, the mountains of southern Colorado. We were about 570 miles from Offerle, and we would need to find another night of lodging before our arrival. It was about mid-day when we left Mesa Verde. With all the high mountain roads ahead of us, and pulling a trailer with a sail boat on top of the car, we had a travel time of about 20 hours ahead of us.

There was not much elevation change from Mesa Verde to Durango, Colorado, but east of Durango we climbed steadily from about 6,000 feet to Wolf Creek Pass, an elevation of 10,850 feet. There was snow on the sides of the road at the high elevations, and the temperature at night was in the 40s. We connected with old Highway 50 south of Pueblo near my 1941 Boy Scout camp, Camp Birch. A few more miles and we were out of the mountains and on the plains of eastern Colorado and western Kansas. On entering Kansas, we passed very near Mt. Sunflower. At a height of 4,039 feet, Mt. Sunflower is the highest point in Kansas. Since western Kansas is so flat, remember Kansas is flatter than a pancake; this high point is not noticeable to the casual observer, as it blends with the rest of the landscape. As you would expect, the Kansas high point is close to the Colorado low point.

We had a great reunion with Grandma and Grandpa Boehme. In 1966, Grandpa was 87, a year younger than my current age (2017) and Grandma was 77. Now, at the time, I didn't consider my grandparents to be old, but I certainly thought they were much older than I am now. I don't know how to explain it; I just simply feel much younger than they seemed to be in 1966. The high point for Eddie, Diane, and David was the Boehme farm; they could get near the horse and cattle and chase the farm cats. They also liked to climb on the old farm machinery stored in a nearby field. Much of this old machinery was still stored in this field when we had the 2013 Boehme family reunion in Offerle. A collector asked Uncle Elmer if he could purchase some of this machinery. Uncle Elmer would not part with it. This old machinery was the fa-

Boehme (mother's family) family reunion, 2013

Eddie and David Dempster; Nicole Phillips; Greer, Reagan and Darrell Dempster; Holly Phillips; and Cody and Dawn Dempster, 2013

vorite photo spot of the reunion, as families of 10 to 20 persons posed on tractor seats, fenders, wheels, and hoods.

We stayed overnight with Grandma and Grandpa and then drove east 130 miles to Wichita. I always experience bouts of nostalgia when I am in Kansas, and sometimes, when I read about or remember events of my past. You can take the boy out of Kansas, but you cannot take Kansas out of the boy.

It was good to see the Wichita family. Wilma and John were living in Wichita, and Dee, who was 15, was home with Mom and Dad. Eddie, Diane, and David had seven cousins living in Wichita, and a good time was had by all. After four days, we packed our trailer and said farewell. We left one thing behind in Wichita — we gave our sailboat to Wilma's four boys. It was a sad farewell, but just as well, as we no longer had the time or inclination to take this boat to sea.

We had one more stop in Perry, Missouri, to see Shirley and Roy Fishback, who introduced me to Sally. We had experienced many new adventures during our two weeks on the road, but we were anxious to end this odyssey and eager to establish a new hone in the Washington, D.C. area.

We camped at Sally's folks in Baltimore, as we searched for a new house. We settled on renting a small, two-story house on Kenilworth Street in Arlington, Virginia, about seven miles from my new office in Washington, D.C. Our street and the streets around us were lined with the same type of houses. I learned that we were in a Broyhill home. M. T. Broyhill built tens of thousands of these homes in the post-war era in northern Virginia. They were solidly built and near Washington. They became more valuable later because of their location. M. T. Broyhill's son, Joel, was an 11-term Virginia congressman. By coincidence, the daughter of Congressman Joel Broyhill, Jane-Anne Houser, is a member of our church, St. Martin's in Annapolis.

CHAPTER 19: WASHINGTON, D.C.

My new office was in the Main Navy Building at Constitution Avenue and 17th Street. The National Mall Reflecting Pool was behind Main Navy. Main Navy was located between 17th and 19th Streets, and the companion Munitions Building was located between 19th and 21st Streets, adjacent to the Lincoln Memorial. Small temporary wooden buildings were located across the Reflecting Pool. All of these buildings were, indeed, in a prime location of our nation's history. Also, those "temporary" buildings were within a short walk of the White House. They were built in 1918 to provide temporary space for the military. The Department of War needed additional space, and in 1939, moved from the Old Executive Office Building, next to the White House, to the Munitions Building. In 1942, when the Pentagon was being built, the Department of War was the first tenant to be relocated to the Pentagon. The Department of War was renamed the Department of Defense in 1947.

When I was stationed at the Pentagon in 1976, I attended a meeting in a conference room that had a sign, titled Department of War, stored in a corner. I often thought about that sign and intended to retrieve it as a souvenir, but I never did.

My Aunt Virginia and two of her cousins from New Albany, Indiana, visited us when we were stationed in Philadelphia. One of her cousins came to Washington, D.C., in 1917 to find work and help with the war effort. She worked in the newly constructed Main Navy Building and lived in a rooming house near the White House with other young women, who also worked at Main Navy.

Speaking of the Department of War reminds me of the memory jogger I used in high school to remember the names of the president's cabinet — St. Wapniacl. The cabinets, in order of the letters of St. Wapniacl, were State, Treasury, War, Attorney General, Postmaster General, Navy, Interior, Agriculture, Commerce, and Labor. You will note that there was no Secretary of the Army — the Secretary of War served as the Army secretary.

This also reminds me of my memorizing the square roots of the numbers two, three, four, and five. In the case of two, I simply memorized 1.414, for three, 1.732, the birth year of George Washington, and, again, memorizing 2.236 for the square root of five. I now put this feat in the category of useless information, but it was fun at the time.

This view of the National Mall, looking from the Washington Monument towards the Lincoln Memorial, shows the Main Navy and Munitions Buildings on the right, the Reflecting Pool in the center, and the small temporary wooden buildings to the left and right of the Reflecting Pool. The small buildings to the right of the Reflecting Pool had been demolished by the time I reported to Main Navy. These buildings were expeditiously planned and constructed on limited space in 1918, when there were few cars and most occupants used public transportation. In 1966, 48 years later, parking was limited to car pools and high ranking officers and civilians. I frequently used public transportation.

National Mall Reflecting Pool and World War II buildings

Since I had recent education in computers, I was assigned as branch head of the Uniform Inventory Control Point (UICP) program. We were assigned the duty of designing and implementing a uniform data processing system to be used at all Navy Inventory Control Points (ICPs) located across the United States. One of these ICPs was my former duty station, the Aviation Supply Office in Philadelphia. The Navy was moving from semi-automated control of repair parts and supplies to a centralized automated system. I literally went from the frying pan at Monterey into the fire in Washington D.C. We faced the challenges of computer and peripheral equipment selection, computer procurement, central design, computer programming, system implementation, evaluation of recommended system changes, and implementation of these approved changes. It seemed as though we were always on the hot seat to do it quickly and do it right. I did a lot of traveling to Philadelphia and Mechanicsburg, Pennsylvania, Great Lakes, Illinois, and various Navy Supply Depots across the US. I met officers, enlisted personnel, and civilians that would become my associates and lifelong friends. I was in a position to learn all aspects of the Navy supply system.

Naturally, we did a lot of sightseeing in Washington, Maryland, and Virginia. We saw all the museums and monuments in Washington and went on excursions to the Shenandoah Mountains and to the beach at Ocean City, Maryland. You can see in the picture that Sally, with Holly on the way, doesn't want to go into the water. She is crossing her heart and telling David to watch out — what do you think happened to David? He came through in good

Sally, Ocean City, Maryland, 1967

David, Ocean City, Maryland, 1967

shape, but he waited awhile before he wanted to go back into the water.

My mother came to Washington, D.C., for a visit in 1967 and we took her to all the sights, including a visit to John F. Kennedy's gravesite.

Catharine Dempster, Sally, David, Eddie, and Diane, Kennedy grave, Washington, D.C., 1967

One of our favorite activities in the winter time was ice skating. We skated on the Chesapeake and Ohio Canal and at the small pool off 17th Street, adjacent to the Reflecting Pool. The World War II Memorial is now on this site.

Diane and David, "Hello Officer, wanna skate with us?" 1968

On a really cold day in January 1968, we were ice skating on this small pool, when a policeman came by and talked to us. A photographer was there, and he took a picture of us. The next day we got a call from Sally's cousin, Regina Wenchell. She told us that Diane's picture was in the **Washington Star.** Sure enough, there was a picture of Diane, David and the policeman with the caption "Hello, Officer, wanna skate with us?" David was looking up at the officer and asking the question.

Bethesda Maryland Naval Hospital, birth of Holly, 1967

Our daughter, Holly, was born on December 29, 1967, in the Bethesda Naval Hospital. We now had a balanced family, two sons and two daughters. Holly was soon ready to join us on our weekend visits to historic sites. On Easter Sunday 1968, we loaded our refurbished antique baby carriage into the car, went to church, had some lunch, and drove to the National Mall. In those days, even on the National Mall, it was not difficult to find parking on weekends. We were all in our Easter finery and we considered ourselves to be the most photogenic family on the Mall. We strolled on the Mall, fully expecting a newspaper photographer to take our picture. But, it was not to be. I guess we were just an average family, so we took pictures of ourselves and enjoyed the magnificent spring weather.

Holly, Eddie, Diane, Sally, and David, National Mall Washington D.C., Easter, 1967

Diane, Eddie, David, and Sally, Lincoln Memorial, Easter, 1968

On another occasion, we went to the west end of the Mall, climbed the steps of the Lincoln Memorial, and visited our dear friend Abe.

In 2015, I went on a diet of clear jello and popsicles for a day to prepare for a medical procedure. As I went through that day, my memory drifted back to a salad called "shivering Jimmy" that was a Dempster favorite and present at every family get-together. It was one of my favorites, and I always took a big helping. I considered it a dessert, whereas the adults ate it in smaller portions as a salad or relish. I wanted to experience those memories again, so the next day, when I had a real appetite, I made it using lemon jello, rather than the clear jello I had been eating. I added walnuts and sweet gherkins. Aunt Geraldine's recipe used almonds instead of walnuts. It was a delicious throwback, and I'll do it again when our family comes to Annapolis.

We joined the nearby Westover Community Pool. It was great fun for all of us. By one of those unbelievable life circumstances, Eddie's future spouse, Eva Alakanian, and her family were also members. In 1968, Eddie was nine years old and Eva and Diane were seven years old. Despite the difference in ages, I am sure Eddie splashed water on Eva, as he did on Diane, as a way of having great fun. We probably sat at the pool with Micha Alakanian, not knowing that we were enjoying the company of our future dear friends and in-laws. Life is full of surprises.

Eddie started the second grade in Arlington in 1966, and Diane was in kindergarten. Virginia, being a southern state, did not integrate public schools until forced by the court in 1959. Eddie attended second grade at Robert E. Lee Elementary in our community, but, in the third grade, he went to an all-third-grade school on Lee Highway. He returned to Lee for fourth grade. Diane's school, exclusively for kindergarten students, was on Lee Highway. Diane needed a ride to school, so Sally and another lady took turns taking Diane and another child to school. The next year, Diane transferred to the nearby Robert E. Lee Elementary School. Diane and Eddie were in different elementary schools during our first two years in Arlington, but they were together at Lee our last year. The changing of schools was caused by the gradual integration of Virginia schools.

When I drove the car to work, the only available parking was a good distance from Main Navy. There was generally parking available near the Potomac or the Tidal Basin. Since it was a long walk, I took my bicycle in the car and rode it to the office. I could also drive to Ft. Myer, park, and then ride the Army bus to Main Navy.

In 1968, I saw Washington burning. No, this was not when the British burned the White House in 1814. This was 1968 and was an aftermath of the assassination of the Rev. Martin Luther King on April 4. There was some looting that evening. The next day, Washington was ablaze with fires set by the city's own residents. I could see these fires from our office windows. It was a tragic sight. President Lyndon Johnson called in over 15,000 regular and National Guard troops to help the police control the rioting. This was the largest occupation of an American city since the Civil War. At one point, the rioters were within two blocks of the White House (about five blocks from the Main Navy Building) that was guarded by Marine and Army troops. When the rioting was brought under control on Sunday April 7, over 1,000 buildings and stores had burned. The only "success" the rioters achieved was to destroy their own homes, welfare, and livelihood.

When we returned to Washington in 1976, the 14th Street corridor had still not returned to its former vitality, with many abandoned buildings and vacant lots visible. With similar riots occurring over the years caused by actual or perceived injustice, these actions fit the definition of insanity — doing the same things over and over, expecting different results.

I actually enjoyed riding my bicycle along the Potomac River, the Tidal Basin, the National Mall, and the Washington Monument and to the Main Navy entrance on Constitution Avenue. I experienced history on my early morning and afternoon rides.

One event that I did not expect was the construction of "Resurrection City" in May 1968. The purpose was to house the "Poor Peoples Campaign" protesters. It was constructed on the south side of the Reflecting Pool on the National Mall. The 3,000 Resurrection City inhabitants lived in small plywood buildings and tents. There was a lot of rain during the six weeks of the life of Resurrection City (yes, I sometimes rode my bicycle in the rain). As I rode by the site, I often saw standing water. There was a six-week permit for the use of the Mall by the protestors, and they didn't seem to be taking any action to depart. The permit expired on Sunday, June 23, and on Monday, June 24, the D.C. police evicted the protestors and removed the lodgings. Most of the protestors had gone to another site to protest. When they returned, there was no Resurrection City. I can assure you that Resurrection City was gone.

We were returning from a vacation at Assateague National Park, Maryland, and when we drove north on 17th Street on the evening of June 24, I was shocked to see a muddy piece of land with large piles of trash. It looked as if dozens of semi-trailers had used the site as a roadway. It took the National Park Service about a year to restore the site.

David, Assateague Island, Maryland, 1968

Campsite, Assateague Island, Maryland, 1968

By the way, you can see from these pictures that we had a good time at Assateague. With our new tent, we had almost luxurious sleeping quarters, and we had a fine cooking area in the trailer. We even saw a few of the wild horses that have made Assateague famous.

Robert F. Kennedy, the younger brother of President Kennedy, was assassinated in the early morning hours of June 6, 1968, the 24th anniversary of D-Day. He was shot by Sirhan Sirhan, a Palestinian, who, purportedly, was displeased by Kennedy's support of the Israelis during the Six-Day War, one year earlier. Kennedy's mass was held at St. Patrick's Cathedral in New York City on June 8. The train carrying Kennedy's body left New York after the mass and was scheduled to arrive in Washington at about 4:30 PM. With this information, Eddie, Diane and I went to Arlington Cemetery to view the arrival of the procession. Sally stayed home with David and

Holly. We waited and waited at the cemetery with no sign that the procession was near. It was difficult to determine the new expected arrival time, since we had no way to communicate. Eventually, new arrivals gave us information on the train's location

The burial site, near the grave of President Kennedy, was adjacent to the section of Arlington Cemetery that used to be a part of Ft. Myer. This Ft. Myer site was later turned over to Arlington Cemetery. Since it was nearing dinner time, we went to Ft. Myer and had a meal at the snack bar. When we returned to the burial site, we learned there was another delay, so we went back to Ft. Myer and went to a movie. After another wait at the cemetery, we returned to Ft. Myer for some ice cream. We were told that the train had arrived in Washington at 9 PM, so we hustled back to the cemetery. Finally, the cortege arrived at about 10 PM. Candles were passed out, and we held lighted candles as the cortege passed. There was a large crowd of guests and dignitaries, and it was not possible for us to get near the grave site. Eddie, Diane, and I had a long day, but it was an historical occasion. We were grateful that we had access to Ft. Myer and did not have to stand in the cemetery for six hours without nourishment.

Eddie and Diane, Robert F. Kennedy burial, Arlington Cemetery, 1968

Eddie, Falls Church, Virginia, 1968

In 1968, when Eddie was nine years old, he joined a Pop Warner football team. Eddie liked to play defense, and he was a real disrupter. He was always in the other team's backfield.

The typical Kansan has a mindset of owning land. I had lived at home and in Navy quarters. After I was married, we lived in rented houses in Annapolis, Japan, Philadelphia and Virginia and in Navy quarters in Japan and Monterey. I had a dream of owning land. Sally and I looked at rural properties in Virginia in about a one-hundred-mile radius of Arlington. We settled on 112 acres of wooded land. We called our farm "Culpeper," as it was near Culpeper, Virginia. The land consisted of 15 acres of pasture and the rest was wooded with a good number of mature trees and a large cedar grove. Cedars also grew along the fence lines where the birds "dropped" seeds.

Our only neighbor was Mr. Landis, an elderly, retired farmer. We had a creek across our property that had water only when it rained and a running creek at the back edge of the property. We obtained fresh water from a well on the property of Mr. Landis, who welcomed us as a neighbor. We established our "home place" near the woodland, built a wooden fence, erected a small shed, put up a large tent, and with our trailer for cooking and sleeping, we were "home sweet home." Culpeper was located near Cedar Mountain, the site of two Civil War battles. Unfortunately, we enjoyed our vacations at Culpeper for only two years, as we moved to California in 1969 and did not return to Virginia for seven years.

About March of 1969, my division head advised me that he was going to request that my tour in Washington be extended for another year. Since I enjoyed the job and my family was well situated and enjoying their schools in Arlington, I did not object. This request was denied, and I was told that I would be going to an aircraft carrier assigned to our forces in Vietnam. I was given the choice of the **Coral Sea** or the **Ranger**. **Coral Sea** was a smaller carrier and her schedule for the next two years called for one eight-month deployment to Vietnam and one year in the Naval Shipyard Hunter's Point, San Francisco, California, with a home port of Alameda, California. The **Ranger**, also home ported in Alameda, would have two eight-month deployments. Caring for our family, when I was absent for two eight-month periods, seemed like a daunting task for Sally, so I chose the **Coral Sea.** This choice lasted about two days; I was called by my friend, Captain Bobby Hatch, who was on the staff of the Commander, Pacific Fleet in

Hawaii. Captain Hatch told me that I was going to the **Ranger** and to get ready to go. Captain Hatch considered the **Ranger** to be a more demanding assignment and that was where he wanted me to go. I said "Aye Aye, Sir" and we began to prepare ourselves for a June departure for California.

My assignment to the **Ranger** was the only time, thus far, in my Navy career that I had been given a choice of assignments, and I made the wrong choice. This was corrected by Captain Hatch. My tour of duty on the **Ranger** turned out to be the most enjoyable, rewarding, and successful of my Navy career.

Sally, Bedford Springs, Pennsylvania, 1967

Eddie, Sally, David and Diane, Bedford Springs, Pennsylvania, 1967

Eddie, David and Diane, Ocean City, Maryland, 1967

David, Eddie, Holly, and Diane, Arlington, Virginia, 1968

Sally, Eddie, David, and Diane with trailer at farm home site, Culpeper, Virginia, 1967

Holly, Eddie, Sally's father and mother, and Sally, Assateague, Maryland, 1967

Dempster and Van Scoyoc families, Nixon Inauguration, 1969

"Ike" funeral, Pennsylvania Avenue, Washington, D.C., 1969

CHAPTER 20: USS RANGER (CVA-61)

Our household goods were packed and shipped, and we loaded our travel needs and supplies in our station wagon and travel trailer, said farewell to our relatives and friends, and hit the road for California. We traveled through Virginia, West Virginia, Pennsylvania, Ohio, and into Indiana where we stopped to see Aunt Virginia (my grandmother's sister) in New Albany. We drove through Kentucky, Missouri and into Kansas for a reunion with the Boehme and Dempster families. After a visit with my parents in Wichita and Grandpa and Grandma Boehme in Offerle, Kansas, we headed north through Nebraska to South Dakota. We drove through Badlands National Park. When I see expansive views such as these eroded buttes and pinnacles splashed with a variety of colors of layered rock, I want to walk a distance into the splendor. However, our walking was limited by our four children, with Holly

Sally, Holly, Diane, David, and Eddie, Badlands National Park, South Dakota, 1969

one and a half years old. Also, the children were anxious to see Fred and Wilma and the rest of the Flintstones at the Flintstone Park in Custer, South Dakota. The children were exhausted from our 600-mile drive through Kansas and Nebraska, and to Rapid City, South Dakota. I couldn't imagine a better place to build this park than in this rocky area of South Dakota. Fred and Wilma Flintstone were wonderful hosts. They allowed our children to pose with them and climb on all the animals, pets, and Flintstone furniture, as well as ride in all their stone conveyances.

David, Eddie, Diane, Holly, and Sally, Flintstone Park, Rapid City, South Dakota, 1969

The highlight of our South Dakota adventure was Mt. Rushmore. We traveled a curvy, mountain road, emerged from a forest, and saw majestic Mt. Rushmore with sculptures of Presidents George Washington, Thomas Jefferson, Theodore Roosevelt, and Abraham Lincoln. Construction of the sculptures began in 1927, but due to lack of funding, the work ended in 1941. The original intention was to show each president from head to waist, but the final sculptures show only heads and shoulders.

Mt. Rushmore, South Dakota, 1969

Eddie, Diane, Holly, David, and Sally, Mt. Rushmore, South Dakota, 1969

I saw pictures of the monument many times in **Collier's**, **National Geographic**, and other magazines over the years.

Mt. Rushmore, like the Statue of Liberty, is a national icon. We had a nice view of the 60-foot high faces with 20-foot noses and 11-foot wide eyes.

Our son, David, and his family visited Mt. Rushmore in 2013, and there were mobs of people. There was a large visitors' center and parking lot. Our visit was during simpler times — we had a simple viewpoint and small parking area with no crowds — we could enjoy one of the wonders of the world in peace and tranquility.

We completed our sightseeing in South Dakota and continued our westward journey through Montana, Utah, Nevada, and into California. For such a long drive, we always tried to combine cultural attractions with some "fun" things for the children. It was an exciting trip for them and, to this day, they often comment on things they had seen. They are taking the same adventures, when traveling with their families, as we did as a family for so many years.

We stopped in Pleasant Hill, California, near the **Ranger** home port in Alameda. We stayed with our friends from our days in Japan, the Hohensteins, while we looked for a house. Pat Hohenstein helped us find a nice house in a cul-de-sac in a Mormon community in Pleasant Hill. The house had three bedrooms, a garage, and a swimming pool. Our household goods were delivered, and I reported for duty on the **Ranger**.

The **Ranger** was in the Hunter's Point Naval Shipyard undergoing repairs when I arrived. I commuted to Alameda and took a **Ranger** boat across San Francisco Bay to Hunter's Point. The commute to Alameda took about 30 minutes, and the boat ride took about 15 minutes. I had to get an early start to arrive on the **Ranger** for the morning muster. I soon joined a carpool with the **Ranger** executive officer and air boss, so Sally would have the car during the day. We were in the shipyard for about 40 days and then went to the dock at Alameda. For about three weeks, we went to sea off the northern California coast during the week and then went to San Diego for about three weeks for refresher training. Our air wing from various West Coast air stations flew aboard, and we conducted air operations and exercised all the ship's equipment to verify that we were ready for our deployment to Southeast Asia.

We had about two weeks back in Alameda before our eight-month deployment. David had learned to swim, but we were worried that Holly might open the door to her bedroom, that opened to the patio and pool, and wander into the pool. I installed a lock on her bedroom door as a safety precaution. This would be the first time that Sally would be alone with the kids for an extended period. She would be left to care for the children, personal finances, and other household duties — she would be in charge of everything. But, it came time to depart, and I departed. I didn't want to leave the family, but I was looking forward to the challenge and responsibility of being the supply officer of a United States Navy attack aircraft carrier.

We paid a port call for a day at Pearl Harbor, Hawaii, and some of the crew took the opportunity to tour Hawaii. I spent most of the day with Captain Bobby Hatch from the Pacific Fleet staff. Of course, I had already been briefed by our immediate superior, the Naval Air Force, Pacific staff, on ship and aircraft readiness reporting procedures and how to report problems and requests for assistance. Bobby, as well, went over these procedures and gave me some fatherly thoughts on how to succeed and stay out of trouble. The most common advice to all supply officers was to beware of the ship's store operations, particularly shortages of cash and merchandise. Without proper control and attention to detail, more than one supply officer had his career derailed by shortages of merchandise and cash of a few thousand dollars.

The **Ranger** had a complement of about 3,000 ships' company personnel and about 2,000 air wing personnel. The **Ranger** carried about 90 aircraft. There were seven divisions in the Supply Department: Stores, Food Service, Retail Sales, Disbursing, Wardroom, Aviation Stores, and Data Processing. There were about 400 personnel in the Supply Department and 200 more serving as "mess cooks." The duties of the mess cooks were assisting cooks and bakers, serving food, and cleaning the mess decks (kitchens and dining areas). All the **Ranger** junior enlisted personnel were available for temporary assignment from their divisions to the Supply Department on a three-month rotating basis.

There were two mess decks on the second deck (one deck below the main deck), one forward and one aft. At least one of the mess decks was open for meals 24 hours a day. There were three wardrooms: the senior officers' wardroom, the junior officers' wardroom, and the "dirty shirt locker." The first two wardrooms had regular dining hours, and all officers were served at the same time and were required to wear the "uniform of the day," generally a khaki uniform without a tie. Those dining in the third wardroom were mainly pilots and other flight officers who generally wore their flight suits. However, there were many other officers supporting flight operations, and they could always eat in the "dirty shirt locker." It was open about 20 hours per day. Of course, the same meals were served in all wardrooms except that sandwiches were always available in the "dirty shirt locker."

Enlisted personnel received their meals free as part of their enlistment contract. There was a food allowance budget, and I received a report every month of spending versus budget. The Food Service Officer did a good job, and we never went over budget. The officers received a basic allowance for subsistence of $47.88 per month. The Wardroom Officer established a mess share (members' equity) based on the inventory of provisions in stock. This amount was paid by each officer when he reported to the ship. The mess share was returned to the officer on his departure from the ship. Each officer was charged the cost of food served on a monthly basis. The objective was to stay within the officer budget of $47.88 while serving high quality meals. The number of officers in the officers' mess more than doubled when the air wing came aboard.

One of the cautions that I received was to be cognizant of the mess share paid in and the amount paid out when the air wing came aboard and left the ship. It was best to pay out a bit more than was paid in. This was accomplished by having a monthly mess bill with a little "cushion" during the last part of the deployment. The air wing officers felt better if they were paid a bit more at the end of the deployment than they paid in at the beginning. This strategy fulfilled our objective of good will and hospitality to the air wing and ship's officers, but in the overall picture, the food served was either paid for by the monthly mess bill or the increase or decrease in mess share. In the overall management picture, this was a minor detail, but if it was important to the officers to "get their money back," it was an important detail to be managed.

The principal role of the **Ranger** was to conduct flight operations in support of its mission in Southeast Asia. The hours of flight operations dictated when those directly involved in operation and support of the ship and aircraft were on duty.

The **Ranger** generally conducted flight operations over a 30-day period, followed by a week in port. Flight operations were conducted 12 hours a day with the other 12 hours on standby duty. The flight operations were conducted from 12 noon to midnight or from midnight to 12 noon. The daily flight operations consisted of seven cycles of one hour and 45 minutes each. We launched aircraft the first cycle of the day followed by five cycles of recovery and launch and the last recovery. Of course, the ideal was to have the same number of recoveries as launches.

The worst situation was to have an aircraft and crew shot out of the sky over Vietnam. If these aircraft could fly over the Vietnam coast, the crew could be rescued by destroyer or helicopter. In the worst case, the crew bailed out over Vietnam and became prisoners of war, or they went down with their planes.

In some cases, due to maintenance problems, planes were diverted to land at Cubi Point, the Philippines, or flew to Cubi Point to drop off mail and pick up mail and supplies. Many of the **Ranger** officers and crew and most of the air wing were at their stations during flight operations. They got very little sleep during this hectic schedule. The captain had a small stateroom on the bridge where he could take catnaps.

As all of us know, carrier flight operations are inherently dangerous. The pilots, flight crew, squadron support personnel, flight deck crew, catapult and arresting gear crews, the captain, and all ships operators are highly skilled and undergo rigorous training. All equipment settings are checked, double checked, and triple checked to verify that things that can go wrong, will not go wrong before "pushing the button." But, things are things, and things do go wrong, whether by personnel failure, equipment failure, enemy fire, or acts of nature. We had what was considered "good" deployments, but we did have losses. I will mention four incidents.

The C-2 Carrier Onboard Delivery (COD) aircraft was used to transport mail, personnel, and supplies to and from the ship. In 1971, the COD was taking off from the **Ranger**. The C-2 stalled just after being catapulted off the deck, lost air speed, went nose up, and dropped into the sea with nine souls on board. The **Ranger** and its supporting ships went into full emergency action. I was in my stateroom and felt the hard turn of the **Ranger** as it maneuvered to avoid colliding with the wreckage and get into position to rescue survivors. There were no survivors. It was determined that the most likely cause of the accident was the shifting aft of a heavy radar generator that was being sent to Subic Bay for repair. Filipino technicians had previously been sent from Subic to repair the generator, but repair of the generator was beyond their capabilities. The Filipinos and the generator were onboard the C-2. I will never forget that day.

In another instance, in March 1971, a flight deck crewman was blown over the side during flight operations. He was recovered by the **Ranger** plane guard, a Navy destroyer that always followed the **Ranger** during flight operations.

We lost a Grumman A-6 aircraft on a dead catapult shot in broad daylight. The aircraft shot forward about 200 feet and dropped into the sea. Despite rescue attempts by a helicopter that was in the air standing by and supporting ships, the aircraft and both pilots were lost. This was particularly nerve shattering to me, as I knew one pilot quite well. He was a commander and served as executive officer of the A-6 squadron. He was one of the few Air Wing senior officers to regularly have his evening meal with us in the second deck wardroom. It was a sad loss. I am sure that he planned to be back on deck soon and have his evening meal with us.

We lost a few aircraft over North Vietnam and one I remember, in particular, was a lieutenant missing over Vietnam. Right after he was shot down, we departed the Tonkin Gulf for Subic Bay. On the way to Subic, we learned that he had been rescued, and when we arrived in Subic, he was there. Some of his fellow air wing officers commandeered a flat-bed truck and formed a parade to the Cubi Point Naval Air Station Officers' Club, where they staged a grand celebration.

Although we had several losses during our deployments, nothing could compare to the **Forrestal** flight deck fire in 1967. The **Forrestal** was preparing to launch a strike over Vietnam when a rocket on an F-4 Phantom aircraft accidentally discharged. Although the rocket did not detonate, it struck an external fuel tank on another aircraft, causing explosions and fire. The rocket also dislodged two 1,000-pound bombs. One of them exploded less than two minutes after the start of the fire.

The **Forrestal** ordinance crew had been reluctant to use these bombs, due to their age and corrosion. These bombs had been taken aboard the day before from an ammunition ship after many years storage in Subic Bay. They were sent to the **Forrestal,** as a last resort, due to the shortage of ammunition caused by the very high level of strikes over Vietnam. The safety mechanisms built into the bombs were unreliable due to their age. These bombs were not supposed to detonate from the heat of a fire before a 10 minutes exposure. The explosions tore two holes in the flight deck, causing fuel oil to flow into the crew's living quarters below and all the way down to the hangar deck. Eight of the nine bomb explosions were caused by the older 1,000-pound bombs. The specially trained fire-fighting team estimated they had 10 minutes to control the fire, but the bombs cooked off in less than two minutes. Most of the fire-fighting team was killed in the first explosion.

The pilots, who were in their aircraft, were in extreme danger. The two 1,000-pound bombs that provided the impetus to the fire and explosions were next to future US Senator John McCain's aircraft. The aircraft crews had less than two minutes to exit their aircraft and get over the side of the flight deck.

McCain left his aircraft, jumped off an external fuel tank and was helping another pilot to escape when the first bomb exploded. He was hit by shrapnel in the legs and chest, but managed to escape. Three months later, McCain was a North Vietnam POW. Talk about bravery: in three months McCain had recovered from his **Forrestal** injuries, volunteered for another squadron combat assignment, and was shot down over North Vietnam. He became a guest of the North Vietnamese for five and a half years.

When the prisoners were released by North Vietnam, McCain was offered to be among the first to be released because his father was a four-star admiral. McCain refused early release and waited his turn as the prisoners were released in the order of the length of time that they had been held prisoner.

In 2015, a Presidential candidate was "stupid" enough to say that he did not think McCain was brave because he had been taken prisoner. Flying from an aircraft carrier is brave enough. McCain exhibited bravery during his Navy career. He was also heroic.

Robert Timberg in **John McCain: An American Odyssey** wrote: "When a reporter was questioning whether McCain was a carpetbagger when McCain was running for Congress from the first district of Arizona when he had only lived there a short time, McCain responded, 'Listen, pal, I spent 22 years in the Navy. My father was in the Navy. My grandfather was in the Navy. We in the military service tend to move a lot. We have to live in all parts of the country, all parts of the world. I wish I could have had the luxury, like you, of growing up and living and spending my entire life in a nice place like the First District of Arizona, but I was doing other things. As a matter of fact, when I think about it now, the place I lived longest in my life was Hanoi.' "

One of my **Barton** shipmates from 1955 and 1966, Lieutenant Commander Herb Hope was farther aft in an A-4 on the **Forrestal**. He survived the explosion, exited his aircraft and rolled on the flight deck to a safety net on the starboard side. After he had made his way to the hangar deck, he stated that the port quarter of the flight deck was no longer there. I saw Herb Hope in 1970 when he was commanding officer of an attack squadron on the **Constellation**. I flew by helicopter from the **Ranger** to the **Constellation** in the Tonkin Gulf to exchange spare parts and ideas with the **Constellation** supply officer. I had lunch with Herb. As we toured the ship and visited his squadron spaces, Herb was wearing a flamboyant jungle-type hat that he bought in Thailand. That was Herb, always the dashing naval aviator. That is when I got the idea of purchasing some of these hats in Thailand for resale on the **Ranger.**

The 1967 **Forrestal** fire and explosions killed 134 officers and men and injured 161. **Forrestal** made its way to Subic Bay, and later to the US, where it was dry docked for eight months for repairs. Twenty-one aircraft were lost.

Aircraft carriers suffered two other serious fires. **USS Oriskany** had a fire in 1966 that killed 44 men and injured 138. **USS Enterprise** had a fire in 1969 that killed 28 and injured 314. Aircraft carrier operations are, indeed, a dangerous business.

One of the most famous rest and recreation areas for Navy personnel in the Pacific was the Cubi Point Officers' Club. It was a place where the crews of Navy ships, returning after

Aircraft catapult for amateurs, Cubi Point, Officers' Club, the Phillipines, 1970

many days of aircraft carrier combat operations, could relax and unwind. One of the high points for frivolity, especially for aviators, was the catapult apparatus. It consisted of an open cockpit cabin on rails with a slight decline that ended in a pool of water. The cabin was propelled by nitrogen that provided acceleration from zero to 15 mph in two feet. It was said that this was the equivalent G force of World War II hydraulic catapults. The "pilot" was secured in the cabin by shoulder straps and a safety belt. If all went well, the cabin cockpit was arrested by a jerk on the joy stick and, hopefully, the tail hook caught the wire before the pilot went into the water. It would seem that if the hook was released immediately on launch, it would be easy to catch the wire, but there was a bar just before the wire that would cause the hook to jump over the wire if the hook was released too soon.

This caper was available to all comers, but was mainly used by aircraft carrier pilots. I observed the catapult dunk, and almost every participant went into the water, some several times; most of the participants never caught the wire. One of the participants was the **Ranger** Carrier Air Group Commander (CAG) Captain "Boot" Hill. CAG arrived at the club in his dress-white uniform and was promptly installed in the cockpit. There was a full house of his fellow naval aviators — the place was jumping. CAG was dumped in the water, and he was dumped a second time. Finally, he caught the hook and emerged triumphal from the cockpit to the raucous cheers of his fellows. CAG's participation in this frivolity was his way of displaying leadership by example. Captain Hill was a famed naval aviator flying over 400 combat missions in Korea and Vietnam while logging 620 carrier landings. Captain Hill, later Rear Admiral Hill, returned to the **Ranger** later as commanding officer.

Having observed many catapult shots at Cubi Point, I was now ready to join the fray. Not wanting to attract undue attention, unlike Captain Hill, I wore civilian clothes. The only part I had to play in this caper was to release the tail hook. I had calculated my point of release to be when the forward point of the cabin passed the arresting gear, thus allowing for my reaction time, and permitting the hook in the rear of the cabin to catch the arresting gear. I was dunked on my first try. After drying off a bit and analyzing my failure, I was ready to have another go. I caught the wire and was now a member of the small, select group to have my name on the wall of the club. Air Force F-4 pilots from Clarke Air Force Base tried, but never caught the wire.

An analysis of those who missed the wire led me to conclude that the catapult operators had some latitude in "setting" the apparatus. For example, if the gap between the bar and the wire was small, the catch would be more difficult than if there were a large gap. It doesn't really matter. Maybe the operators gave me a break, or maybe I was just lucky. In any regard, my name was on the wall, and I was a legend in my own mind.

The Navy operations at Cubi Point and Subic Bay were closed in 1992 and much of the memorabilia at the Cubi Point Bar was relocated to the Naval Aviation Museum in Pensacola, Florida, where the old naval aviator scene has been recreated. I am told it is a must see for all Cubi Point habitués. I visited the museum in the 1980s, but haven't been back to see the old Cubi Point Club exhibit.

Cubi Point, Philippines bar

During the Vietnam War, 530 Navy aircraft were lost in combat, and there were 329 operational losses. There were 377 Navy officers and crew killed, 64 missing, and 179 prisoners of war. Not only is flying from an aircraft carrier dangerous, but many duties aboard the carrier are also dangerous.

One night, as we were being resupplied with ammunition, a working party was unloading ammunition from pallets to ammunition carts on the elevator off the main deck. When the job was done, one person was missing. After muster and search of the ship's spaces, it was determined that the sailor was lost overboard. It was sad, but it happened. Maybe a buddy system could have prevented the loss. Using heavy equipment, testing aircraft engines, moving aircraft by their own power or by aircraft handling equipment, and a myriad of other tasks are dangerous, and one must always be alert to the dangers aboard a fighting ship. The **Ranger** safety officer was constantly on the move around the ship, noting and correcting unsafe procedures. One of his observations directly affected me.

On the first deployment, I jogged on the flight deck every day we were at sea. This was not easy. There was a 45-minute period between launches when the flight deck was available for jogging. I generally ran six lengths (about one thousand feet per length) of the flight deck; one length with the wind — the next against the wind. There was generally a 30–40 mph effective wind over the deck. There was never a cross wind. All launches and recoveries are made with the carrier running into the wind. At the time I ran on the flight deck, the **Ranger** was going down wind to recover its position to turn into the wind for the next series of launches and recoveries. When running in the same direction the ship was heading, I had to hold back to keep from going too fast. When running in the opposite direction, it was a real effort to move forward — excellent exercise. It helped me in two ways: I felt better and the running decreased my appetite; I took in fewer calories at the evening meal. However, my exposure to the noise of jet engines, both on the flight deck and the main deck, seriously affected my hearing. I was told, after my first physical upon leaving the **Ranger,** that I had hearing loss. I put up with this hearing loss for about 18 years, but it gradually worsened. I started wearing hearing aids in 1990. This hearing loss could have been easily avoided by wearing "Mickey-Mouse ears," sound suppressors worn by all aircraft-handling and flight deck personnel. We see them worn by all aircraft-handling personnel at airports during take-off and landing. It was my responsibility to protect my hearing, and I failed. I did not pay attention to this "detail."

Early in my second deployment, the **Ranger** safety officer ruled that there would be no running on the flight deck, and he was right. Running on the flight deck and dodging vehicles, aircraft, working personnel, and hopping over the arresting gear cables was dangerous, and I had to find other ways to maintain my fitness. I found other ways to exercise, but none of them were as effective as jogging on the flight deck.

We conducted underway replenishments of ammunition, fuel, provisions, and supplies almost every day when we were not having flight operations. Since we were flying so many sorties over North Vietnam, we replenished ammunition about every third day. The ammunition and supplies came aboard by highline and helicopter from ammunition and supply ships that came alongside and paralleled our course during the transfer. Fuel oil and aircraft gasoline were transferred by hoses passed from a fleet oiler about once a week. We, also, frequently replenished smaller ships with fuel oil.

The supply department was directly involved with the replenishment of provisions and supplies, the most important being toilet paper — a "never out" item. Woe to the supply officer who runs out of toilet paper. The replenishment of provisions and supplies by helicopter was labor intensive, as the pallets had to be quickly removed from the flight deck and transferred to the storeroom hatch on the main deck and then manhandled to a storeroom, sometimes four decks below. Working parties from other departments were assigned to assist in this process. There was always a chance of pilferage, especially the ship's store supplies, and supply department supervisors always had to be on the alert. Some sailors did not consider this as theft — after all, it was just borrowing from the government.

Our C-1 aircraft frequently flew to Saigon, Vietnam, to transfer our pilots and other officers for temporary assignment to the various commands in Saigon. On return, they generally brought back large ceramic elephants that had a non-repeatable nickname. After seeing several of these shipments, I turned them into a "must have" and ordered two elephants. They were packed in wooden crates, weighing about 50 pounds each. They are about two feet tall and serve as perfect end tables. Mine were a metallic green with gold marking.

These elephants have moved with us four times — one now serves as our outdoor elephant, and the other is our indoor elephant — similar to indoor and outdoor cats. The elephants have now been with us in Annapolis for 29 years. The indoor elephant is like new, but the outdoor elephant has lost some of its sheen — the gold has faded due to the harsh Annapolis winters, but the green is in good shape. I had to have those elephants, and fortunately, Sally agreed. That has not always been the case with my "one-of-a-kind" purchases.

Among my worldly purchases, now long gone from the Dempster household, is a 36-inch-round brass plate, handmade by Moroccan craftsmen, my camel saddle, previously mentioned and also from Morocco, and a desert-fighting man's or pirate's 36-inch sword from Algeria. These are but a few examples of spur-of-the-moment purchases that were too great a temptation to pass up. Whether it was a change in taste, my wife didn't want it, it wasn't what it was cracked up to be, it smelled bad, or whatever — they're gone, and life goes on without them. Maybe I'm being a little hard on myself. Some of my purchases have become Dempster heirlooms. I'm batting about 50/50.

I flew to Vietnam twice on our C-1 aircraft. I went to Da Nang to obtain critical ship and aircraft repair parts from the Da Nang supply department. The Navy facility at Da Nang was a very large operation. I was met by the supply captain, whom I knew from my assignment in Philadelphia. We drove around the large compound in a jeep. I was amazed by the size of the supply department and the broad range of support that was available. My second trip was to Chu Lai, about 100 miles south of Da Nang. I agreed to go there at the behest of the **Ranger** operations officer to obtain a replacement wing for one of the Air Wing's F-4 aircraft. Chu Lai was a fully functioning Marine Corps Air Base from 1965 to 1970. The F-4 spare wing was available and was later shipped to the **Ranger**. The flight time from **Ranger's** position in the Tonkin Gulf to these bases was from one to two hours.

I also flew from the **Ranger** to the Royal Thai Air Force bases in Ubon and Udorn, Thailand. Although designated Royal Thai Air Force bases, in actuality, they were US Air Force bases. There were six such bases in Thailand and about half of

USAF missions flown over Vietnam originated from the Thai bases. The purpose of our flight was to take **Ranger** aviators to the Thai bases, where they served as forward spotters for Navy missions over Vietnam.

My purpose was to purchase Thai merchandise for resale to the **Ranger** crew. We stayed overnight in Thailand and left about five in the morning for return to the **Ranger**. As we flew over Laos, the night sky was filled with flares and, maybe, missiles. A spotter returning with us to the **Ranger** was not too comfortable being a passenger in an unarmed aircraft. Having had little sleep that night, I dozed off and was jarred awake when we landed in Da Nang. We were scheduled to fly directly to the **Ranger**, but had missed the first landing cycle and had to wait for the next cycle. We made a successful arresting-gear trap on the **Ranger**. That was my third take-off and landing on the **Ranger**. I also had two other take-offs, as I flew twice from the **Ranger** in the Tonkin Gulf to Hong Kong to arrange for port facilities for the visit of the **Ranger.**

Charles and Lillian Strott (Sally's parents), David, Eddie, Sally, Holly, and Diane, Christmas 1969

Meanwhile, what was happening back home? Sally's parents came to California for a Christmas visit in 1970. Our home was in a Mormon community and Sally had many Mor-Mormon friends, and the children had Mormon playmates. David attended a school program at the Mormon Temple. Sally and the children attended a Mormon benefit and meal at the Temple. Sally entered a raffle, and "Sister Sally" was announced as one of the winners.

Sally and the children often went out to dinner with Pat Hohenstein and her family. Their favorite was a Chinese restaurant. About the third time they were there, the manager suggested to them that they have takeout, but Sally and Pat said they would rather eat there. Apparently, the manager thought the six children were a bit disruptive, but Sally and Pat stood their ground and enjoyed their meal.

A big event was the arrival of a pure-black cat. Midnight was a stray cat, and after she was around the house for a few days, the children wanted to keep her. So, Sally had Midnight checked by a vet. After a short time in our home, Midnight had her eye put out by a feral cat. She didn't seem to have any problems as a one-eyed cat. Midnight traveled with us to San Diego, and when we went to Virginia, Midnight flew by herself to Dulles Airport to join us in Falls Church, Virginia. Midnight was a great pet, but after 18 years, Midnight just wore out. She walked into our den, fell over, and died in 1987.

My stateroom was directly across the passageway from the supply office — the shortest commute I ever had — about six paces. I had a small desk, a couch that folded into a bunk, and I shared a head (bathroom) with the weapons' officer. I had a small TV where I could watch flight operations and movies that operated off the **Ranger** closed circuit. It was a small but comfortable room and more than suited my needs.

There was no such thing as a routine day. I was generally up by 6 AM, followed by a review of overnight message traffic. After breakfast, I toured some of the supply spaces concentrating on items I had picked up from the morning message traffic. I told the office staff where I was going, and I am sure that they told the personnel in the various spaces that I was on my way. When my morning tours became routine, the division officers would be prepared for my visit.

We submitted an evening report on the operational status of our aircraft from a supply point-of-view. The critical area that measured readiness of aircraft with regard to available repair parts was the number of parts that were not immediately available, making the aircraft unable to perform its mission. In most cases, the aircraft were still flyable but could not perform their mission with inoperable weapons' systems.

During the first part of our deployment, the number of critical items on order hovered around 200. After considerable attention, we decreased this number to 100 with about ten aircraft down for parts. My goal was to always stay below

100 and have no more than five aircraft down for parts. There were generally three aircraft carriers deployed, and there was an informal competition among the three carriers. One of my good friends was the supply officer of another carrier. He had the same background that I did, and I knew that he would pay attention to the same things. Our deployments overlapped by about five months, and our aircraft-awaiting-parts statistics were pretty even, whereas the third carrier statistics were two to three times our numbers.

A major part of getting repair parts quickly was the **Ranger's** intermediate repair capability. I worked very closely with the Aircraft Intermediate Maintenance Department (AIMD) officer. I advised him of the repairable assemblies needed to make aircraft operational, and he, in turn, would expedite the repair of these items and order any required repair parts from the supply department. The smooth functioning of these two departments was critical to our operational mission.

About five or six times a day, I would review and approve approximately 50 priority requisition messages. Early in the deployment, I would hold five to ten requisitions for further review. Key review points were when a quantity of more than one was ordered, and when a non-stocked item was ordered. When the Navy provisions support for a new item, the estimated failure rate is investigated and the higher failure rate parts are stocked in the supply system. Items with low estimated failure rates are not stocked. It is rare that two of the same item fail at the same time. I was suspicious that the repair shop was ordering extra items on a priority basis. For the non-stocked item, the lead time could be more than a month, and in some cases, the item would have to be manufactured by a vendor with a lead time of several months. I would alert the AIMD officer of the need to review the requisitions, and he would set up a time during the day or evening for us to visit the applicable repair shops. In the case of over ordering, the quantity would be reduced, and for part-numbered items, we would often find that the part wasn't really needed, or that it could be manufactured by another repair shop on the **Ranger**.

One example was an order on a priority basis for an ash tray for the **Ranger's** C-1 aircraft — a single-engine, propeller aircraft. The ash tray would have had to be manufactured and would have cost at least two to three hundred dollars. It had a lead time of several months, and it was not mission essential. The crew could do without this ash tray, manufacture one onboard, or use a tin can. This vigilance paid off in the elimination of bogus requirements, and the aviation stores' office had more time to expedite those items that affected aircraft readiness.

Another way of obtaining more operational aircraft was by removing a part from an aircraft that was already not operational and installing it on an aircraft to make it operational. The term used for this is "cannibalization." This had to be carefully controlled. The supply department had to be involved, so the required part on order could be reassigned to the cannibalized aircraft. The squadron commanding officer was usually involved in this process. No one wanted an aircraft to be in a lengthy down status. An aircraft in this status was called a "hangar queen." The assemblies being repaired in the intermediate repair shops could also be cannibalized, if they were awaiting other parts. Again, the status of needed repair parts had to be carefully controlled, or we could later find the replacement part was not really on order.

Our main liberty port was Subic Bay in the Philippines. We called there six times during each deployment. Our main supply point while deployed was the Naval Supply Depot, Subic Bay. The supply department was always busy replenishing supplies and repair parts while in port. All supply department officers called on their counterparts in Subic Bay to expedite critical items and to have personal contacts that could be used while at sea to request special handling of essential items.

Subic Bay had excellent recreational facilities: picnic areas, golf course, basketball and tennis courts, baseball fields, handball courts, sailing, and snorkeling. Of course, there were other "recreational" facilities in the nearby town of Olongapo that the crew enjoyed very much. The golf course at Cubi Point was both flat and hilly. There was a rope tow, similar to rope tows used at skiing areas, to assist in walking up a 30 degree incline from a green to the next tee. In the flat areas, it was best to stay in the fairway, as there was a plethora of snakes in the tall, grassy, rough areas. There was a mango grove behind one of the greens, and my golf bag was always heavier after I picked a load of the tasty fruit — I ate only one mango per round.

Grande Island, located just off the beach at Subic, was a recreational area with cabins and cooking facilities. I went there for an overnight stay with a group of officers and enlisted personnel from the **Ranger**. The water was warm, and we snorkeled early in the morning and late in the evening to avoid too much exposure to the sun. I had foolishly snorkeled from a friend's boat earlier in the deployment and was treated to sunburn, similar to what I experienced 22 years earlier at Santa Cruz, California. A lesson learned, but repeated — insanity. We snorkeled at Grande Island when Sally was in Subic. It wasn't Tahiti, but to us, it was a honeymoon experience.

Darrell and Filipina girl, Mayor's party, Olongapo, the Phillipines, 1970

Several of us were invited to a celebration hosted by Mrs. Gordon, the mayor of Olongapo, in the town square. The ladies were dressed in traditional attire — a long gown with high shoulders. We had a traditional Filipino meal and were entertained with Filipino dancing including tininkling, where two bamboo poles are held just above the ground. The poles are pulled apart and then slapped back together with the dancers jumping in and out between the poles without getting their ankles broken.

During our first deployment, we were in port at Subic Bay for Christmas. I attended the Christmas celebration at the Subic Bay Officers' Club with the depot officers and wives. It was a formal affair and very festive with the officers wearing their dress uniforms. We were at sea for Christmas on our second deployment and were hosts to Bob Hope and his USO troupe. It was a great affair with Bob Hope at his best. Bob Hope's son celebrated his birthday while they were onboard and we baked a cake for him. The celebration was held in the wardroom after the show, and Bob Hope mingled with all the officers and men. Neil Armstrong, the first man on the moon in 1969, accompanied Bob Hope. Bob Hope gave me an autographed copy of his Vietnam story, **Five Women I Love**. Neil Armstrong autographed a copy of the special crew menu.

We had great chaplains on the **Ranger**. During my conversations with men of the supply department, if I thought a talk with one of the chaplains was in order, I did not hesitate to set up an appointment. They were always available. Our senior chaplain was Father Patrick Grace. Father Grace was selected for captain in 1970, and we had a celebration for him giving him the title of Chaplain Captain Father Patrick Grace. Church services were held in the **Ranger** forecastle (pronounced fowk-sul). On sailing ships, the forecastle was on the forward part of the ship and was used for sailors' living quarters. On aircraft carriers, it is a very large area on the forward part of the main deck and is used to house the ship's anchor chains. It is a very clean and shipshape area.

I heard from Pacific deployment veterans about the golf course at Camp John Hay in the mountain town of Baguio, north of Subic. Baguio is known as the summer capital of the Philippines, since the government moves there during the oppressive heat of the summer months in Manila. We arranged with our executive officer to fly a foursome to Baguio in the **Ranger** C-1 aircraft. The flight of about one hour had good scenery of hillside rice terraces and small villages. The Camp John Hill runway was built on a mountain plateau with about a ten-degree angle from one end to the other. Our executive officer skillfully landed the aircraft, and we deplaned for a two-day stay in Baguio.

Our first stop was the Army Exchange to stock up on food and drinks. We transferred our luggage into our two-bedroom cottage and went directly to the golf course. After an enjoyable round of golf, we returned to our cottage to find that we had been robbed. Our cameras and other valuables, including the adult drinks, were gone. We discovered that our cottage, in a wooded area near the base perimeter fence, was an easy target for any observant thief who may have been watching from outside the fence. We took this experience as a lesson learned and enjoyed the rest of our stay in Baguio.

Our other liberty ports were Hong Kong and Sasebo, Japan. Hong Kong was a British colony that was transferred to China in 1997. Hong Kong is truly a city where East meets West. Hong Kong definitely has a British influence, but it is a Chinese city. You could isolate yourself in a British enclave, but if you go about the city, you are in China with streets filled with vendors selling an immense variety of items that excite the senses of sight, hearing, smell, taste, and touch. They sell everything from 1,000-year-old eggs to handfuls of diamonds carried in suit pockets and everything in between. The senses are bombarded with a cacophony of noise, colors, and aromas.

By the way, the 1,000-year-old egg isn't really 1,000 years old. The fresh egg is preserved in clay and buried in the ground for several months. The yolk turns black and the white turns brown. It has an ammonia smell and is salty. It is hardly a pleasant sight to see, an example where an unpleasant sight minimizes the desire to partake of the "delicacy," but to the Chinese, it is a delicacy.

I purchased very little on the street — there were enough small shops and stores to deplete my resources. Most of the crew did the majority of their shopping in Hong Kong.

I met an Indian merchant, and as we were chatting, he told me that he played squash. I had played some squash at the Naval Academy, and I considered myself a below average player. Nevertheless, when he asked me to join him at the Royal Squash Club for a game, I readily agreed. He seemed to be a bit out of shape, but he gave me a lesson in humility on the squash court. The ball used in Hong Kong was a bit softer that the American squash ball and had very little bounce. I couldn't get to the forecourt fast enough to hit the ball.

After the game, I went to the hotel where the **Ranger** officers had a hospitality room. As I approached the hotel, the Sikh doorman saw my racket and asked me to play a game of squash with him. I agreed to meet him the next day. I completely forgot the squash date, and when I went to the hotel again, he reminded me that I had missed my squash date. These Sikh doormen are large men, and they wear Indian military attire with an unsheathed sword and other armaments. When I saw him, my life flashed before my eyes, but he accepted my apology, and we left as friends. I regret that I missed the opportunity to play squash with him, but I undoubtedly avoided another Indian waxing.

I was returning to the **Ranger** late one evening, and my route took me through the butchering district. The profession was carried out on the street, and I had to dodge around the butchering process. I spotted a pair of longhorns. The horns were as large as Texas longhorns. On the spur of the moment, I decided that I had to have a pair. I offered a small amount of money for the longhorns, had them washed, and carried them back to the ship. I had a few stares from the **Ranger** officers and crew, but I withstood the scrutiny. When I arrived on the **Ranger**, I stored them in a sponson on the side of the ship. The sponsons are open spaces not used for any purpose except for my longhorns to "cure" and get rid of the unpleasant smell. I checked on the longhorns periodically, and the smell almost went away, but after about two months, I tossed the longhorns over the side into Davy Jones' Locker (bottom of the sea). I got rid of something I wanted but didn't really need. This is a lesson that I often forget.

During our second deployment, Sally and a plane full of **Ranger** wives came to Hong Kong. We purchased teak end tables, a carved teak coffee table, three carved teak (cedar) chests, jade and pearl jewelry, and linens. Sounds like a lot of bulky items, but they were delivered to the ship, placed in safe storage, and transferred to us when the **Ranger** made a port call in San Diego later in the year.

Sally and I did all the mandatory sightseeing trips in Hong Kong, including Victoria Peak, Tiger Balm Gardens, and a trip across the harbor to Kowloon, the New Territories, and the Chinese border. We could look across the border, but we could not cross the border. We also had a chance to meet Sally's former assistant pastor in the New Territories. The Rev. and Mrs. Singer were Lutheran missionaries. It was a joy to hear of their work with the Chinese and foreigners of all nationalities living in the New Territories.

We learned in Hong Kong that the **Ranger** was going directly to Subic from Hong Kong and would be there about five days before returning to the Tonkin Gulf. Sally and I decided this would be a good time for her to visit the Philippines. I called my parents, who were with our children in Pleasant

Hill, and they agreed to stay for another week. I rebooked Sally's return flight to include a stop in Manila. Sally then flew from Hong Kong to Manila with some other wives, including the captain's wife. Sally was already in Subic when the **Ranger** arrived two days later. We had a great time in the Philippines, going to the Cubi Point pool, snorkeling, boating, and meeting many of my friends at Subic.

We rented a car with a driver for a three-day trip to Baguio. Although only about 175 miles from Subic, the roads were all two lane and congested with traffic — go with the flow, enjoy life, and the opportunity to really see and understand the Filipino people, their customs, and way of life. The drive took about six hours. There were many villages along the way with ample opportunities for shopping. As in my previous trip to Baguio, we stayed at Camp John Hay. We stayed two nights and did a lot of sightseeing and played a round of golf. After we returned to Subic, Sally stayed one more day, and I saw her off in a taxi to Manila and her flight back to San Francisco.

We had many Filipino vendors call on us while in port in Subic. One of the vendors that I became acquainted with was Joe Sarmiento, known as Filipino Joe. Joe was a hard worker, and, although he didn't have the resources to handle a wide variety or large quantities of items, he did have a small workshop in Angeles and had access to several home workshops. His specialty was special orders. We could order on one port call and pick up the next port call. Joe told me about where he had grown up in Barrio Dila Dila, Santa Rita, Pampanga Province. I went there with a group of supply department personnel to attend a festival held at the local church. The community greeted us at the secondary school. We were treated to a meal cooked by the culinary students. We presented the school with a monetary gift and some school books. I told them we would provide more books. We later obtained more books and went to the school again to present the books. We had a great time at the festival posing for pictures with the community, riding water buffalo, and participating in community games. The most pleasant part of the journey was the attention we received from the children. They particularly liked our buffalo rides and our participation in their games.

This was a rural community, and although there were a lot of western people in the Philippines, very few visited this rural setting.

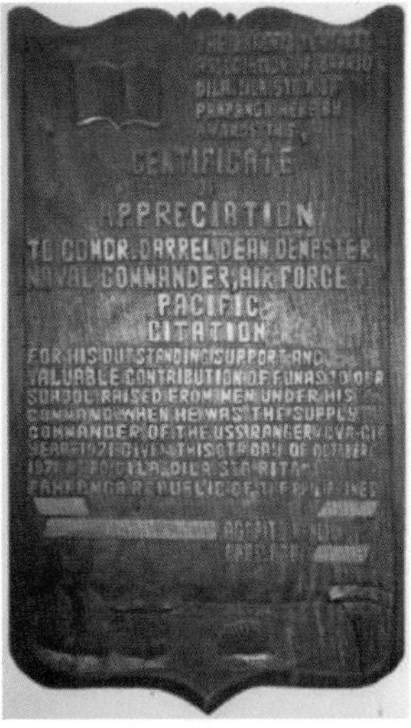

Presented to Commander Darrell D. Dempster by Parent Teachers Association, Barrio Dila Dila, Pampanga, the Phillipines, 1971

The Parent Teachers Association of Barrio Dila Dila presented me with a plaque in recognition of funds and support given to their school from the **Ranger** crew. Later, after I had departed the **Ranger,** I visited Dila Dila and posed for a picture with Joe Sarmiento, his family, and the teachers.

Darrell, teachers of Barrio Dila Dila, and Sarimento family, 1971

I couldn't have been more proud of the **Ranger** crew and their willingness to sacrifice their valuable and limited time of shore leave to participate in this memorable cultural exchange.

Our visits to barrio Dila Dila laid the framework for a cultural relationship between the **Ranger** and Dila Dila, including the surrounding Santa Rita community. One of the crew members who went with us to Dila Dila was Seaman Lawrence, later Petty Officer Second Class, who was the supply department yeoman. He was a pleasant and efficient young man and on future **Ranger** deployments coordinated friendship and cultural visits of the **Ranger** crew to Dila Dila.

Petty Officer Lawrence later sent me a letter noting that the **Ranger** captain had taken a group of **Ranger** crewmen to Dila Dila in a helicopter. They took gifts to the school, had a meal prepared by the culinary school, and toured the community. Petty Officer Lawrence also noted that one of the school buildings had been named the Commander D D Dempster Building. This was an unexpected honor, but all the credit goes to the crew, and, as usual, we got more out of it than we put into it.

USS Ranger school building, Barrio Dila Dila, Pampango, the Phillipines, 1971

Later I took a tour of the countryside around Subic with Joe. We drove south on the western side of the Bataan Peninsula to Mariveles and then north on the eastern side of the peninsula along the route of the famous Bataan death march. Immediately after Pearl Harbor, the Japanese invaded the Philippines with an overwhelming force. Manila fell on January 2, 1942, and the American and Filipino forces retreated south on the Bataan Peninsula. General McArthur left the Philippines in March 1942, leaving the command of allied forces to Lieutenant General Jonathon Wainwright. Wainwright and his forces fought a delaying action as they retreated south and escaped to the island of Corregidor in April 1942, where they surrendered a month later. The captured US and Filipino troops numbered from 60,000 to 80,000. The prisoners were force-marched north on the eastern side of the Bataan Peninsula to San Fernando, near Joe's hometown, where they were taken by rail to Capas. The number of prisoners who did not survive the march is unknown, but it was in the thousands. They suffered from the heat, Japanese cruelty, such as bayoneting sick and fallen men, and lack of food and water. There were summary executions, as many of the Japanese believed that a man who would surrender was not really a man — he was sub-human. Tens of thousands of American and Filipino prisoners were sent to other Japanese POW camps in Japan,

Manchuria, and Taiwan for use as forced labor. About 2,500 Americans were transferred from Capas to a prison near Cabanatuan City.

Filipino house, 1971

In early 1944, the American public was belatedly informed of the extreme cruelty inflicted on American and Filipino POWs. Magazines, such as **Life,** published articles with photographs of this cruelty. I remember, to this day, the photos of emaciated men with protruding ribs. Americans were incensed. General of the Army George Marshall stated: "These brutal reprisals upon helpless victims evidence the shallow advance from savagery which the Japanese people have made. We serve notice upon the Japanese military and political leaders as well as the Japanese people that the future of the Japanese race itself, depends entirely and irrevocably upon their capacity to progress beyond their aboriginal barbaric instincts."

General McArthur returned to the Philippines October 20, 1944. Soon after, the Japanese transferred about 1,500 US prisoners from Cabanatuan to camps in Japan, leaving about 500 of the weakest prisoners. After hearing from a survivor of the burning alive of 150 US prisoners at an island camp, the US plotted and carried out a rescue of the 500 remaining prisoners at Cabanatuan City. US Special Forces launched a daring rescue attempt that freed all prisoners at Cabanatuan.

It was a very hot day when Joe and I drove north from Mariveles on the very same road as the death march. The road was congested with chickens and other farm animals. Joe didn't seem to mind the congestion, as he experienced it every day. The road was very much the same in 1971, as it was in 1942, although the children who witnessed the scene in 1942 were now grandmothers and grandfathers. The photos that I saw in 1944 flashed through my mind, and I relived the horror. After about 15 miles, Joe turned west over the mountains.

As we were driving through this mountainous area, I saw caves high on the hillside where many Japanese soldiers had hidden for several years after the end of World War II, unwilling to surrender.

It was in this mountainous area that I spent a Saturday with a group of pilots at a Survival, Evasion, Resistance, and Escape (SERE) refresher course. My comrades all had SERE training in the states, and I was a rookie — I was also a few years older than they were. I wanted to have the experience. SERE was instituted to counter the abduction of Americans, and for military personnel in combat situations, to avoid capture and, if captured, to withstand severe interrogation techniques. We had military trainers in most phases, but the jungle survival phase was taught by indigenous Negrito people. They were natives of this mountainous jungle area, dark and small in stature and not inclined to mingle with other Filipino people. They taught us to find water from jungle plants, to start a fire with sticks, to traverse dense jungle areas, and to blend with the natural habitat. They were skilled in many areas, one of them surprising. They used junked cars to make machetes from car springs and, as you would expect, I purchased a machete. Also, as you would expect, I disposed of this treasure in a few years, but it was fun to use it to trim tree branches while I had it.

We passed a roadside workshop where a group of men were making sidecars for motorcycles. I observed their construction process and decided I had to have one. I ordered one with fittings for a Honda-100 motorcycle. The manufacturing lead time meant the **Ranger** would complete its deployment and depart for the US before completion of the sidecar. It would need to be delivered to Subic for loading on another carrier and then delivered to me in San Diego. I asked that "Dempster" be painted on the front and selected a color scheme. I paid the purchase price of $400 in advance.

Early in the years of 1970 and 1971, we made trips past the coast of Korea to the southern Japanese port of Sasebo. We made some flights over Korea on missions that were beyond my need to know. The first year we were in Sasebo, I stayed busy on the ship and calling on officers at the supply department in Sasebo. Our retail stores division ordered a variety of Japanese items for resale to the crew. The crew enjoyed liberty in Japan, but the prices were much higher than in the Philippines. The best purchases in Japan were electronic items.

During the second deployment, a number of the crew had expressed interest in the purchase of motorcycles. The retail sales division asked for bids from local vendors. We selected the best offer that provided for delivery to the Sasebo Supply Department for delivery to the **Ranger** when in port in Subic. We also accepted orders for electronics and other items not available in sufficient quantities at the Navy Exchange in Sasebo. The **Ranger** order was to be delivered to Subic in April, when we were in port. In April, we learned that we would be extended on the line in the Tonkin Gulf and would not be in port when the shipment arrived. This scenario did not look good for one hundred thousand dollars of ship's store items that were stored in vans and sitting at the Subic Bay Depot.

Visions of the caution that Captain Hatch had given me raced through my mind — beware of mismanagement and theft of ship's store items. After discussions with the supply department officers, I decided to send the retail stores' officer and two of his staff to Subic to provide a 24-hour a day watch over the vans with instructions to make a daily log entry in the supply depot log as to the security of the vans. It all worked out, and after 58 days at sea, we arrived in Subic and took possession of the vans.

The handling of the motorcycles was also a complicated process. The crew placed orders while we were at sea. The orders were then sent to the vendor in Sasebo for delivery to the supply department in Sasebo for further shipment to Subic. The delivery was not expected until our last port call of the deployment in Sasebo. As it turned out, I was transferred from the **Ranger** in June of 1971, five days before this port call, and my Honda-100 and Honda-70 motorcycles were not delivered to me until the **Ranger** made a port call in San Diego later in the year.

I had some spare time during my 1971 visit to Sasebo, and I decided to go to Expo 70, held in Osaka, Japan. This would also give me the opportunity to see my friend, Sen Soshitsu, Urasenke Master of Tea Ceremony. I took a flight on March 31 from Sasebo to Osaka via Fukuoka. Shortly after landing in Fukuoka in mid-morning, I found myself in the middle of a hijacking. Japan Airlines Flight 351, flying from Tokyo to Fukuoka, was hijacked by nine persons from the Japanese Communist League Red Army Faction. The hijackers took 122 passengers and seven crew members hostage. I could see the aircraft on the tarmac, but it didn't seem to me that much was happening, as I didn't see anyone board or depart the aircraft. Finally, late in the afternoon, several passengers departed the aircraft, and the aircraft departed Fukuoka. Our aircraft then departed for Osaka late in the afternoon. I learned later that all the passengers were allowed to depart the aircraft in Fukuoka and Seoul, South Korea. The aircraft then flew to Pyongyang, North Korea, where the hijackers were granted political asylum.

I had a grand experience at Expo 70. It turned out that Urasenke had an exhibit in the Japanese Pavilion and I was able to meet Sen Soshitsu. He was quite surprised to have me turn up at Expo 70. I was also invited to Kyoto where I stayed in Urasenke lodging. I couldn't have asked for more hospitality, and I had a memorable adventure in meeting people and being involved in the history and skill of tea ceremony.

There is the inevitable sense of monotony that occurs after long periods at sea, even though you are working long hours and feel that what you are achieving is important. Food is an important part of the morale of the crew. In the service of food, we always aspired to serve a variety of food and often surprised the crew with something unusual. One example was Baked Alaska Flambé. It took some time to prepare, but the presentation with a burning flame created the aura of fine dining, and it was very tasty. It was served once during each at-sea period. We had other recipes with fancy names that appealed to the crew. We also had ice carvers who created statues of splendor on special occasions.

The food service division purchased frozen cups of mango and papaya in Hawaii on our first deployment. They purchased about 12,000 cups — enough for two meals. This was such a hit that on our second deployment, we obtained about 60,000 cups. One of the biggest problems that we could not solve was the availability of fresh milk. The supply of fresh milk lasted for about the first ten days at sea. After that, we had to serve reconstituted powdered milk. I sort of got used to it, but after about two weeks, the crew ate less cereal.

The famous **Ranger** donut machine produced 5,000 to 10,000 donuts a day. We always had glazed donuts ready for the other ships — it was an important duty that we could not fail to perform. After one late delivery of donuts, we established a procedure where everyone responsible for the donut production and delivery signed a checklist. The donuts were transferred by highline that was also used for exchange of mail and movies. The donut machine was so important that the engineering department assigned trained repairmen to keep it operational. I didn't go so far as to declare the donut machine as mission essential equipment, but it almost had that status.

About March of 1971, the Naval Air Force, Pacific Fleet (AirPac) admiral and others came aboard the **Ranger** to observe operations. The assistant supply officer was among those accompanying the Admiral. During our many conversations, he asked me if I wanted to be transferred to the AirPac staff as the fleet supply support officer. I readily agreed, as I was sure Sally would agree to live in the beautiful San Diego area. The AirPac staff was a desirable assignment, and I would be in the perfect position to utilize my many years of experience in the field of aviation support.

During our deployment, we had about five days at sea with no flight activity, a chance to catch up on sleep, except for the food service division. We had to have some type of caper that made the day seem like a real holiday. Our solution was to have a cookout on the hangar deck — hamburgers and hot dogs — the whole nine yards. We had about five charcoal cookers made from 50-gallon drums. It was always a huge success. The captain, executive officer, department heads, and leading chief petty officers cooked and served the food. The food service officer and his staff always did an excellent job.

Despite all our efforts, every once in a while, we had problems with a menu item, and I always heard about it during my meals in the wardroom. I learned early to go with the flow — don't be defensive, be positive and laugh with the rest of them.

One of our engineering officers had a thin skin. He was an excellent officer and quick to take action to correct problems, but he liked to eat his meals in peace and not be subjected to jovial slander of his person. Having a sufficient supply of fresh water and air conditioning were two of his many responsibilities and were obviously important to all the **Ranger** personnel. If there was a shortage of fresh water, we were required to take salt-water showers. After about a week of salt-water showers, there was a crescendo of griping. The engineering officer stopped taking his meals in the wardroom to avoid the "feedback." If you can't take the heat, get out of the kitchen.

About 10 days before the end of our deployment, my relief came aboard while we were in the Tonkin Gulf. After about five days of turn-over briefings, I departed the **Ranger** for home. Since we were at sea, my transportation from the **Ranger** was by C-2 — the same type of aircraft that crashed on take-off from the **Ranger** six months earlier. The seats face towards the tail of the C-2, and I was seated in the last row. I said farewell to those who had gathered at the rear of the aircraft. The loading ramp was closed. I was on my way home.

Holly, Sally, Diane, Eddie, and David meet Darrell when he arrives at Travis Air Force Base, California, 1971

We landed safely in Cubi Point. I obtained transportation to Clarke Air Force Base and was on my way to Travis Air Force Base in California the next day. Sally and the children met me at Travis, and we had a grand homecoming.

How did Sally cope during my long absences from home in the last two years? She told me recently that she had a good time. She took charge of her life and did a good job. I was not needed for changing diapers, helping with cooking and doing the dishes, going grocery shopping, helping the kids with homework, taking them to school and sports activities, doing household chores, or taking out the trash. The bottom line was that Sally took charge, performed in the highest traditions of the United States Navy, and had a good time. What more could I ask?

My tour of duty on the **Ranger** was extremely rewarding and full of life-changing experiences, but the most important was how my decisions influenced the capability of the **Ranger** to perform its mission. The two most important measurements that the supply department could impact were morale and ship and aircraft operational readiness. Many functions of the supply department affected morale: food service, pay, ship's retail operations, laundry, barber shops, "gedunk" items (ice cream and popcorn), and special events where special food was available to the entire crew. All members of the supply department supporting these well-being activities were attuned to their importance and performed admirably. Their suggestions were accepted and incorporated to enhance morale and well-being.

The stores and aviation divisions had as their primary objective the mission readiness of the **Ranger** and its aircraft. They worked the long hours necessary to maintain the fighting capability of the **Ranger**. I was rewarded by the feeling of a job well done, and also by "pats on the back" by the captain, the executive officer, the department heads, and the air wing personnel. I was awarded the Bronze Star and Navy Commendation medals. I departed the **Ranger** with deep gratitude for the opportunity to serve on the **Ranger** and with awe of the bravery and skill demonstrated by all the **Ranger** and Air Wing personnel.

Chapter 21: Back to San Diego — After 23 Years

I didn't get much rest after I arrived home in Pleasant Hill, as we were busy preparing for our move to San Diego. Sally and the children bid farewell to their many friends, and we departed with our small trailer in tow. We did some camping and sightseeing en route, but not too much, as we were anxious to locate a new home in San Diego. We had decided that we wanted to live in Coronado, near my new station, the North Island Naval Air Station. After a couple days, we bought a house about three blocks from the base and three blocks from the Pacific Ocean. It was in an area called Country Club Estates, a misnomer, as the area was neither a country club nor an estate. However, it was a nice house with three bedrooms and a big garage and yard. Most of our neighbors were either active or retired Navy.

North Island is not currently an island, but it used to be an island. It was separated from the city of Coronado by a body of water called the Spanish Bight. About 1917, when the first naval aviation pioneers were flying aircraft on North Island, a causeway was built for ease of commuting to North Island. The Spanish Bight was prone to silting, and the city often dredged the bight and filled an area on the southern side of Coronado that became the Coronado Golf Course. Another area filled was adjacent to the bight. This area became Country Club Estates, where we were to live. In 1943, the Navy needed more land, and they filled in the Spanish Bight and built warehouses, barracks and other facilities.

The Navy shared North Island with the US Army Air Corps. The Army site was called Rockwell Field. Charles Lindberg's aircraft, The Spirit of St. Louis was built by Ryan Aircraft in San Diego. Lindberg took off from Rockwell Field (North Island) for New York City on May 10, 1927 where he would start his record-breaking transatlantic flight. Lindberg left New York for Paris on May 20, 1927 and flew nonstop to Paris, landing in Paris on May 21, 1927.

Lindberg (second from right) and his aircraft, the Spitit of St. Louis, prior to departure from North Island to New York

Our Coronado home was three blocks south of the North Island boundary. There is a grove of eucalyptus trees on a slight rise to the north of the seven North Island warehouses. This was the edge of North Island before the Spanish Bight was filled. The southern edge of the old Spanish Bight is Alameda Avenue. There also are eucalyptus trees alongside Alameda Avenue. I relate this historic development of North Island and Coronado because, if you are going to live somewhere, you will enjoy it more if you are aware of why it is there — don't tear down the fence before you know why it was built.

Coronado was a haven for jackrabbits in the early 20th century. As Coronado became more populated, there was no place for the rabbits to go except to the barren sand dunes of North Island. The rabbits remain there to this day.

North Island Naval Air Station and Coronado, California

It was about a 10-minute commute from our house to my office on North Island. Since there were many neighbors who also worked on North Island, I often got a ride to work, so Sally would have the car for errands.

The schools were very convenient. Eddie was in the seventh grade and he went to the high school, a distance of about six blocks. Diane was in the fifth grade, David was in the second grade, and Holly was in pre-kindergarten. David and Holly went to the Christ Church Episcopal School in downtown Coronado. Holly attended school in the morning and Sally took her to and from school. David attended Christ Church through the 4th grade and Holly started kindergarten at the public elementary school near our house. David later attended this public school. They could ride their bicycles or walk to the public schools. The Coronado School System was excellent, and the kids quickly settled in, as if they were lifelong Coronado residents.

The downtown area on Orange Avenue was six blocks distant and within an easy walking or bicycling distance. The kids often went to the Coronado beach with their friends. One day, when I went to the beach to look for them, I found them some distance away at the Hotel Del Coronado. They had gone into the Del game room right off the beach and were playing pin ball. They had no idea they were visiting one of the most historic and famous landmarks in America.

My position at Naval Air Force, Pacific Fleet was challenging, as we supported deployed aircraft carriers that had a very high operational tempo in supporting the Vietnam War. Resources were also strained by the tempo of stateside carriers and squadrons preparing for deployment. Most of the staff worked on Saturday morning and some Sundays.

The climate in San Diego was exceptional — not too cold — not too hot. It was often foggy early in the morning in the summer months, but it usually burned off by late morning. The evenings, even in the summer, could be cool. For outside events, we always carried a sweater. Also, the ocean temperature never seemed to get above the 60s. We did go swimming, but it was not an everyday occurrence. Eddie quickly became a surfer. A neighbor gave him a surf board, and he spent many hours preparing his board for surfing. He became a very good surfer, but not to the detriment of his studies. Eddie also loved to fish, mainly off the North Island seawall and piers. He went by himself and often encountered Filipino fishermen who took him under their wing and taught him the skill of fishing.

I did some fishing but never took it up as a hobby; however, I did participate in grunion "fishing." Grunion are a sardine-sized fish that leap from the ocean onto the beach in a mating ritual. They are unique to southern California. The grunion run is within two hours after a high tide on the first four days after a full moon. The season is March through August. The North Island beach was the ideal place for a grunion run, as there was no light, and it was not crowded. Since the high tide varies, we went only if the run was before midnight. It was a social event, as we went with other families from North Island. The fish can only be caught by hand, so the whole family participated by being constantly alert and looking for the sparkle of the silver fish. Grunion are edible, but I don't remember eating them — maybe we ate them once. We went about twice each year and caught grunion about half the time.

Late in 1971, my motorcycles arrived in San Diego, as did my Filipino sidecar. The placement of the attaching mechanism on the sidecar was perfect, and the sidecar was easily attached to my Honda-100 cycle. I was a bit concerned that the power of the Honda was not sufficient to run both the cycle and the sidecar, but, since the speed limit in Coronado was 30 mph, and often less on the base, it had more than enough power to pull the sidecar. I did make one trip out of Coronado to Imperial Beach, about 10 miles south, to get the motorcycle and sidecar licensed. I was a bit worried because there was no brake connected to the sidecar, but the contraption was readily registered. The driver had to compensate for the lack of brakes on the sidecar by turning the handlebar to adjust for the pull or drag of the sidecar depending on whether he was

Phyllis Dempster Kasenberg and family
with Dempster family, Coronado, 1974

accelerating or decelerating. I used the sidecar for commuting to work and parked in an enclosure behind my office. The sidecar, the only one in Coronado, and maybe even in California, and the US, definitely attracted attention.

The children loved it, and I used it often to transport them to and from events. I also drove it for the Coronado Garden Club in the Coronado July Fourth parade.

Darrell riding Filipino sidecar in Coronado July 4 parade, 1974

We took many excursions while in Coronado. My favorite trip was to the desert during the winter to relax, hike, and see the wild flowers. We could pick out any camping spot we wanted, park our trailer, unload our small Honda-70, and the kids could ride it into the wild-blue yonder.

We also liked to go to Mexico. Even then, we were cautioned to be careful when driving in Mexico. It was recommended that you purchase Mexican auto insurance at the border. We often went to Tijuana to shop and have dinner. Our favorite dinner spot was La Speciale, a hole-in-the-wall diner. The staff got to know us, and we always had a good meal, complete with the typical Mexican ensemble playing "dinner" music. When we crossed the border to return home, I always asked Sally and the kids not to say anything when customs asked us if we had anything to declare. We didn't buy much, but I generally thought the best strategy was "loose lips sink ships" (reference to World War II caution regarding talking about ship schedules). The less said the better. This strategy almost backfired, so to speak, when David suddenly had some fireworks for the Fourth of July. He had carried this contraband across the border with him.

We took Sally's mother to Ensenada to see the famous blowhole, La Bufadora, a marine geyser, and to see Rosarita beach. On the way home, we made the obligatory stop in Tijuana to have dinner at La Speciale and to do some shopping. About half of our buys were made from street-side vendors, as we waited in line to cross the border. We bought such things as serape blankets, ceramic or cast iron piggy banks, and, oh well — you get the drift, things that would soon be discarded. Haggling with the sales people was expected with the final price less than half the initial asking price. Even at a young age, Diane was an expert haggler, never paying more than what she thought the item was worth.

Just before we crossed the border, I reminded everyone that I would be the only one to talk to the US customs officials; however, Sally's mother could not contain herself. She mentioned the serape blanket, the pig, the knick-knacks, and the bread and pastries we always bought at our favorite bakery. We passed customs.

Another exciting excursion was from Tijuana to Tecate along the border and then back into the US. This was a completely different Mexico from the tourist areas of Tijuana, Rosarita, and Ensenada. It was more mountainous with farmland wherever one could farm. We drove next to the farms, villages, and homes of the real Mexico. I wasn't thinking about it at the time, but we drove just north of the rail route that I took from Kansas City to San Diego through Mexico in 1948.

I made several trips to the Naval Air Stations Whidbey Island, Washington, and Lemoore, Miramar, and Alameda, California, for supply assistance visits. I also sometimes accompanied our admiral on periodic inspection visits. My favorite air station was Whidbey Island, located in the northern part of Puget Sound, near the Olympic Peninsula, and about 30 miles north of Seattle. We had some spare time on one of the trips, and I played golf with a Navy captain from Washington, D.C., who was assigned to the inspection team. The golf course was located on Puget Sound, and some of the holes bordered the sound. I observed an abundance of driftwood, and resolved to do some beachcombing the next time I was at Whidbey. I spent about three hours beachcombing and found some treasures. Puget Sound is famous for king crabs. A friend took me out in his boat, and we caught about a dozen king crabs. I steamed six of them in the Whidbey galley and put them in the freezer. They were part of my luggage on my flight home.

I also was a regular beachcomber at North Island. On one occasion, I accidentally entered a restricted area and was told of this restriction by base security. I discussed this with the base security officer, and he presented me with his unofficial/official beachcomber's pass, so I could continue my hobby. Sally and I visited North Island, along with our daughter, Holly, and granddaughter, Nicole, in 2015. One end of the beach had a no trespassing sign. There was also a restriction on driving on some roads. I learned the area is restricted due to ammunition storage. You can no longer drive the entire perimeter of North Island.

The most exciting and all-encompassing flight I made was a Far East tour as part of the AirPac inspection team. Our first stop was Hawaii and then to Midway Island, made famous by the World War II decisive Battle of Midway, where four Japanese aircraft carriers were sent to Davy Jones' Locker. Midway is a tiny speck in the vast Pacific Ocean. It is very flat and surrounded by a blue lagoon and coral reef.

Midway is home to the black-footed albatross, known as the gooney bird. Gooney birds are everywhere on Midway. The young fly away and return after about seven years and nest where they were born — on lawns, roads, runways, everywhere. Vast amounts of sea debris, including mountains of plastic, wash up on the Midway shore line. The plastic is especially dangerous to gooney birds. I saw some Japanese fishing-net-glass floats that the Midway inhabitants had salvaged from the debris, just as I had done in Japan. We were on Midway less than a day, so I couldn't do any beachcombing.

We departed from Midway to the northwest to Adak, Alaska, in the Aleutian Island chain. Adak is 1,200 miles west of Anchorage, Alaska. Adak is known for its cold, very windy, foggy, rainy, and snowy climate — what more could I ask for? The cold is not extreme, with a record low temperature of three degrees Fahrenheit and record high of 73. Fortunately, we arrived at Adak on a "nice" day. I went by car to the interior with an Adak civilian. The terrain gradually rose in elevation, and the ground cover was mostly tundra with few trees, and no inhabitants. We came to an abandoned World War II wooden hut. Due to the Adak climate, it was perfectly preserved. I went on this excursion about 10 in the evening, and when we returned to the base, there was still daylight remaining. We departed Adak for the island of Guam, a distance of 3,400 miles.

The distance to Guam meant that we would do some sleeping on the aircraft. Our aircraft was a P-3 Orion anti-submarine patrol aircraft. There were sleeping accommodations for four, and the rest of us had at least double seats for sleeping. I slept OK, and we had meals on board, so I was ready to go when we reached the Naval Air Station, Agana, Guam. As usual, I met with the air station supply and maintenance personnel to discuss supply support and to propose action on critical items.

One of our secretaries at North Island was a native of Guam. She had recently resigned and returned to help take care of her father. She met me at the base and took me on a tour of the island, including a visit to her grandfather's farm. We passed through a jungle-like area with palm trees and bamboo groves and arrived in a clearing. There was a house and some out buildings. Her grandfather was at the top of a palm tree, where he was tapping the tree for its juice to make into wine. He was bare-chested and didn't use a line and tackle to climb — he climbed the old fashioned way. I was pleased to be invited to his home and to share his hospitality. After some socializing and a taste of the local wine and tidbits, we departed and passed near the area where a Japanese soldier, Shoichi Yokoi, hid until 1971 — 28 years after US forces defeated Japanese forces on Guam. The capture of Yokoi was national news in the US. After only a day and night on Guam, we departed for the Naval Air Station, Cubi Point, Republic of the Philippines, a distance of 1,574 miles.

When we arrived at Cubi Point, I was met by my friend, Filipino Joe. I didn't have time to go see my friends in Dila Dila, but I delivered some school books for Joe to give to the Dila Dila School. After a good night's sleep at Cubi Point, we departed for the Tonkin Gulf and the carrier **Hancock**. We flew in an A-3 aircraft, configured with five passenger seats. I, being the junior officer, sat in the rear single seat. My view was up the middle of the aircraft, and I could see between the pilots and out the cockpit window. As we approached the carrier **Hancock**, I braced myself for the sudden stop of the aircraft, as it caught the arresting wire. It was sudden, and it was gut-wrenching, as my stomach was restrained by the seat belt and my upper body snapped forward.

A Rear Admiral with a specialty in aeronautical engineering was with us. His staff recommended and reviewed aircraft design changes, supervised aircraft maintenance, and investigated aircraft accidents. We worked as a team in meeting with supply and maintenance personnel. It was good to be back aboard an aircraft carrier and get a feel of what was really going on in the fleet. We toured squadron spaces and met with supply and maintenance personnel. We departed the **Hancock** for the carrier **Kitty Hawk**. By now I was a veteran in carrier take-offs and landings, but the forward snap of my upper body got me again, as the pilot landed our A-3 on the **Kitty Hawk**. We went through the same routine on the **Kitty Hawk** and departed the same day for Cubi Point. I visited the Officers' Club and witnessed some young aviators enjoying the catapult shots into the water.

We departed for Taiwan, a distance of 725 miles. The main reason for going to Taiwan was to discuss aircraft repairs. Some of the Navy aircraft in the Far East were repaired in Taiwanese aircraft factories. We had almost two full days in Taiwan, and I was free one of the days, as the senior members of our entourage met with senior Taiwanese military officers. One of our Taiwanese Navy counterparts told me about a mountainous area two hours from Taipei that had many scenic attractions and mountain views. I was furnished with a car and driver and had a magnificent sightseeing day, including close-up contact with the Taiwanese culture and people. I also saw a lot of Taipei, with colorful pagodas, Buddhist temples, and festivals. We departed Taipei early in the morning for a 500-mile trip to Hong Kong.

On our first day in Hong Kong, I accompanied the Admiral to a business luncheon in the New Territories. We went by helicopter and had a wonderful view of Hong Kong, Kowloon, and the New Territories. After the luncheon, our Admiral and some of the staff had a meeting with the host, and since my presence was no longer required, I departed in one of the government staff cars for a delightful drive back to Hong Kong. I had time to walk the busy and exciting streets of Hong Kong and to take a tram to Victoria Peak again. Our next and last stop was Japan, 1,800 miles distant.

We landed at the Naval Air Station, Atsugi, headquarters of Commander Fleet Air, Western Pacific. I was met by my good friend, the staff supply officer, who quickly unloaded on me all that he thought should be done by AirPac to support our deployed carriers and aircraft. Of course, he was right for doing that, I was used to his style, as he called our office in San Diego every morning the minute we arrived at work. He was a dedicated officer, and I readily took notes for further action when I returned to San Diego. We departed Atsugi by helicopter for the Naval Base at Yokosuka where we stayed the rest of the day and a night. I met with the commanding officer of the Naval Supply Depot to discuss actions to improve aircraft support. I had alerted one of my Japanese friends at the supply depot, and he gathered some other friends, and we had a wonderful dinner at a restaurant in Yokosuka. It was a treat to be with them and to reminisce about all the wonderful times we had from 1959 to 1963.

We departed Japan on the last leg of our trip to San Diego via Hawaii, a distance of 5,630 miles. It was good to be home, but I had no time to relax. The people in my division knew that. We had to get to work on our many action items and be prepared to brief the admiral periodically on our progress.

The total distance traveled was over 20,000 miles, 5,000 miles short of the approximate 25,000 miles around the world. We made 10 landings and take-offs in the P-3 and three in the A-3, two of these being to and from carriers. We also made several trips by helicopter.

I made another trip with the Marines to the Far East to evaluate supply and maintenance support of their air stations and squadrons in the Pacific. I flew by commercial aircraft from San Diego with two Marines from the Air Pac staff. We were met in Hawaii by Marines from the Fleet Marine Forces Pacific and the Third Marine Air Wing. We conducted our first evaluation at the Marine Corps Air Station, Kaneohe, Hawaii.

We then flew in a Marine C-130 transport aircraft to Taiwan. Our destination was really Japan, but we flew via Taipei,

Taiwan, to deliver an aircraft engine. We arrived in Taiwan early in the morning and were expected to depart for Atsugi, Japan, in two hours, but our aircraft also had engine trouble. We waited and waited at the terminal, expecting to depart at any time. One of the Marines in our group was aviation major. He had flown over 100 helicopter missions in Vietnam, and his campaign ribbons and medals almost covered his chest. He was always on the move — he couldn't relax or sit down. He was a real character with a lively sense of humor, conversing with all the Chinese in the waiting area. Observing his activity helped me pass the time. Finally, at about 8 PM, we were told we would not depart that evening.

We obtained transportation to Taipei and stayed in a hotel for the night. I had some time for shopping and bought a four-panel mahogany screen with each panel depicting one of the four seasons. Each panel was 30 inches by 72 inches. It was a bulky and heavy item to handle. There were hinges for folding the panels. Each panel floated in the frame, meaning that it could expand without cracking. It is a beautiful piece of art and great for a room backdrop or room divider. It graced our homes in San Diego and Falls Church, but when we moved to Annapolis in 1988, there was no room for it in our town home. It now graces the home of our son, Eddie, in Virginia.

We returned to the Taipei Airport early the next morning, and we were faced with another delay — our aircraft was still not prepared to depart. We evaluated other options and decided to take another aircraft to Atsugi, Japan. When it came time to board the aircraft, we were told other travelers had priority over us, and we were bumped. After another delay, we boarded an aircraft to Atsugi via the Marine Corps Air Station, Iwakuni, Japan. When we arrived at Atsugi via Iwakuni, the passengers who bumped us at Taipei were waiting to go to Iwakuni.

This was a true SNAFU, a military acronym for Situation Normal All F****d Up. It was developed from the tendency of the junior reporting to his superior that the situation was normal, whereas the real situation was all messed up. The all-messed-up situation became the normal, thus SNAFU.

This entire hullabaloo gave us a chance to bond and to have some nice aerial views of Taiwan and Japan. We eventually arrived at Atsugi where we met with the Commander Navy Air Forces, Western Pacific and his staff and attended a two-day support conference. I had some time to travel to Yokosuka for another reunion with my Japanese friends.

We left Atsugi and went back to Iwakuni where there was a large concentration of Marine aircraft. We spent a lot of time with the squadron maintenance personnel and came away with several action items. I had some time to visit the historic city of Iwakuni that I had previously visited in 1962.

Our last stop was Okinawa, a Japanese prefecture. Okinawa was the site of one of the last battles of World War II, the only inhabited part of Japan to experience a land battle. There were about 120,000 combatants and 300,000 civilians, one third of the population, killed in the battle that started on April 1, 1945. Due to the history of native Okkinawans, their cultural differences, and animosity to mainland Japanese, the US expected the Okinawans to welcome them as liberators, but Japanese propaganda led the Okinawans to expect that they would be cruelly treated by the Americans. Consequently, many of them joined local militias and fought against the Americans, causing the high civilian losses. The Japanese and militias fought to the bitter end, refusing to surrender. The Americans finally secured the island on June 23, 1945. The manner in which the Japanese fought in the battle for Okinawa led the Americans to believe that an invasion of the Japanese homeland would result in unacceptable losses for both the Americans and the Japanese. An analysis of this scenario helped President Truman make the decision to use the atomic bomb to compel the Japanese to surrender.

The Marine Corps Air Station Futema on Okinawa was a large, self-supporting facility. The Marines welcomed us to the base, and we found that the supply and maintenance departments were professional and mission oriented. We were only there a short time, and I had no opportunity to visit the nearby town of Naha. As we were waiting in the terminal for departure for Hawaii, I observed an example of the traditional marine self-deprecating humor. There were two jars of hearing plugs for placement in the ears to suppress aircraft noise. Although both jars contained the same plugs, one was marked for the right ear and the other was marked for the left ear. After a long hop to Hawaii and a short ride to San Diego, I submitted an action item report and was gratified that I had this opportunity to work closely with my United States Marine Corps counterparts.

When I returned to North Island, I was promoted to Captain and I assumed the number two position as assistant force supply officer. I was assigned the task of evaluating the readiness of the P-3 anti-submarine aircraft of the Atlantic and Pacific Fleets. I went to the Naval Air Station Moffett Field, near San Francisco, home station of the Pacific Fleet P-3s. I visited with the P-3 squadrons and the P-3 wing commander and staff. My next stop was the Naval Air Station, Jacksonville, Florida, where I met with the Jacksonville P-3 squadrons and the P-3 wing commander and his staff. I was accompanied by my counterpart from the Commander Naval Air Force, Atlantic Fleet (AirLant). The difference in the readiness reports of the two commands was traced to the daily maintenance actions taken by one command as opposed to those not taken by

Darrell's promotion to Captain, Rear Admiral Baldwin, David, Eddie, Sally, Holly, and Diane,1973

the other. The staff and squadron maintenance personnel of one command reviewed the status of all aircraft at the end of each day and took the necessary maintenance actions to put the aircraft in an up-status prior to submitting their operational report. The other command, although ensuring they had the available aircraft to perform their mission, did not take action that day to maximize the up-status of their aircraft. Both commands met their mission requirements, but one maximized the daily operational status report by working the necessary hours that day to maximize the aircraft in an up status while the other did not.

As a result of this investigation, our admiral made a presentation to the aviation staff of the Chief of Naval Operations at the Pentagon in Washington, D.C. I accompanied the admiral and made a report of my findings. I had to be careful in my report to credit the excellent mission performance of both commands, while still documenting the corrective action necessary to improve the operational aircraft status report. I did not know it at the time, but three years later, in 1976, I would be assigned to the aviation staff at the Pentagon.

My time on the AirPac staff was drawing to a close, and in June 1974, I was transferred about three blocks distant as supply officer at the Naval Air Station, North Island. It was a prize assignment, and although I did not request this assignment, I was in a position to know that there were others vying for this posting. Also, this meant that our family would remain in our home, and the children would attend the same schools for two or three more years.

North Island was home base for the Pacific Fleet helicopters and anti-submarine aircraft. The Navy was introducing the new S-3A Viking anti-submarine aircraft. Introduction of a new aircraft to the fleet was always a highly anticipated event, and this was no exception. I went to the Lockheed plant in Burbank, California, to see the rollout and Navy acceptance of the first S-3A aircraft. I knew that the Navy brass would have their eyes on us, and I spent a lot of time verifying that the S-3A was receiving top-notch support. We had an excellent intermediate maintenance facility at North Island, and we also were co-located with the Naval Aircraft Rework Facility (NARF) that had the capability to rework (overhaul) aircraft and repairable sub-assemblies. There was a long lead time to obtain necessary repair parts, test and support equipment, publications, training manuals, and to train all repair technicians in the testing and repair procedures. Consequently, the aircraft manufacturer assigned Lockheed personnel to North Island to assist in the transition to full Navy support. All these assets had to be properly integrated and managed to guarantee quality support.

I was assigned additional duty to the S-3A and helicopter air wing staff. The air wing commander was Rear Admiral Stockdale, former prisoner of war (POW) in Vietnam for over seven years. Stockdale was released as a POW on February 12, 1973. He was assigned to the AirPac staff on a temporary basis, while he recuperated. I saw him occasionally in the AirPac offices, while he was writing about his imprisonment and specifically about two officers who he felt had given aid and comfort to the enemy. These charges were dropped by then Secretary of the Navy, John Warner. I occasionally attended Admiral Stockdale's staff meetings and briefed him when the occasion warranted.

One of the responsibilities of the supply department was storage, handling, and delivery of aviation fuel at North Island. We also managed a small fuel facility at San Clemente Island, about 70 miles west of San Diego. As part of my duties, I flew to San Clemente to review the fuel facility. It was a 25-minute flight. After touring the fuel operation, I had a chance to see some of the island and the Navy facilities. I learned that they had two small houses available for visitors, so I arranged for a weekend family visit. There was a regular Friday flight to return island personnel to San Diego. The flight to San Clemente was mostly empty. There was a regular flight on Monday to return personnel to San Clemente and the return flight to North Island was mostly empty; thus there were seats for space-available personnel.

We found a free weekend and were on our way to San Clemente for a three-day weekend. The house was on the waterfront with two bedrooms and a couch that could be made into a bed. The Navy had a small dining facility, a recreation building, boats, and a Navy van was available to us. San Clemente Island is 23 miles long and about two to three miles across. It is hilly with a flat area in the center. There are two mountain peaks, the highest being about 2,000 feet in elevation.

Sally and Holly off
San Clemente Island, 1974

The first thing we planned to do was go deep-sea fishing. We checked out the necessary fishing gear. A two-man boat crew took us about ten miles south along the shore. We fished about a mile off shore. We had three fishing poles with enough line to drop our six hooks on each line 600 feet to the ocean floor. We enjoyed the sunshine and gentle sea swell for about thirty minutes, and then reeled in our lines, sometimes having as many as six lingcod fish on a line. We dropped our lines to the sea floor two times and had enough fish to satisfy our needs.

Eddie reels in lingcod,
San Clemente Island,
California, 1974

Since it took us some time to drop and reel in the lines, we decided to head back to the harbor, as the boat crew was helping us on their free time. One of the San Clemente sailors showed us how to fillet the cod. We stored the fillets in the freezer. We decided not to have a fish dinner on the island. Instead, we gave the dining room staff advance notice and had our meals there, except for box lunches that we had for our noon meals.

We took one of the Navy vans on a day-long tour of San Clemente. We went to several beaches and small coves where we sun-bathed and fished. The water was clear and we could see the fish. There were a lot of abalone on the rocks and the beach. We were more interested in the abalone shells with their vivid colors. We tried to eat abalone a couple times but were never able to pound it enough or to cook it so that it was tender and a pleasure to eat — it was always more like an endurance test. There was an area near the runway that had hundreds of abalone shells. We called it the abalone graveyard. There were not many trees on San Clemente. The exception was a stand of three trees near the main road that was called the San Clemente National Forest.

At the time we visited San Clemente, the feral goat population of 11,000 was causing major problems for the native plants. The goat population was reduced by capture and removed by helicopter. By 1980, the goat population had been reduced to 4,000. Despite this large number, we saw only a few during our visits from 1974 to 1976. After our family trip, Eddie, David and I made another weekend trip. We didn't do any fishing, but we did a lot of exploration to all parts of the island.

Our friends, the Greens, whom we had known in Japan, were stationed at Ford Island on the island of Oahu in Hawaii. They invited us for a visit, and we made plans for a space-available flight from Norton Air Force Base to Hawaii. On the evening of the scheduled flight, we drove to Norton and boarded the flight. After departure, we were told we would make an unscheduled stop at Travis Air Force Base in central California. When we arrived at Travis, six of us were told to disembark. We were told that higher priority passengers would take our seats. An Air Force colonel pulled some strings, and he and his wife reboarded. We were certainly aware that space-available travel has risks, but this was a little too much; however, there was absolutely nothing we could do about it. After a three-day wait and no flight, we went to San Francisco and caught a commercial flight to Hawaii.

The Greens met us in Honolulu. Since we were late for our booking at the Kilauea Military Camp on the island of Hawaii, we immediately boarded a commercial flight to the big island. We picked up our rental car and started to enjoy our first day in this beautiful paradise. Since our lodging was in the Volcanoes National Park, our obvious first stop was the Kilauea volcanic area, an awe inspiring sight. We could see steam rising from the Kilauea crater and surrounding area. We saw solidified-lava streams leading to the sea. We could only imagine the fear of being there amid a not uncommon volcanic eruption. Hawaii is a huge island, with cattle ranches the size of those in Texas. Our travel took us along the seashore, through small villages, to mountain top vistas and steep seaside cliffs. We walked through a rain forest full of plant life, birds, and flowers of all shapes and colors. We visited the beach where the famed British explorer and navigator, Captain James Cook, was killed by islanders in 1779. After three days and nights, we returned to Oahu to spend some time with the Greens and see the sights of this fantastic island.

I had some conversations with the personnel office in Washington about a pending new assignment. A good friend in the Office of the Chief of Naval Operations was due to be reassigned, and he told me that he had recommended me as his relief. I, of course, told him that I would rather complete my three-year assignment at North Island, but I knew that my personal desire would probably be to no avail. Eventually, I received orders to report to the Office of the Chief of Naval Operations. It was time to relocate, and we began planning for our cross-country move to Washington, D.C. We contracted to have a special trailer manufactured to haul our motorcycle and sidecar, sold our house, packed our household goods, and we were on our way. Eddie and Diane still had one more week of school, so they remained with friends in Coronado.

Our plan was for Eddie and Diane to fly to Wichita, Kansas, when school was out. In the meantime, Sally, David, Holly, and I would have time for sightseeing in the great Southwest United States. Our first stop was the Marine Corps Air Station, Yuma, Arizona. We stayed at a Marine Corps recreation camp on the Colorado River. We had a cabin right on the river. We had been there once before on a five-day holiday from San Diego. Yuma is on the Mexican border, and being in the desert, is very hot. We rented a boat and cruised on the Colorado River. There was a slight down-river current that made for pleasant swimming. We landed on sand bars where we ate our lunch and relaxed. We continued our travel and visited my Aunt Opal and Uncle Kollis in Black Canyon, Arizona. We continued north and stayed overnight at the Grand Canyon Lodge. We drove along the canyon rim and made many stops to view the Grand Canyon. We drove west and made several stops in Arizona and New Mexico. We went to Canyon de Chelly National Park, Seven Corners, and Durango, Colorado. We stopped in Offerle, Kansas, to visit Grandpa and Grandma Boehme and other relatives.

When we arrived in Wichita, Kansas, we had a few days before Eddie and Diane arrived. Sally decided that she would rather fly on to Baltimore, so she and David flew to Baltimore ahead of us. The rest of us had a three-day drive to Baltimore where we stayed with Sally's parents until we found a place to live in the Washington area.

Chapter 22: Washington, D.C. — Redux and Finale

Some Navy friends suggested Lake Barcroft in Falls Church, Virginia, as a place to live. We visited the area and liked the schools, the lake, and the commuting distance to the Pentagon. We found a house at a price that we could afford. It was across the street from beach number one on the lake. The house was about one block from Columbia Pike and a five-mile straight shot to the Pentagon. The house had four regular-size bedrooms and two small bedrooms, so all the children had their own bedroom, and we had one bedroom to spare, where I placed my old roll-top desk and had a bedroom office.

The house was definitely a fixer-upper. The first time one of the children took a shower in the downstairs bathroom, water leaked into the hallway. Later, when Diane saw a former resident on the beach, he asked her if she had taken a shower downstairs. You might say we had some undisclosed, hidden surprises, but we went to work, and with everyone helping, we soon had a manageable house. The kids, outside of helping bring the house under control, made new friends and enjoyed the beach and swimming in the lake.

Eddie was a senior and Diane was a sophomore at JEB Stuart High School. David was in the seventh grade, and Holly was in the third grade. They all took buses to school, but since Eddie and Diane were on sports teams; they had to be picked up after their practices.

I occasionally took the car to work, but most of the time, I caught a bus on Columbia Pike to the Pentagon. An admiral friend from our days in Philadelphia saw me standing at the bus stop and offered to pick me up and drop me off each day. This was very convenient, and it gave me a chance to listen to some wise advice and get some Pentagon news.

My first boss at the Pentagon was Rear Admiral Bill Lawrence, USNA class of 1951, and former POW in Vietnam for six years. Admiral Lawrence was one the finest officers I ever met. His management style was calm and deliberate. He was a friend and a true Tennessee gentleman. My main responsibility was to assist Admiral Lawrence

I researched background information in the areas of aviation supply and maintenance support and coordinated recommendations that led to policy decisions. These decisions led to improved aircraft operational safety and supply and maintenance support.

Fortunately, and unlike many of my previous assignments, my position at the Pentagon did not require much travel outside of Washington. However, I was often out of the office coordinating actions with the systems commands and other Pentagon offices. As with previous assignments, I worked very closely with our aircraft maintenance branch. I was a one-man supply staff. I was alone, and being alone, I often informally enlisted help from the Naval Air and Supply Systems Commands. I would brief them on the requirement, and they would staff the answers and recommendations.

The Naval Aviation Logistics Command Management Information System (NALCOMIS) was being developed, and I kept an eye on its progress. It automated the Navy and Marine Corps aviation organizational and intermediate maintenance systems, as well as the logistics support systems, including supply support.

A new computer system was being procured to be placed in all squadrons, air stations, and ships. The lead development command was the Naval Sea Systems Command. I kept abreast of progress by reviewing periodic reports and attending policy meetings and conferences. My maintenance counterpart and I verified that budgets were funded.

Aircraft engine procurement recommendations were made by the Naval Air Systems Command, and, after staffing through our office, were presented to the Secretary of the Navy and Secretary of Defense for approval. My responsibility was to review aircraft engine usage and rework and procurement lead times. This data was then used to formulate the budget. With engines costing about $1,000,000 each in 1977, these budgets received a lot of attention. During budget approval times, we worked long hours, much of this time briefing the Navy comptroller, reworking the budget, and briefing the comptroller again. We spent a lot of time waiting for our turn in the budget "pit."

This was the first time in seven years that we were close enough to spend time on our 110 acres of land in Culpeper, Virginia. We often went there on weekends and for longer periods in the summer. We bought a riding mower and cleared areas where we could participate in sports and other activities, and we cleared paths where we could ride our motorcycles. We often had friends accompany us, and a Girl Scout troop often camped there.

In 1977, while discussing vacation plans, Sally suggested we save our money and go to Europe over the Christmas holidays. All of us agreed on the European travel plan — this included no Christmas presents. Our plan was to travel space-available from Dover Air Force Base to the Rhein Main Air Force Base in Frankfort, Germany. We would then travel by car from Frankfort to Innsbruck, Austria, where we would meet our friends, the Greens. The Greens were stationed in Rome, Italy, where Captain Green was the Naval Attaché at the US Embassy.

We packed one suitcase with our ice skates, hoping we would skate on lakes and canals. As it turned out, we never found places to skate; the result was transporting a heavy suitcase of unused ice skates throughout Europe. We had a two-day delay in Dover waiting for a flight. When our names were finally called, there were only five seats — we needed six. A commander I had known in San Diego did not get on the flight; he was prepared to fly commercially from Philadelphia.

I quickly gave Eddie money and asked the commander to take Eddie to Philadelphia, where Eddie would fly to Germany commercially, and we would meet him in Frankfort. At the last minute, the plane commander must have heard of our plight, and he added a seat by not counting a baby as needing a seat. We rejoiced and boarded the flight to Frankfort.

We arrived on December 23. We rented a van, bought some snacks and drinks at the base commissary, and acclimated ourselves by spending the night at quarters on the Frankfort base. The next day, we drove to Heidelberg and visited the famous castle on the Rhine. We then visited Sally's cousin, whose husband was stationed at an Army base near Heidelberg. We proceeded on to Munich after a stop at Neuschwanstein Castle, the Disneyland Castle. You might say we were sightseers — yes we were. We didn't want to miss anything.

We arrived in Munich about 10 PM, checked into the military hotel, and went to the center of Munich to find a place to eat. We had already realized that Germany takes Christmas seriously — many businesses were closed. We went to the famous Hofbrauhaus Beer Hall, thinking that surely they would serve us a meal. But, it was nearly midnight, and all we got for our effort was the smell of stale beer. Desperately hungry, we walked the streets looking for a street-side vendor. We found a food cart that sold bratwurst "hot dogs" but we had only enough German marks for three bratwurst — the vendor would not take our dollars. We loaded the bratwurst with mustard, relish, and onions and ate our midnight snack — three "hot dogs" for six people.

We returned to our quarters where we had three rooms. Diane and Holly made a Christmas tree out of a tree branch, and we sang some carols. After a wonderful night's sleep, we had a bountiful breakfast and hopped into our van for a drive to Innsbruck to meet the Greens for skiing. The most obvious sight driving through the magnificent Austrian Alps was the absence of snow. The Greens were not in Innsbruck, so we called them. They, of course, knew that there would be no skiing, as there was not much snow. They insisted that we drive on to Rome for a visit. We did some sightseeing in Innsbruck, including the site of the 1976 Winter Olympics. It was mid-afternoon as we drove over the Brenner Pass to Bolzano, Italy, where we would stay the night. Bolzano is more a German or Austrian city than an Italian city — many people speak German.

We always carried lunch meat, cheese, bread, and drinks that we purchased in local markets, so we mostly ate our lunch while driving. We also purchased pastries and cookies to "test" the skills of the German bakers.

We departed Bolzano for a stop in Verona where we visited the site memorialized in the famous Shakespeare play **Romeo and Juliet.** We made a short stop in Florence and saw several landmarks, including the famous statue of David by Michelangelo. We still had a long drive to Rome, and it was now time to stop sightseeing along the way and reach our unplanned, but desirable destination. After maneuvering our van through the crowded streets of Rome, we reached the Green residence.

The Greens were anxious, as we were, for us to see the glorious city of Rome. After a quick dinner, we boarded our van about 10 PM for a nighttime tour. The Coliseum was lighted like a Christmas tree. We went inside and could visualize Nero's spectacle, when he released the lions to attack Christians. We toured Rome nonstop the next day — December 29, Holly's birthday. We saw many sights. The highlights were the Vatican and the magnificent St. Peter's Cathedral.

Marge Green made a birthday cake for Holly, and after celebrating her birthday, we departed early the next morning for Leysin, Switzerland. Why Leysin? Eddie and Diane had a friend, Len, who was attending the American School in Leysin. His father was Naval Attaché in Moscow, Russia. Captain Green contacted the Moscow attaché, confirming that Len was in Leysin and further asked him to advise Len that we would meet him in Leysin on New Year's Day. Now, we had some tall driving ahead of us — about 700 miles from Rome to Leysin. But, obviously, we could not drive straight through — we had to do some sightseeing, and we selected as our primary stop, the city of Pisa and the Leaning Tower. Pisa was wonderful — super sights and a great meal. I held Holly's hand as we climbed the tower's narrow steps. I held her tighter, as we stepped to the rail on the low side. It was as I remembered from my visit 23 years earlier — scary.

Diane, Sally, Holly, Eddie, and David, Pisa, Italy, 1977

Holly on top of Leaning Tower of Pisa, 1977

After satisfying ourselves that we had absorbed the sights of historic Pisa, we headed north, bypassing sightseeing at the historic Italian port cities of La Spezia and Genoa with its Columbus connection. We had driven quite a distance over several hours and stopped for the night at Alessandria, Italy, with a distance to travel on the morrow of about 200 miles to Geneva and 100 more to Leysin. We had trouble finding an open store to buy something for our New Year's celebration, but we finally found a plum cake — it turns out it was soaked in rum, but everyone ate some.

We were off early the next morning for the last leg of our trip to Leysin. After driving an hour, we were blessed with a stunning view of Mont Blanc, the highest mountain in Europe, with an elevation of 15,778 feet. We passed through the seven-mile-long Mont Blanc tunnel, and we were in France. After several miles of winding downhill mountain roads, we entered Switzerland, and soon we were in Geneva. Being mindful of the distance we had to travel for our New Year's Day commitment to meet Len in Leysin, we did a cursory drive through Geneva, stopped for some pictures, and drove east along the north side of Lake Geneva. After a short drive, we were in Lausanne, where we had lunch at a rather nice lakeside restaurant. The meals were quite expensive, and, as we lingered over the menu, the waiter graciously suggested that he would let all four children have the children's menu, even 18-year-old Eddie. We were then afraid that they would get small portions, but we all had the same portions and enjoyed a magnificent meal. We stopped again to see the Chateau de Chillon at Montreau on the eastern end of the lake — my second visit, as I went there from Marseille, when I was on the **Randolph**.

Departing Montreau to the south along the lake, we gradually climbed, and after a few miles, turned east and started the real climb into the snow-covered mountains surrounding Leysin. We climbed about an hour in the dark on mostly snow-covered roads and arrived in Leysin. We went to the American School and found that Eddie and Diane's friend was downtown. We drove along the Leysin main road, and Eddie spotted Len walking with some friends on the sidewalk. Eddie and Diane got out of the car and greeted Len in a casual manner, as if they had run into each other back in Falls Church, Virginia. I had driven over 700 miles through Italy, crossed over the Alps, drove through France and into Switzerland, and these kids thought it was a normal two days — **please show a little respect**. Eddie and Diane stayed in the school dormitory, and the rest of us found lodging in a magnificent mountain lodge. That was New Year's Day, 1978.

The next day was ski day, and we all held up remarkably well, as we progressed from the beginners' slopes and joined the more advanced, but not too advanced, skiers. We were not prone to take risks, as any injury would have ended our vacation, making the trip back to Frankfort and the flight home very difficult. On the second day, Sally decided she would rather spend the day relaxing in Leysin. Eddie, Diane, and David skied with Len and his friends, and I skied with Holly. Holly and I skied on the gentle slopes with gorgeous vistas, while the others selected the more rigorous slopes. We all had a great time.

It was now time to wind up our European vacation and return to Frankfort for a flight home. Our route, of about 400 miles, took us through Basel, Switzerland, and Strasbourg and Manheim, Germany. We made a short sightseeing stop in Basel. Basel is on the Rhine River at the point where the borders of Switzerland, France, and Germany meet. Basel, the third largest city in Switzerland, has suburbs in France and Germany. I can certainly imagine that Basel was a major escape route for those fleeing Nazi Germany and occupied France during World War II. As we approached Strasbourg, we could see the outline of the mammoth Strasbourg Cathedral at a height of 466 feet. It was the tallest structure in the world from the 17th to the 19th centuries. It is the tallest church in the world completed during the Middle Ages. The inside of the cathedral is awe-inspiring; we marveled at the architects, engineers, and artisans who had performed these everlasting feats centuries earlier. Later in the 1990s, when I began studying my genealogy, I learned that I had an ancestor, Jacob Conrad, born in 1717, who came from the small town of Miekeshiem, near Strasbourg.

It was late in the afternoon when we departed Strasbourg for the drive to Frankfort. We checked in at the terminal and caught a flight early the next morning, and we arrived late in the day at Dover. We were exhausted but at home. It was a glorious trip with many memories.

With our Switzerland skiing experience behind us, we decided to purchase some ski equipment and proper clothing and take to the slopes. We did most of our skiing at Round Top, a less than two-hour drive to Pennsylvania. We also did a lot of ice skating in front of our house on Lake Barcroft. The winter was cold, and the lake was frozen from end to end. We even joined some hockey games. Because of the cold winter, we decided to seek a warmer climate for our Christmas vacation in 1979 — the choice was Puerto Rico.

Our flight would be from the Air Force Base at Charleston, South Carolina. Diane was on the JEB Stuart High School basketball team, and the coach insisted that if she wanted to be on the team, she would have to attend practice over the Christmas holidays. She chose to remain in Falls Church and stay with friends. We drove to Charleston and stayed overnight at base quarters. We caught a flight the next day to the Roosevelt Roads Naval Station in Puerto Rico. We rented a car and settled into our quarters on the base. Our first stop was a small sheltered beach on the base with good snorkeling. We went there almost every day and saw some beautiful coral. We rented a small motor boat and cruised many coves and sheltered beaches on the base. We stopped on beaches frequently and scavenged for sea shells. We found a coconut that had sprouted, and Holly decided that it would make a good Christmas tree, so we took it to our room. Holly decorated our Christmas tree, and we put our small presents around the tree. These presents were mostly made from things we had collected along the beaches.

We celebrated Christmas with a nice dinner at the club and, naturally, by going to the beach. There was a nice golf course on the base, and I played a couple rounds of golf. We went to San Juan and toured this historic city, as well as El Morro Fort, completed in 1587. Eddie had brought his old and very large surfboard, and, since part of the deal was to surf at the famous Rincon Beach, we made the long trip to the other end of the island. The surf was not at the high level that made Rincon a famous surfing area, but it was good enough. The pleasant conditions made for nice swimming and snorkeling amidst the rocks and small coves. We had a pleasant two days at Rincon. We also went to the Rain Forest, located not too far from Roosevelt Roads.

It was now time to celebrate Holly's birthday away from home, and we wanted to do something special. I talked to the base dining room manager, and he agreed to bake a cake for her. It was a Friday noon, and there were not many diners on this New Year's weekend. We had a nice meal, and the baker brought out the cake. Several diners joined us in singing happy birthday, and they all had a piece of the cake.

The flight home surprised us, as it took us to Norfolk instead of Charleston. Since our car was in Charleston, some extraordinary planning had to be quickly accomplished. Sally and the children could not fly space A in the continental US. I called a friend in Norfolk just before departing Puerto Rico, and asked him to reserve two rooms at the bachelor quarters for Sally and the children, where they would stay overnight. I would continue from Norfolk to Charleston on the same plane and retrieve the car. I stayed in Charleston overnight and drove to Norfolk the next day. Having had a good night's sleep and enjoying their stay in Norfolk, my family joined me, and we drove home to Falls Church — another delightful and memorable winter vacation.

During my time at the Pentagon, I had three different bosses. At the end of my second year, I could have petitioned for a commanding officer assignment or an executive officer assignment at one of our inventory control points, but I was reluctant to leave Washington and relocate the kids.

I had been watching the progress of the S3-A aircraft that was now out of production. I talked to my boss, a naval aviator, about the position as the S3-A Program Manager, a position equivalent to that of a commanding officer. My argument was that since the S3-A was now out of production, the main problems would be with logistics support — my specialty. After some time to mull it over, he just could not break the mold of having an aviator in this assignment. I then decided to wait for the personnel people to make a decision, when out of the blue, my rear admiral friend, whom I had accompanied on the Western Pacific inspection tour, asked me to become the NALCOMIS Program Manager. I cleared this with the Commander, Naval Supply Systems Command, and he enthusiastically endorsed this assignment.

I still had about six months at the Pentagon and a lot of work to do as well as to plan another winter vacation. We decided that our destination would be Spain, possibly flying to the Naval Air Station, Rota, near Seville. We went to Dover to catch our flight. When we arrived, we were told that the flight to Rota was not scheduled, but there was a flight to Frankfort. We decided to go to Frankfort, and if we could not fly from there to Spain, then our vacation would be in Germany.

Shortly after arriving in Frankfort, we boarded a medical flight to Rota via Torrejon Air Base near Madrid. We were met by a friend who was the supply officer at Rota. We had three rooms at the base quarters. With a bit of jet lag, we discussed our plans for a Spain vacation with my friend, and he made a few suggestions.

Our first stop was Cadiz, about an hour from Rota. Cadiz is the oldest city in Spain and one of the oldest in Europe. Columbus sailed from Cadiz on his second and fourth voyages. It is the home port of the Spanish Navy. Cadiz is a beautiful walking city with narrow and hilly streets. In 1980, after a fire burned some warehouses, a Roman forum, the second largest Roman forum in the world, was discovered. The Cadiz visit was slightly marred, as I became ill and had to sleep in our car, while the rest of the family enjoyed Cadiz. Not being ready to venture too far from Rota on the second day, we went to Palos de la Frontera, the port where Columbus departed on his first voyage of discovery.

Now ready to venture further afield, we went to Algeciras, near Gibraltar. Algeciras is now the largest container port in Spain and one of the largest in the world. We went on to La Linea, adjacent to Gibraltar. In 1954, when I was on the **Randolph,** I walked from Gibraltar to La Linea. I wanted the family to see the iconic Rock of Gibraltar. The crossing was now closed, due to conflict between England and Spain, but we walked up the road to the border fence and took some pictures. We then went to the beach on the Mediterranean Sea and walked up the beach to the Gibraltar border fence. It was an amazing place to be during that Christmas season in 1979.

It was now December 23 and time for us to venture farther afield. We were going to Granada. We drove south to the Mediterranean Sea and along the Costa del Sol to Malaga. It was a magnificent drive, and we made many stops to walk on mainly deserted beaches and to see small villages and farms. We took a horse and buggy ride and then drove north to Granada, with a stop at the famous Moorish palace and fortress, the Alhambra. I was reading Washington Irving's book, **Tales of the Alhambra**, and was anxious to see this historic complex and relive some of Irving's tales. It was all that I imagined — full of unbelievable splendor. We saw some of the sights of Granada, including the ever-present Roman ruins — this time a coliseum.

Sally skiing in Sierra Nevada mountains, Granada, Spain, 1979

We were going to ski the next day, Christmas Eve, and we wanted to get an early start, so we were early to bed in our hotel in Granada. Arising early, we drove south in the Sierra Nevada mountains to the ski slopes. Arriving at the ski lodge, the parking lot was almost empty, and for a moment, we were worried that the slopes might be closed. They were open, and we rented our ski equipment and hit the slopes. It was wonderful — no crowds, no waiting for lifts — just ski and ski. We were tired from the continuous skiing and were ready to stop by mid-afternoon. This gave us the opportunity to get back to our lodging early, have dinner, a good night's sleep, and an early start for our return to Rota on Christmas Day. However, Sally and I hadn't had enough, so we went to midnight mass at the large Granada Cathedral. We thought the church would be crowded, and, when we arrived at 11:30 PM, the church was almost empty. We waited and waited, and about 11:55 PM, the crowds arrived, and the cathedral was full. The splendor, ceremony, and music of the mass were superlative. We were blessed to be in that place.

The drive from Granada to Rota was about 180 miles. We were not on a main road, so it was a drive of about six hours. However, we made several stops, Ronda being the main attraction. In **For Whom the Bell Tolls**, Ernest Hemingway relates how the republicans murdered nationalists by throwing them over the cliffs in the Spanish Civil War, supposedly the El Tajo Cliffs in Ronda. It is unbelievable to see houses built into these cliffs that have survived for hundreds of years. We saw very similar cliff-side houses in Cuenca, Spain, when Sally and I visited there in the 1990s. We saw several smaller mountain-top villages that required short visits. We arrived back at Rota about 11:45 on the evening of Christmas Day. When we entered the lobby,

Dempster family, Christmas Eve, Naval Air Station, Rota, Spain, 1979

there sat a Christmas tree, a delight to our weary eyes. We could not help ourselves — we posed for a picture in front of the tree. We were, indeed, a bedraggled lot.

Rock of Gibraltar, 1979

When we were in Algeciras, we investigated the possibility of taking a ferry to Tangier, Morocco. We decided to make the voyage. Departing Algeciras early in the morning, we arrived in the exotic port of Tangier about 10 AM, having crossed the Mediterranean Sea from the continent of Europe to the continent of Africa. My thoughts on entering Tangier Harbor were of the Barbary Coast pirates, who had sailed from this city. My ancestor, Jan Jansen, was a Dutch pirate who sailed the Barbary Coast, and, after being captured by the Moors, transferred his allegiance to the Sultan of Morocco. After about 20 minutes of aimless meandering and being accosted by innumerable "guides" and peddlers, it became obvious that if we were to be safe, comfortable, and enjoy this magnificent city, we would need protection by a local from the locals. We hired a burly guide to usher us in and about Tangier. His name was Abdul, a name selected by many of the "guides." Abdul assigned Eddie to bring up the rear of our convoy, and we were off to see the wizardry of Tangier. Abdul guided us through the mazes of this ancient city. We were not completely free of the hassle of beggars and vendors, but his imposing presence minimized the danger of probably non-existent bodily harm. The early fear soon subsided. You can see that Holly is discussing a pur-

Holly contemplates a purchase with Diane, Darrell, Eddie, Abdul, and Sally, Tangier, Morocco, 1979

chase with a vendor. Abdul took us to a merchant of his choice, where he would receive his sizable commission — dependent on our haggling prowess. We were seated amid expensive Moroccan carpets and glassware in the medina, while being served tea and pastries. The medina is the ancient, non-European part of the city, sometimes called a souk or casbah. However, casbah originally meant a walled portion of the city that housed the local leader, and a souk is a market place.

We also viewed the mosques and historic sites in Tangier. In late afternoon, we walked back to the ferry terminal. Our last purchases were brassware sold by vendors who followed us to the terminal.

We met six Irishmen on the ferry — three from Ireland and three from Northern Ireland, who ordinarily would not mix. Having completed a memorable day by traveling between continents, we relaxed on the ferry and were entertained by the Irishmen. When we arrived in Algeciras, it was dark, and we could not find our parked car. After a long search, along with the Irishmen, whose car was also missing, we learned that our car had been towed. We had parked in a zone where parking was illegal after 6 PM. Diane had studied Spanish and served as our translator, but I could not blame her. I should have read the signs, as they clearly indicated the parking rules. It took us some time to determine the location of our car, and since we had spent almost the last of our Spanish pesetas, we thought it best that we save taxi fare and walk to the storage lot, guided by a map that had been drawn for us by a helpful security guard.

After trudging through the darkened streets, burdened by our Moroccan purchases, we arrived at the lot. As we arrived, our Irish friends were departing. I asked them to exchange some dollars for pesetas, but suddenly they were not our friends, and they hurriedly departed the lot. The parking attendant, an elderly Spaniard, was drowsy from drink, spoke no English, and insisted that he would not accept any payment but pesetas. I had more than enough money in dollars and German marks, but he spoke peseta only. Sally became frustrated and called him a bandito. He understood this and closed the window on his small shack and ignored our pleas. Holly saved us, as she suddenly fell asleep. The "bandito" observed this, took mercy on us, and accepted American dollars. In his defense, he knew little about the exchange rate. I paid him about 50 per cent extra in dollars. Again, we arrived back at Rota at a very late hour.

We had a free day in Rota to wrap up our Spanish trip. We did our last minute shopping, packed our bags, and departed the next day for Dover Air Force Base. We had a short rest at home before all the kids went back to school.

I had several loose ends to finish, and with the daily input of new "problems," I had a busy five months before transferring from the Pentagon to the Naval Air Systems Command in Crystal City, Virginia, about a mile from the Pentagon. My new job was Program Manager Air 270 (PMA 270). I had a small staff: a Navy commander, a Marine major, and three civilians. We obtained program support from other Washington offices and Navy field activities. Our software support activity was located at the Naval Supply Depot in Mechanicsburg, Pennsylvania, and our computers were being procured by the Naval Sea Systems Command. Since our customers were ships and air stations, we received policy guidance from the fleet commanders. My direct superior was the Commander Naval Air Systems Command. He ensured that I met the requirements of the fleet within the available budget. I did get some program assistance from a contractor in the form of program design and documentation. In summary, I had one boss, but I had many people who thought they were my boss. If I did not meet their "needs," they would talk to my boss, and it would roll downhill to me. I was usually aware that this was going to happen and was prepared to respond that the "needs" were not reasonable, or that I was making changes. These were not burdensome situations, but they were certainly a nuisance and time-consuming.

As stated previously, my staff was minimal and the real workers were located in various agencies around the country. Each of these agencies had a mission to support various program managers, and it was up to me to make sure that our requirements were met. Feature yourself as being commanding officer of a ship and the operations officer reported to another command, and your orders to him had to be cleared by the other command. This would never work in the dynamics of a shipboard environment, but in my environment, I had to make it work. It could work only if my requirements were clearly stated, and the receiving command understood that completion of these requirements was within their stated mission, and they would complete the stated requirements in a timely and quality manner. I often found myself facing an admiral and explaining that improvements had to be made by field activities, if we were to meet our stated goals. I could not operate with kid gloves, and I could not go to the other extreme and operate with brass knuckles. I had to operate from firm ground.

We were testing our software at Mechanicsburg, Pennsylvania. I was satisfied that we were far enough along to conduct a field test, but we had no field computers. Our computers were in the procurement stage with deliveries at least two years away.

We obtained authorization to procure a single test computer with external terminals. I investigated three activities that were recommended for testing. The Marine major on our staff recommended the presidential Marine helicopter squadron in Quantico, Virginia. Although the proximity was an advantage, I ruled this out. This was more visibility and risk than I wanted. The two others were the Naval Air Station in Key West, Florida, and the reserve Naval Air Station in Willow Grove, Pennsylvania. I visited both activities and selected Willow Grove. Although Willow Grove was a reserve activity, it had a dynamic command environment with knowledgeable personnel, who were willing to take on this task. We provided funds for site preparation, procured a test computer system, and were off and running our field test.

I had significant help from the command master chief of the Air Systems Command, who ran interference for us, and became one of our biggest boosters. He had enough clout to get tasks done, and by talking to the systems users in the field, he provided us honest and useful feedback. Our project had expended a lot of money over the four years from concept to testing, and we had not implemented anything. We had to show some real progress, and our systems field test was progress.

After about two months, we took our show on the road to the Marine Corps Air Station at Cherry Point, North Carolina. Our objective was to demonstrate functionality for maintenance and supply personnel of the Atlantic and Pacific Fleets. The personnel who attended were experts in the subject matter. It was also important to have the design and systems programming personnel present, so they could interact directly with the system's users. The interaction between designers and users was extraordinary. We received positive feedback, but, more importantly, we documented many areas where the interaction between supply and maintenance personnel could be improved. Also, improved management reports were suggested that would enable supervisors to monitor backlogs and performance and take action to increase aircraft readiness. The operation was a resounding success, and we resolved to continue direct liaison with the fleet.

As a result of the exposure to multiple fleet users, we received many requests for software changes. The first step was to analyze these recommended changes. As with any large software program, the requests for change always exceed the capacity to make these changes. The next step categorized the changes from critical to nice to have. Once the changes were accomplished, we tested the changes, and implemented them in our test system at Willow Grove.

In the future, when our system was implemented at multiple activities, we would send the changes to all activities at the same time. This procedure is called configuration control. It is necessary for all activities to run the same system, not only because it is the optimum system, but also for training, documentation, and management control. In order to assist activities with problems, we had to know what version of the system they were running.

NALCOMIS was now operational, but it could not be implemented system-wide because the hardware computer systems were not yet available. Our hardware was being procured as a part of the Shipboard Non-Tactical Automated Data Processing (SNAP) computer system. SNAP computer systems would be installed on ships and activities to support automated logistics support systems.

In January of 1981, we invited fleet personnel to our development facility at Mechanicsburg, Pennsylvania, to perform hands-on testing. We simulated four organizational maintenance sites interacting with supply and intermediate maintenance activities. As usual, we received requests for changes, but we were well satisfied with the performance of the system. We were now ready to implement at our first site, the Marine Air Group at the Marine Corps Air Station at Cherry Point, North Carolina.

Our 1980 Christmas voyage to Europe was going to be a bit different. Eddie was 21 and not eligible for space-available transportation, so he would have to fly commercial to Frankfort, Germany. The rest of us left from Dover Air Force Base two days before Eddie's departure. After our arrival at Rhein Main Air Force Base in Frankfort, we rested one day and then made our way to Huebach, Germany, to visit Sally's cousins, the Strotts. Huebach is near Fulda, a famous cold war defensive point known as the Fulda Gap, where North Atlantic Treaty Organization (NATO) forces established defensive positions against possible Soviet aggression. As we drove north from Nuremberg to Huebach, we drove along the East German border fence that separated East Germany from

East German/West German border fence

Diane, Sally, Karl Strott with wife and daughter, David, and Holly at Strott house, Heubach, West Germany

West Germany. We had an eerie feeling, as we drove along the border that, if we did something wrong, we could end up on the wrong side of the border.

When we arrived in Huebach in the late afternoon, we inquired at a pub as to the location of the Strott farm. The pub owner immediately escorted us to the Strott home, and we knocked on the door of Sally's cousin. Sally's great-grandfather, George Heinrich Strott, emigrated from Germany to Baltimore, along with two brothers, in 1853, to avoid conscription into the German army. Despite our unexpected arrival, Karl Strott, and his wife, immediately invited us into their home. We had an obvious language problem, but the Strott's 16-year-old daughter spoke some English, and we managed to communicate. Karl's brother, Reinhold, and his family, also lived in a section of the farm house. We met Reinhold at the door to his home, but he did not seem to be interested in visiting with his third cousin, Sally, who had traveled such a long distance to visit with her family that had been separated for 127 years.

Karl was wearing his working overalls that had patches on patches, a garb that I was familiar with from the days of the Great Depression. Karl and Reinhold's father, Johannes, Sally's father's second cousin, was bed-ridden and very frail. We greeted him, and he shook our hands with a firm grip. Some folks, such as Reinhold, have no interest in their ancestors, but I have always had an interest in genealogy. I think it is important to be knowledgeable of the lives of our ancestors. It is important to understand their lives, their environment, the risks they took in crossing oceans, and the work they did to support their families and communities. My ancestors are not famous and known worldwide, but they are known to me, and I have a responsibility to make their lives relevant and to relate their hardships and accomplishments to my descendants.

After a delightful and historic visit with the Strotts, we went back to the pub, had a sumptuous German meal, and then drove to Nuremberg, where we stayed at the military hotel. We went to the famous Nuremburg Christmas market and Diane and I shared a bratwurst. We also visited the famous Nuremburg Castle before departing for Frankfort to meet Eddie.

Diane and Darrell eat bratwurst, Nuremburg, Germany, 1980

We picked up Eddie and hit the road for Brussels, Belgium. We stopped in Saarbrucken to see the old city and some Luther sights. We made another stop in Luxemburg. It was late in the afternoon, and most shops were closed, so we went to the Luxembourg rail station and bought some snacks and souvenirs. When we returned home, one of Diane's classmates told Diane that he thought he had seen her at the Luxemburg rail station. Diane confirmed that she was there — small world.

We stayed in Brussels with our friends from Falls Church, the Malones. Dan Malone, an Army colonel, was stationed with NATO in Brussels. We arrived in Brussels on December 23. We toured Brussels the next day and went to Christmas Eve Mass at the Brussels Cathedral. We visited the famous Belgium seaport of Bruges and went to the North Sea. A must see was Waterloo, site of Napoleon's final defeat by the British and German armies in 1815. The defeat was so decisive that it is used as a phrase to this day. When someone is defeated, it is said that they have met their waterloo. After saying a thankful farewell to the Malones, we left Brussels for Paris.

Eddie, Sally, Darrell, and David posing as Napoleon, Waterloo, Belgium, 1980

We made a stop in Compiegne, France, the site of the signing of the armistice that ended World War I at 11 AM on November 11, 1918. The armistice was signed in a railway car in the Forest of Compiegne. President Wilson established Armistice Day on November 11, 1919. Armistice Day honored those who died in World War I. Armistice Day was renamed Veterans Day in 1954, and the scope was changed to honor all veterans. I remember the celebration of Armistice Day, particularly from 1937 to 1941, when my family lived in Kinsley, Kansas. I put red, white, and blue crepe paper on the spokes of my bicycle and rode in the parade down the main street. Of course, at that time, we had both Spanish American War and World War I veterans, and they marched and rode in the parade.

We arrived in Paris in mid-afternoon and obtained hotel rooms through the Paris USO. We did some sightseeing in the afternoon, and Sally and I were ready to retire for the night, but Eddie and Diane were eager to see Paris by night. David wanted to go with them, but being just 16, we thought it best that he stay with us. He looked at it a different way — he was 16 and felt he was perfectly qualified to go out on the town, even if the town was Paris, France. We finally relented, since he would have such stellar companions in Eddie and Diane.

Eddie, David, Diane, Holly, and Sally, Eiffel Tower, Paris, France, 1980

Our highlights in Paris were the Louvre, Notre Dame Cathedral, and the Eiffel Tower. After a day of sightseeing, we decided to return to Frankfurt in hopes that we would get a hop home and arrive before New Year's Day. It was a 260-mile drive from Paris to Frankford. About 50 miles east of Paris, we saw an American flag on a sign indicating the direction to the Chateau Thierry American Monument. We turned off the main road, and soon we were at Chateau Thierry, also the location of the Aisne-Marne American Cemetery and Belleau Wood. The Chateau Thierry Monument is massive and is said to be the nicest American monument in Europe, celebrating American victories and sacrifice in World War I. General Pershing said the Battle of Belleau Wood, fought by US Marines, "was the most considerable engagement American troops had ever had with a foreign enemy." He also said, "The deadliest weapon in the world is a United States Marine and his rifle." Belleau Wood is forever embodied in Marine Corps lore. There was a bronze relief of a fighting Marine at the entrance to the cemetery. We stopped for a group picture, and I saw that the bronze was sculptured by Felix de Weldon.

Belleau Wood Monument, 1980
Sally, Darrell, Holly, Diane, and Eddie

This was of interest to me, as I met Felix de Weldon the previous year, when I accompanied the Chief of Naval Operations from Washington, D.C., to Pascagoula, Mississippi, to attend the christening of the **USS Leftwich**. The **Leftwich** was named after my Naval Academy classmate and friend, Lieutenant Colonel William Groom Leftwich, who was killed in Vietnam. Bill and I served together at the Naval Academy in 1957–1959. Felix de Weldon, who also sculpted the Iwo Jima Monument in Washington, D.C., was on the plane, as he had sculpted a statue of a fighting Marine that was to be presented to the **Leftwich.** Additional statues were made to present to the Marine Ground Officer of the year. Incidentally, Ross Perot, another classmate, was on the plane, as he was a close friend of Bill Leftwich.

As we were leaving Belleau Wood on December 29, the cemetery superintendent wished us bon voyage and warned us of the dangerous road conditions, as the roads were covered with black ice. We proceeded with caution, and made a short stop at Metz to celebrate Holly's 13th birthday. We had a nice meal and a birthday cake and continued our drive to Frankfort in darkness. I drove until about 10 PM and turned the driving over to Eddie. We arrived in Frankfort after midnight and boarded a flight about 6 AM for Dover.

We arrived home to be met by a frozen driveway. A water pipe had burst in a downstairs bathroom, and water had flowed through a hallway, into the garage, and down the driveway. Our neighbor, across the street, managed to turn off the water. Although the downstairs was a mess, we were happy to be safe and sound at home after some memorable European experiences.

As I write this in 2017, we are experiencing the same thing that our parents experienced in 1977 through 1980. We were not at home to celebrate Christmas with our family. Our children, maybe because they had the opportunity to travel during their Christmas holidays, are now going to other states or countries during their children's Christmas school breaks. What goes around comes around — C'est la vie.

In the summer of 1981, I requested retirement. This request was granted, and I retired from the United States Navy

Navy Retirement, 1981: Edwin Dempster, Lillian Strott (Sally's mother), David, Catharine Dempster, Diane, Sally, Holly, Darrell, Dee Dempster (brother), and Eddie

on September 30, 1981 — after almost 30 years on active duty. In reality, I had been on active duty from the day I joined the Navy, in January 1948, but my four years as a midshipman did not count for retirement purposes.

I took a position with a small company in Norfolk, Virginia, for two years and then formed a sole proprietor company — Three D Dynamics. I worked in logistics and information management for various companies and was an instructor in several different areas of logistics. I had consulting contracts in Washington, D.C., California, Florida, Switzerland, Indonesia, and Thailand. After about 15 years, I gradually decreased my workload and completely retired about 2000.

Sally and I continued to travel throughout the world. We have made several trips to Finland, Estonia, Denmark, India, and Tanzania in conjunction with the Global Mission Division of our church. We have traveled to over 50 countries, islands, and possessions. But, that is another story of our lives that is not yet completed.

I am now where I didn't know where I was going.
I AM THERE!

El Tajo Cliffs, Ronda, Spain, purportedly where republicans murdered nationalists by throwing them over the cliffs in the Spanish Civil War in Ernest Hemingway's **For Whom the Bell Tolls** (see page 304)

ACKNOWLEDGEMENTS

My wife, Sally, who managed our home front during my Navy career and, with the help of God, gave birth to five children and instilled in them the blessings of Christianity.

My cousin, Dr. Galen Boehme, who painstakingly edited this memoir, starting with a few chapters at a time, and then the entire document. Galen, who has a Ph.D. in English, was a high school teacher in Kinsley, Kansas for many years. Galen lives on the Boehme homestead, and, along with his brother, Jary, farms the land where I worked for my Grandfather and mentor, John Boehme, during my teen years.

My Aunt Geraldine Dempster Collins, my father's sister, who helped me describe my early years, especially life on the Dempster farm and how the Dust Bowl and the Great Depression affected our family. Her memory was excellent, and she answered many questions that I should have asked my parents much earlier. She died in 2016 at the age of 98 and was helping me to the very end.

Martha Hollenbeck of Annapolis, Maryland, who has worked with me on this memoir for the last year. Martha did all the document layout, formatting, and photo sizing and placement. Martha never chastised me for my many errors and iterations, as I progressed through the document. Martha is also an excellent editor and gave me many suggestions.

Martha also designed the front and back covers. I will also add thanks and praise to Martha's husband, Glenn, who is a computer guru extraordinaire and kept my computer running when it was running out of gas.

My children, Eddie, Diane, David, Holly and daughter-in-law, Eva, who painstakingly read portions of the book and significantly enhanced the readability.

Navy Storekeeper Jim Hoffman (later Lieutenant Commander), **USS Ranger (CVA-61)**, shipmate and valued friend, who reminded me of some of our experiences in the Tonkin Gulf. Although Jim was a junior sailor on **Ranger**, his expertise was valued by all hands.

Navy Storekeeper Andy Anderson, **USS Barton (DD-722)**, shipmate and long-time friend, who provided material related to the **Barton** mine incident in 1952. Andy also helped me immensely during my tour as a novice supply officer on the **Barton**.

My neighbor, Ruth Wexley, self-described "comma-maniac," provided last minute expert assistance in reviewing and commenting on my writing.

Note: I have had a lot of help in the preparation of this book. Any remaining errors are mine and mine alone. Thank you to everyone, named and unnamed, who helped me.

IN MEMORIAM

Parents Edwin Dempster (1907-1986) and Catharine Boehme Dempster (1911-2006), infant daughter Deborah (1961-1961), sister Phyllis (1936-2016), and brother Dee (1950-2013). Sally's parents John Charles Strott II (1904-1973) and Lillian Heubner Strott (1903-1983), and brother, John Charles Strott III (1929-2012).

EPILOGUE

Our nation suffered tragedies of war and my family suffered tragedies of war and on the home front: my father's aunt, Blanch Laib Lydick, died at age 28 in 1909, five days after childbirth; Donald Boehme, my mother's brother, died when he fell down the cellar steps at eight months of age in 1926; John Lightcap, my mother's cousin, drowned in a sand pit at age 20 in 1932; Kenneth Stinson, husband of my mother's sister, Ramona, died in a truck fire at age 23 in 1938; my Uncle Elmer's son, Donald, died in a tractor accident at three and a half years of age in 1945; my father's cousin, Forest Lydick, died in Chicago at 38 years of age in 1947; our daughter, Deborah, died at childbirth in 1961; my mother's cousin's son, Wayne Proberts, was killed in Vietnam at age 23 in 1965; Edgar Jackson, the second husband of my mother's sister, Ramona, died in a tractor accident at age 65 in 1969; my 2nd cousin, Virginia Armstrong Engel, died from a blood clot in 1974 at age 43, leaving her husband and six children; my cousin, Keith Jackson's son, Clark Jackson, was killed in a car accident at age 21 in 1982;my 2nd cousin, David Armstrong, died from cancer in 1984 at age 52: my mother's sister, Thelma, died when she fell down the cellar steps at age 82 in 1992; my cousin, Larry Jackson, died from cancer at the age of 45 in 1996; my cousin, Bill England, died at age 47 in 2004; and my cousin Sally Gorum's son, Blayne Gorum, died from a stroke and heart attack at age 47 in 2015. Are these more than enough tragedies for one family? Yes, but the survivors were SURVIORS—they went on with their lives on the plains of Kansas.

Are the risks of living on the Western Plains a relic of the past? I think not. In March 2017, wildfires spread across the plains. Over 650,000 acres were burned in Kansas, from Wichita to the Colorado border, a distance of over 250 miles. Farmers lost their homes and hundreds of cattle — they lost everything — sound familiar? Were they now **dead broke**?

The writing of this story has been a pleasure. It is a tribute to my family and forbearers. It is also my hope that it will spark the reader's interest in the events that shaped the history of our great country, the joy of travel, the wonders of nature, and the marvelous creations of man throughout the world.

60TH WEDDING ANNIVERSARY

Eric, Diane, and Carl Stanko, Sarah Aquasvivas Mazanto (fiance of Jason Stanko), Jason Stanko, Sally and Darrell, Eddie and Brooke Dempster, Holly Phillips, Reagan and Dawn Dempster, Nicole Phillips, Greer, Eva, Mitchell, and David Dempster

Pastor David Oravec tells the story of Sally and Darrell and their family. Marlene Lefever and cousin Betty Lou Coursen, to the left and right of Sally and Darrell, were in the wedding.